Chris Bolinger has created an instrument that God will use to change men's lives! *Daily Strength for Men* is a practical, powerful platform for leadership and life change. Nothing moves the heart of a man more than a deep dive into God's Word, and that kind of intentionality is driven home on each and every page of the material. I highly recommend *Daily Strength* for every man, no matter what his particular season of life.

– Dr. Craig Fry, president, Christian Leadership Concepts

If our hearts are the heart of the matter to God, men will find *Daily Strength* to be the spiritual omega-3 they need to heed the admonition in Proverbs 4:23 to "guard your heart because from it flow the springs of life" (ISV).

– Doug Pollock, speaker and author of God Space

Daily Strength for Men helps the men in your church get spiritually healthy by pointing them to God's Word every day.

– Charles Arn, president of Church Growth Inc.
and author of Side Door

A 365-DAY DEVOTIONAL

DAILY STRENGTH FOR MEN

CHRIS BOLINGER

BroadStreet
PUBLISHING

BroadStreet Publishing® Group, LLC
Savage, Minnesota, USA
BroadStreetPublishing.com

DAILY STRENGTH FOR MEN: A 365-DAY DEVOTIONAL

978-1-4245-5753-0 (faux leather)
978-1-4245-5754-7 (e-book)

Stock or custom editions of BroadStreet Publishing titles may be purchased in bulk for educational, business, ministry, fundraising, or sales promotional use. For information, please email info@broadstreetpublishing.com.

Cover design by Chris Garborg at garborgdesign.com
Typesetting by Katherine Lloyd at theDESKonline.com

Printed in China
18 19 20 21 22 5 4 3 2 1

FOREWORD

By David Murrow

Spending consistent time in the Bible can literally turn your life around. Research indicates that men who engage with the Bible at least four times a week are:

- 57 percent less likely to abuse alcohol
- 68 percent less likely to stray from their marriage vows
- 61 percent less likely to view porn
- 74 percent less likely to gamble

These men are also:

- More than twice as likely to share their faith and disciple others
- More than four times as likely to memorize Scripture

Obviously, the Bible is good for men. But how do we get men to read it? Chris Bolinger has written a devotional that guides men into God's Word. *Daily Strength for Men* is unique in three ways:

1. Whereas most devotionals give readers a new passage each day, *Daily Strength for Men* camps out on a single passage for two days. Men read the same passage twice, which gives the "seed" a greater chance to take root in their hearts.
2. Bolinger mixes things up by focusing on devotions and prayer one day, Scripture reading and application the next. I appreciate the variety this brings to my devotional time.
3. *Daily Strength for Men* is drawn completely from the Old Testament. Bolinger mines these "forgotten books" and introduces men to the riches found there.

One more thing: I'm a bit of an odd duck. Most men read their devotions in the morning, but I've always been a "Bible-before-bed" kinda guy. I've found these devotions make great evening reading and serve as a guide for my bedtime prayers.

I hope you enjoy this collection as much as I have.

David Murrow
Director, Church for Men
Author, *Why Men Hate Going to Church*

INTRODUCTION

It was early on a cold Ohio morning in December, and I was meeting with my "CLC brothers," as I did every Friday. We studied the Bible, shared our lives in our prayer requests and our discussions, and encouraged each other, often citing passages of Scripture. I had come to rely on the strength that I drew from these men, strength that I couldn't seem to get on my own. Christian Leadership Concepts stresses the importance of having a daily quiet time, but I had found it difficult to get much out of my own Bible readings, and my devotions had been inconsistent at best.

As I left that December meeting, I decided to find a devotional that would give me a daily shot of strength from God's Word. But I wanted more than that. I wanted to be challenged to go further in my walk with Christ. I wanted stories of men who had overcome obstacles, who had kept their faith under pressure. And I wanted encouragement, because I felt discouraged by the weight of the challenges and stress in my life and the lives of my friends and family members.

After my two-month search for a devotional came up empty, I decided to write my own. I started by listing Bible verses that I found encouraging. Once I had a good set of those, I considered how each verse struck me. Sometimes, a verse made me think of a person who had impacted me. Other times, a verse made me think of a film, a song, or a story.

My notes became devotions. After a few months of work, I stopped to see where I was and discovered two things. First, every verse that I had used was from the Old Testament, thirty-nine books on which I and many other Christian men focus little attention. Second, even though I had written the devotions, each still made me stop and think how I could apply the verse to my life.

I decided each verse needed two days of treatment. The first day would be my thoughts. The second day would include Scripture passages for context and enrichment, and questions for reflection and application.

The result is *Daily Strength for Men*. I pray that it strengthens you and brings you closer to God, the source of our strength.

Check out DAILYSTRENGTHFORMEN.COM for additional resources, including a toolkit, which will help you get the most out of this devotional.

CREATED FOR YOU

In the beginning, God created the heavens and the earth.

—Genesis 1:1

When you read the first verse in the Bible, do you ask why? Why did God create the heavens? Why did God create the earth?

The answer to these "why" questions will astound you.

For decades, or even centuries, we have been told that there is nothing special about the earth. After all, there are 100 billion galaxies in the universe and 100 billion stars in our own galaxy, the Milky Way. Orbiting around many of these stars are planets.[1]

Our planet, therefore, is just one of trillions and trillions of planets in the universe. If there is intelligent life on our planet, then there has to be intelligent life on other planets. In fact, the universe must be teeming with intelligent life.

Earth is insignificant. We, the intelligent inhabitants of earth, are insignificant.

In an interview with Lee Strobel, Dr. Guillermo Gonzales, who earned his PhD in astronomy at the University of Washington, paints a very different picture of our home planet:

> We've found that our location in the universe, in our galaxy, in our solar system, as well as such things as the size and rotation of the Earth, the mass of the moon and sun and so forth—a whole range of factors—conspire together in an amazing way to make Earth a habitable planet. And even beyond that, we've found that the very same conditions that allow for intelligent life on Earth also make it strangely well-suited for viewing and analyzing the universe.

Dr. Jay Wesley Richards, who coauthored the book *The Privileged Planet* with Gonzales, tells Strobel, "And we suspect this is not an accident. In fact, we raise the question of whether the universe has been literally designed for discovery."[2]

God created the heavens and the earth for us, the people of earth. He did it so that we could live and, just as importantly, so that we could study and appreciate every aspect of his creation.

Passage: Verse in Context — Genesis 1:1–2, 26–28

In the beginning, God created the heavens and the earth. The earth was without form and void, and darkness was over the face of the deep. And the Spirit of God was hovering over the face of the waters. ... Then God said, "Let us make man in our image, after our likeness. And let them have dominion over the fish of the sea and over the birds of the heavens and over the livestock and over all the earth and over every creeping thing that creeps on the earth." So God created man in his own image, in the image of God he created him; male and female he created them. And God blessed them. And God said to them, "Be fruitful and multiply and fill the earth and subdue it, and have dominion over the fish of the sea and over the birds of the heavens and over every living thing that moves on the earth."

Related Passage — Isaiah 45:18–19

For thus says the LORD, who created the heavens (he is God!), who formed the earth and made it (he established it; he did not create it empty, he formed it to be inhabited!): "I am the LORD, and there is no other. I did not speak in secret, in a land of darkness; I did not say to the offspring of Jacob, 'Seek me in vain.' I the LORD speak the truth; I declare what is right."

Questions for Reflection and Application

- Why did God create you?
- How do the verse, the passages, and the devotion change your views on God? On yourself?
- How do you demonstrate, to God and others, that you are a special creation, important to God? What are two changes you can make in your approach to life to show more honor to your Creator?
- Who are three people whom you can influence, through your words and actions, to realize that they, like you, are creations of a loving God?

Father, thank you for not only the "what" of Creation but also the "why." Amen.

"LET THERE BE LIGHT"

And God said, "Let there be light," and there was light.
—*Genesis 1:3*

The first time that God speaks in the Bible, it is to create light. Light is essential to life. In the process of photosynthesis, green plants absorb energy from light and use this absorbed light energy to convert carbon dioxide and water into carbohydrates. The carbohydrates feed the cells of the plant, thereby enabling the plant to live and grow. As a by-product of photosynthesis, plants give off oxygen, which people and animals need to survive.

Light, of course, is also essential to seeing. Of the five senses—sight, hearing, smell, taste, and touch—sight is dominant. We perceive up to 80 percent of all impressions by means of our sight.

In chapter 8 of the Gospel of John, Jesus says, "I am the light of the world. Whoever follows me will not walk in darkness, but will have the light of life" (v. 12). That life is not just life in heaven after we die but fullness of life here on earth.

Many other Bible verses mention light. In fact, the word "light" appears over 250 times in the Bible. Some verses that discuss light are:

- "The LORD is my light and my salvation; whom shall I fear?" (Psalm 27:1a).
- "Your word is a lamp to my feet and a light to my path" (Psalm 119:105).
- "The people who walked in darkness have seen a great light; those who dwelt in a land of deep darkness, on them has light shone" (Isaiah 9:2).
- "You are the light of the world. A city set on a hill cannot be hidden" (Matthew 5:14).
- "But if we walk in the light, as he is in the light, we have fellowship with one another, and the blood of Jesus his Son cleanses us from all sin" (1 John 1:7).

God gave us light so that we can live. He gave us the light of Christ so that we can understand and appreciate his goodness. In everything.

Passage: Verse in Context — Genesis 1:3–5

And God said, "Let there be light," and there was light. And God saw that the light was good. And God separated the light from the darkness. God called the light Day, and the darkness he called Night. And there was evening and there was morning, the first day.

Related Passage — John 1:1–10

In the beginning was the Word, and the Word was with God, and the Word was God. He was in the beginning with God. All things were made through him, and without him was not any thing made that was made. In him was life, and the life was the light of men. The light shines in the darkness, and the darkness has not overcome it.

There was a man sent from God, whose name was John. He came as a witness, to bear witness about the light, that all might believe through him. He was not the light, but came to bear witness about the light.

The true light, which gives light to everyone, was coming into the world. He was in the world, and the world was made through him, yet the world did not know him.

Questions for Reflection and Application

- Why do you think that John refers to life as "the light of men"? Why does he refer to Jesus as the "true light"?
- Do you take the benefits of sunlight for granted? What are some other things that you take for granted?
- What strength can you draw from the reminder that God created everything, including light, without which there would be no life on earth?
- How is God calling you to live differently starting today?

God, you are the maker of light and, like light, you are essential in my life. Amen.

THE IMAGE OF GOD

God created man in his own image, in the image of God
he created him; male and female he created them.
—Genesis 1:27

What does it mean to be made in the image of God? In the Merriam-Webster dictionary, the third definition of the word "image" (exact likeness, or semblance) uses Genesis 1:27 as the example of the definition. So being made in the image of God means being made in the exact likeness or semblance of God. The Hebrew root of the Latin phrase for image of God, *imago Dei*, means shadow or likeness of God.

The word "semblance" usually refers to external appearance, but the Bible tells us that no one has seen God. (See Exodus 33:20, John 1:18, and 1 John 4:12.) When he spoke to the woman at the well in Samaria (John 4), Jesus said that God is "spirit", and a spirit does not have physical attributes. The attributes of God that we bear, therefore, must be unseen qualities of God.

In his book *About You: Fully Human, Fully Alive,* author Dick Staub lists some of those qualities:

- **Creative:** Every person has the desire and ability to make things.
- **Spiritual:** Every person has a spiritual nature that, while unseen, is just as real as our physical nature.
- **Communicative:** God spoke creation into existence, and our ability to communicate reflects God's ability to communicate.
- **Intelligent:** Just as God has a logical, orderly mind, each of us has a mind that enables us to think and learn.
- **Relational:** In Genesis 1:26, God says, "Let us make man in our image." This reveals a relational interaction in the very nature of God. We were created for relationship because it "is not good that the man should be alone" (Genesis 2:18).
- **Morally responsible:** Just as there are natural laws that govern the universe, universal moral laws govern human behavior, and these laws are written on our hearts.

You are created in the image of a creative, spiritual, communicative, intelligent, relational, and moral God.

Passage: Verse in Context — Genesis 1:24–28, 31

And God said, "Let the earth bring forth living creatures according to their kinds—livestock and creeping things and beasts of the earth according to their kinds." And it was so. And God made the beasts of the earth according to their kinds and the livestock according to their kinds, and everything that creeps on the ground according to its kind. And God saw that it was good.

Then God said, "Let us make man in our image, after our likeness. And let them have dominion over the fish of the sea and over the birds of the heavens and over the livestock and over all the earth and over every creeping thing that creeps on the earth." So God created man in his own image, in the image of God he created him; male and female he created them.

And God blessed them. And God said to them, "Be fruitful and multiply and fill the earth and subdue it, and have dominion over the fish of the sea and over the birds of the heavens and over every living thing that moves on the earth." ... And God saw everything that he had made, and behold, it was very good. And there was evening and there was morning, the sixth day.

Questions for Reflection and Application

- Why did God make you in his image?
- What are some of your creative qualities? Relational qualities? How do these reflect the image of God?
- Do you think of yourself as a spiritual being? How are you strengthening that aspect of you?
- When are you most effective at communicating? Verbally or in writing? One-on-one or in a large group? Through music? Through visual arts? Do you leverage your communication strengths when you communicate with God?
- Do other people see you reflecting God's image? What are some things you can do to make that happen more often?

Father, thank you for making me a quality creation by bestowing upon me your qualities. Amen.

WORKING TO THRIVE

God saw everything that he had made, and behold, it was very good.
And there was evening and there was morning, the sixth day.
—Genesis 1:31

During the six days of creation recorded in the first chapter of Genesis, God creates, reflects on what he just created, and sees that each created thing is "good." The last thing that God creates is people. After creating us, God reflects on his entire creation and sees that it is "very good."

We are the pinnacle of God's creation. God created the earth for us, so that we would not only survive but also thrive here. Thriving, however, requires effort on our part. It requires work. This is clear from what happened right after God created us.

God gave us a mandate to "fill the earth" and "subdue it" by exercising our dominion over all animals (v. 28). God created the earth to have everything that we need, but nature can be wild, harsh, and unforgiving. Unless we subdue the earth, we may not thrive or even survive.

Even though God put Adam and Eve in a paradise called the garden of Eden, he instructed them to work or cultivate it and to keep or preserve it. The garden had every tree that was good for food and, even with no effort by Adam and Eve, the garden probably could have sustained Adam and Eve and their children for years and years. So why did God instruct them to cultivate it? God foresaw that Adam and Eve would sin, and so their farming efforts in the garden would serve as good training for farming in less hospitable places in the future.

Just as God created the earth for us, he created work for us so that we would maintain the earth for our benefit and for the benefit of the other created beings who share the earth with us. We are not supposed to endure work but to enjoy it.

Work is a good gift from a very good God. He's the best boss you'll ever have.

Passage: Verse in Context — Genesis 1:28–31

And God blessed them. And God said to them, "Be fruitful and multiply and fill the earth and subdue it, and have dominion over the fish of the sea and over the birds of the heavens and over every living thing that moves on the earth." And God said, "Behold, I have given you every plant yielding seed that is on the face of all the earth, and every tree with seed in its fruit. You shall have them for food. And to every beast of the earth and to every bird of the heavens and to everything that creeps on the earth, everything that has the breath of life, I have given every green plant for food." And it was so. And God saw everything that he had made, and behold, it was very good. And there was evening and there was morning, the sixth day.

Related Passage — Genesis 2:15–17

The LORD God took the man and put him in the garden of Eden to work it and keep it. And the LORD God commanded the man, saying, "You may surely eat of every tree of the garden, but of the tree of the knowledge of good and evil you shall not eat, for in the day that you eat of it you shall surely die."

Questions for Reflection and Application

- Why did God want people to fill the earth and subdue it?
- Why did God make Adam work the garden of Eden and keep it? Wouldn't the garden have thrived without Adam's efforts?
- Do you feel that you are working to thrive or working to survive? If the latter, then what do you need to do to change your perspective on the work that you are doing?
- Do you think that you will work in heaven? If so, then what kind of work will you do? How are you training for that work now? How should you be?

Father, let my hands produce good work, glorifying the One whose work is good. Amen.

A PERFECT MATCH

Then the LORD God said, "It is not good that the man should be alone; I will make him a helper fit for him."

—Genesis 2:18

Adam began his life in a paradise. The temperature was perfect. There was "every tree that is pleasant to the sight and good for food" (v. 9). There were animals galore, and none was a threat because, according to the first chapter of Genesis, all animals were vegetarians.

There was just one thing missing: a "helper" who was "fit" for Adam.

The Hebrew word translated as "helper" in this verse is *ezer*. While we may think of a "helper" as someone who is subordinate or inferior to the one helped, the word *ezer* in the Hebrew Bible is used only in reference to a superior or an equal. Nearly all uses of the word are in reference to God in his role as savior, rescuer, or protector.

The Hebrew word translated as "fit" is *kenegdo*. Its meaning is not entirely clear, primarily because it is not used elsewhere in the Bible. When it is used in Rabbinic texts, it applies to things that are like one another, so it means "similar." It also can mean "according to," "corresponding to," or "suitable for," as in an appropriate or complementary match.

Adam was created for relationship, but there was no being with whom he could have a suitable relationship. He needed someone who could rescue him from his life of solitude and complete him. Someone who was different but equal. Someone who had strengths where he had weaknesses and weaknesses where he had strengths. His ideal complement.

That someone was Eve. Like Adam, she was created in God's image. (See Genesis 1:27.) She was of the same "kind" as Adam. Just as she completed Adam, he completed her.

When Adam laid eyes on Eve for the first time, he was overjoyed: "This at last is bone of my bones and flesh of my flesh; she shall be called Woman, because she was taken out of Man" (Genesis 2:23).

It was the perfect match. A match made in heaven.

Passage: Verse in Context — Genesis 2:18–23

Then the LORD God said, "It is not good that the man should be alone; I will make him a helper fit for him." Now out of the ground the LORD God had formed every beast of the field and every bird of the heavens and brought them to the man to see what he would call them. And whatever the man called every living creature, that was its name. The man gave names to all livestock and to the birds of the heavens and to every beast of the field. But for Adam there was not found a helper fit for him.

So the LORD God caused a deep sleep to fall upon the man, and while he slept took one of his ribs and closed up its place with flesh. And the rib that the LORD God had taken from the man he made into a woman and brought her to the man. Then the man said, "This at last is bone of my bones and flesh of my flesh; she shall be called Woman, because she was taken out of Man."

Questions for Reflection and Application

- In general, what are the primary strengths of men? How do these strengths "fill in the gaps" for women and help women overcome their weaknesses?
- In general, what are the primary weaknesses of men? What strengths do women possess that "fill in the gaps" for men and help men overcome their weaknesses?
- If you are married, then what are some areas where you can do a better job of being your wife's *ezer*, or helper? How can you make the team of your wife and you stronger and more effective?
- If you are not married, then what qualities would make a woman your ideal *ezer*? How can you determine if a woman possesses those qualities?

Father, I appreciate the order you have placed in creation, primarily in relationships. Amen.

CLEAVING

> Therefore a man shall leave his father and his mother and hold fast to his wife,
> and they shall become one flesh.
>
> —*Genesis 2:24*

The Hebrew verb *dabaq*, here translated as "hold fast," can be translated as "cling" or "cleave." The latter term is one that we don't use much these days but, because "cleave" rhymes with "leave," you may hear this verse referred to as the "leave and cleave" verse.

What does it mean for a man to hold fast or cling to his wife? It certainly can make for an interesting mental picture!

Let's take a closer look at the Hebrew verb *dabaq*, which is used in fifty-two other Old Testament verses. Here are some examples (with the translation of *dabaq* in italics):

- "You shall fear the LORD your God. You shall serve him and *hold fast* to him, and by his name you shall swear" (Deuteronomy 10:20).
- "You shall *cling* to the LORD your God just as you have done to this day" (Joshua 23:8).
- "Do not go to glean in another field or leave this one, but *keep close* to my young women" (Ruth 2:8b).
- "My strength is dried up like a potsherd, and my tongue *sticks* to my jaws; you lay me in the dust of death" (Psalm 22:15).
- "My soul *clings* to you; your right hand upholds me" (Psalm 63:8).
- "I *cling* to your testimonies, O LORD; let me not be put to shame!" (Psalm 119:31).

Sometimes holding fast or clinging is almost involuntary. At other times, it requires a decision or act of will.

That certainly is true in marriage. Sometimes you are drawn to your wife and have a deep longing to feel the unity that only comes in marriage. At other times, holding fast to your wife requires a significant effort to drown out the din of voices telling you to leave.

There is beauty in all types of holding fast, from magnetic attraction to staying together because of a vow. In the end, it doesn't matter why you cleave … only that you do.

Passage: Verse in Context — Genesis 2:21–25

So the LORD God caused a deep sleep to fall upon the man, and while he slept took one of his ribs and closed up its place with flesh. And the rib that the LORD God had taken from the man he made into a woman and brought her to the man. Then the man said, "This at last is bone of my bones and flesh of my flesh; she shall be called Woman, because she was taken out of Man." Therefore a man shall leave his father and his mother and hold fast to his wife, and they shall become one flesh. And the man and his wife were both naked and were not ashamed.

Related Passage — Matthew 19:3–8

And Pharisees came up to him and tested him by asking, "Is it lawful to divorce one's wife for any cause?" He answered, "Have you not read that he who created them from the beginning made them male and female, and said, 'Therefore a man shall leave his father and his mother and hold fast to his wife, and the two shall become one flesh'? So they are no longer two but one flesh. What therefore God has joined together, let not man separate." They said to him, "Why then did Moses command one to give a certificate of divorce and to send her away?" He said to them, "Because of your hardness of heart Moses allowed you to divorce your wives, but from the beginning it was not so."

Questions for Reflection and Application

- What does it mean for a husband to cleave to his wife?
- Other than his father and mother, what are some other things that a man must leave so that he can cleave to his wife? If you are married, have you left all of those things completely? If not, what steps can you take to leave them?
- What are some of the reasons that Christian couples give for why they get divorced? Do you think these reasons are valid? Why or why not?
- What are three things that you can do to strengthen your marriage or, if you are not married, the marriages of those closest to you?

Father, even when I feel like leaving, help me to hold on. Amen.

THE PROMISE OF THE RAINBOW

When I bring clouds over the earth and the bow is seen in the clouds, I will remember my covenant that is between me and you and every living creature of all flesh. And the waters shall never again become a flood to destroy all flesh.

—*Genesis 9:14–15*

Chapter 6 of Genesis records the fact that, because people everywhere were hopelessly wicked, God decided to destroy "all flesh" through "a flood of waters upon the earth." Only one man, Noah, found favor with God, and so God decided to spare Noah, his wife, their three sons, and their son's wives. To protect Noah's family and every species of land animal from the flood that was to come, God instructed Noah to build a massive ark (450 feet x 75 feet x 45 feet) with three decks, a roof, and one door.

It took Noah and his family at least several decades to build the ark. When the task was finally complete, with Noah and his family, and all of the animals onboard, God shut the ark's door and unleashed the flood. The "fountains of the great deep burst forth" (7:11), and rain fell for forty days and forty nights.

After the rain stopped, it took another 110 days before the waters subsided enough for the ark to come to rest "on the mountains of Ararat" (8:4). It took over seven additional months before the inhabitants of the ark were able to leave the ark and find homes on dry land.

It had been over a year since the flood began. God knew that Noah and his family were not just overwhelmed but also terrified. So God made them a promise: there would never be another flood. The sign of that promise was a rainbow.

The next time you see a rainbow, think about the promise that God made to Noah and his family, and the promises that God has made to you.

God keeps his promises.

Passage: Verse in Context — Genesis 9:1, 8–16

And God blessed Noah and his sons and said to them, "Be fruitful and multiply and fill the earth." …

Then God said to Noah and to his sons with him, "Behold, I establish my covenant with you and your offspring after you, and with every living creature that is with you, the birds, the livestock, and every beast of the earth with you, as many as came out of the ark; it is for every beast of the earth. I establish my covenant with you, that never again shall all flesh be cut off by the waters of the flood, and never again shall there be a flood to destroy the earth." And God said, "This is the sign of the covenant that I make between me and you and every living creature that is with you, for all future generations: I have set my bow in the cloud, and it shall be a sign of the covenant between me and the earth. When I bring clouds over the earth and the bow is seen in the clouds, I will remember my covenant that is between me and you and every living creature of all flesh. And the waters shall never again become a flood to destroy all flesh. When the bow is in the clouds, I will see it and remember the everlasting covenant between God and every living creature of all flesh that is on the earth." God said to Noah, "This is the sign of the covenant that I have established between me and all flesh that is on the earth."

Questions for Reflection and Application

- Does the flood seem out of character for God? Why or why not?
- Have you ever seen something that you knew was a clear sign from God? If so, what was it? If not, do you think that you have missed signals from God, or do you think that God has not given you a sign?
- What promises has God made to you? What evidence do you have that God keeps the promises that he makes to you?
- In what situations is it difficult for you to feel that God is looking out for you? What should you do in those situations?

God, whether I'm in a flood or under a rainbow, help me to remember that you keep your promises always. Amen.

PROMISING THE IMPOSSIBLE

And he brought him outside and said, "Look toward heaven,
and number the stars, if you are able to number them." Then he said to him,
"So shall your offspring be." And he believed the LORD,
and he counted it to him as righteousness.

—Genesis 15:5–6

Have you ever been in a rural area or on a ship—anywhere far from city lights—and looked up at the sky on a clear night? How many stars could you see? Could you count them all? Probably not.

In Genesis 15, God's message to Abraham—then called Abram—was clear: you'll have more descendants, or offspring, than you can count. But Abraham had no children. And he and his wife, Sarah—then called Sarai—were getting old. Really old.

Abraham was seventy-five the first time God promised him that he would be the father of a "great nation" (see Genesis 12). Now when God reassured him by showing him the stars, he was eighty-five. Sarah was ten years younger. The couple had been trying for decades to have a child. It was becoming clear that, even if Sarah was not past her childbearing years, she was barren.

Yet Abraham believed God. Soon after that, Sarah convinced Abraham that because she was barren, he should have a child through her servant Hagar. He listened and Hagar bore a son, Ishmael. When Abraham was ninety-nine, however, God announced that the chosen son was not Ishmael but Isaac, whom Sarah would bear in the next year.

Abraham laughed at the news. And when it was repeated where Sarah could hear it, she laughed too. God knew they would laugh. That's why God said that their son should be named Isaac, which means "laughter."

Sometimes God promises the impossible. He knows that we will find it difficult to believe and trust that he will deliver. When Sarah laughed, God responded, "Is anything too hard for the LORD?" (18:14). The word translated as "hard" also may be translated as "wonderful."

Is anything too wonderful for God? He keeps his promises … even the impossible ones.

Passage: Verse in Context — Genesis 15:1–6

After these things the word of the LORD came to Abram in a vision: "Fear not, Abram, I am your shield; your reward shall be very great." But Abram said, "O LORD God, what will you give me, for I continue childless, and the heir of my house is Eliezer of Damascus?" And Abram said, "Behold, you have given me no offspring, and a member of my household will be my heir." And behold, the word of the LORD came to him: "This man shall not be your heir; your very own son shall be your heir." And he brought him outside and said, "Look toward heaven, and number the stars, if you are able to number them." Then he said to him, "So shall your offspring be." And he believed the LORD, and he counted it to him as righteousness.

Related Passage — Romans 4:18, 20–25

In hope he believed against hope, that he should become the father of many nations, as he had been told, "So shall your offspring be." … No unbelief made him waver concerning the promise of God, but he grew strong in his faith as he gave glory to God, fully convinced that God was able to do what he had promised. That is why his faith was "counted to him as righteousness." But the words "it was counted to him" were not written for his sake alone, but for ours also. It will be counted to us who believe in him who raised from the dead Jesus our Lord, who was delivered up for our trespasses and raised for our justification.

Questions for Reflection and Application

- What promises has God made to you in the Bible? Think of three such promises that seem completely outlandish. Why does it seem ridiculous that God would keep those promises?
- Has God made you any promises outside of those recorded in the Bible? If so, what were they?
- Has God kept all the promises that he has made to you, or are you still waiting for some of them? How does it feel to wait? Do you ever doubt that God will come through?
- What do you have to do for God to fulfil the promises that he has made to you?

Father, I acknowledge that nothing is impossible when the task is placed in your hands. Amen.

HAGGLING WITH GOD

Then he said, "Oh let not the LORD be angry, and I will speak again
but this once. Suppose ten are found there." He answered,
"For the sake of ten I will not destroy it."
—*Genesis 18:32*

Haggling. Some people are really good at it. They always appear willing to walk away from the deal if it's not to their liking, and they never let the other party know their bottom line.

As recorded in Genesis 18, God decided that the people of Sodom and Gomorrah were so wicked that the two cities must be destroyed. The problem for Abraham was that his nephew, Lot, and Lot's family, lived in Sodom. So Abraham decided to haggle with God over the fate of Sodom.

Abraham started with this statement: "Will you indeed sweep away the righteous with the wicked? Suppose there are fifty righteous within the city. Will you then sweep away the place and not spare it for the fifty righteous who are in it? Far be it from you to do such a thing, to put the righteous to death with the wicked, so that the righteous fare as the wicked! Far be that from you! Shall not the Judge of all the earth do what is just?" (vv. 23–25).

God responded that, if there were fifty righteous people in Sodom, then God would spare the city.

Abraham then repeated his request for forty-five righteous people. Then forty. Then thirty. Then twenty. And finally, ten. Each time God responded that he would spare Sodom if there were that many righteous people living in it.

Abraham probably walked away from the exchange thinking that he was a terrific haggler. But God knew Abraham's bottom line: Abraham was concerned only about Lot and his family, who numbered around ten.

The audacity and effrontery of Abraham's haggling is extraordinary. Why did God ignore it and play along?

God would rather have us be concerned and plead for others, even in an impertinent way, than to have us be silent because of fear or self-centeredness. God looks past our rudeness to see our love.

Passage: Verse in Context — Genesis 18:23–26, 28–32

Then Abraham drew near and said, "Will you indeed sweep away the righteous with the wicked? Suppose there are fifty righteous within the city. Will you then sweep away the place and not spare it for the fifty righteous who are in it? Far be it from you to do such a thing, to put the righteous to death with the wicked, so that the righteous fare as the wicked! Far be that from you! Shall not the Judge of all the earth do what is just?" And the LORD said, "If I find at Sodom fifty righteous in the city, I will spare the whole place for their sake." …

"Suppose five of the fifty righteous are lacking. Will you destroy the whole city for lack of five?" And he said, "I will not destroy it if I find forty-five there." Again he spoke to him and said, "Suppose forty are found there." He answered, "For the sake of forty I will not do it." Then he said, "Oh let not the LORD be angry, and I will speak. Suppose thirty are found there." He answered, "I will not do it, if I find thirty there." He said, "Behold, I have undertaken to speak to the LORD. Suppose twenty are found there." He answered, "For the sake of twenty I will not destroy it." Then he said, "Oh let not the LORD be angry, and I will speak again but this once. Suppose ten are found there." He answered, "For the sake of ten I will not destroy it."

Questions for Reflection and Application

- Think of the last time you tried to bargain with God. What were you trying to get? Was it for yourself or someone else?
- It is common practice to ask others to pray to God on your behalf or on behalf of someone else. Why do we do that? If we get more people to pray for something, then is God more likely to listen and respond?
- Can you change God's mind, to get God to make a different decision or take a different action? Why or why not?

God, thank you for looking past my impertinence to see my heart. Help me to be obedient to your plan for my life rather than trying to negotiate my own plan. Amen.

REDEEMING AN EVIL ACT

As for you, you meant evil against me, but God meant it for good,
to bring it about that many people should be kept alive, as they are today.
—*Genesis 50:20*

Joseph's ten older brothers hated him. Hated the fact that their father, Jacob, loved him more than each of them. Hated that he had dreams where they served him. Hated his arrogance in telling them his dreams.

Joseph's brothers hated him enough to kill him. And the brothers were about to kill him when Reuben, the oldest, persuaded them to throw Joseph into a pit instead. Before Reuben could rescue Joseph however, the other brothers sold him into slavery.

Joseph's next twenty years were quite an odyssey:

- He was purchased by Potiphar, the captain of the guard for Pharaoh.
- He was made the overseer of Potiphar's house, in charge of everything.
- He was falsely accused of attempted rape by Potiphar's wife and thrown in prison.
- He was put in charge of all the other prisoners.
- He interpreted the dreams of the king's imprisoned cupbearer and baker. Once freed from prison, the cupbearer forgot to tell Pharaoh about Joseph.
- Two years later, when Pharaoh wanted his dreams interpreted, the cupbearer mentioned Joseph to Pharaoh. Joseph interpreted the dreams: after seven years of plenty, there would be seven years of famine.
- Pharaoh made Joseph second-in-command; Joseph oversaw preparations for the famine and then, when it struck, distribution of stored food.

Among those who came to Egypt for food during the famine were Joseph's brothers; the ones who had sold him into slavery when he was seventeen; the ones who robbed him of twenty years with a father who adored him.

Joseph could have done anything to his brothers to punish them, but instead he forgave them, reconciled with them, and unified a dysfunctional family in the process. When Jacob died, Joseph's brothers feared that Joseph would hate them and pay them back for all the evil that they did to him. Joseph's response: God took your evil and made it good.

God can redeem anything.

Passage: Verse in Context — Genesis 49:1–2, 26; 50:15–21

Then Jacob called his sons and said, "Gather yourselves together, that I may tell you what shall happen to you in days to come. Assemble and listen, O sons of Jacob, listen to Israel your father. …The blessings of your father are mighty beyond the blessings of my parents, up to the bounties of the everlasting hills. May they be on the head of Joseph, and on the brow of him who was set apart from his brothers." …

When Joseph's brothers saw that their father was dead, they said, "It may be that Joseph will hate us and pay us back for all the evil that we did to him." So they sent a message to Joseph, saying, "Your father gave this command before he died: 'Say to Joseph, "Please forgive the transgression of your brothers and their sin, because they did evil to you."'" And now, please forgive the transgression of the servants of the God of your father." Joseph wept when they spoke to him. His brothers also came and fell down before him and said, "Behold, we are your servants." But Joseph said to them, "Do not fear, for am I in the place of God? As for you, you meant evil against me, but God meant it for good, to bring it about that many people should be kept alive, as they are today. So do not fear; I will provide for you and your little ones." Thus he comforted them and spoke kindly to them.

Questions for Reflection and Application

- Joseph's life was a rollercoaster: apple of his father's eye, then sold into slavery; head of Potiphar's house, then imprisoned on false charges; on the verge of getting out, then stuck in prison indefinitely. How often does your life feel like a rollercoaster? Right now, is it on the upswing or heading down?
- Where was God when Joseph was sold into slavery? When Joseph was framed and imprisoned? Why didn't God intervene and help Joseph? Or did he?
- Why do bad things happen to faithful followers of God?
- How was Joseph able to forgive his brothers for their evil act against him?

Lord God, whenever the enemy plans to harm one of your own, you transform the enemy's tactics into something good. Amen.

GOD COMES THROUGH

The Lord is my strength and my song,
and he has become my salvation.
—*Exodus 15:2a*

For hundreds of years, the descendants of Abraham, Isaac, and Jacob—whom God renamed Israel—were slaves in Egypt.

It had started well enough. Israel, his children, and their families had moved to Egypt during the great famine, when Israel's favorite son, Joseph, was second-in-command to the king of Egypt. After Joseph died, however, "there arose a new king over Egypt, who did not know Joseph" (1:8). The king feared that the people of Israel would overwhelm Egypt, so he decreed that they would "work as slaves" (v. 13). And so they did—generation after generation.

Finally, God responded to the cries of the Israelites and selected Moses, a descendant of Levi, to "bring my people, the children of Israel, out of Egypt" (3:10). Moses was a reluctant leader, so God promised Moses that his "wonders" would force Pharaoh to release the Israelites (v. 20).

God unleashed nine plagues on Egypt, but Pharaoh refused to let the Israelites go. Then God sent a final plague that would kill the firstborn son in every non-Israelite household, including Pharaoh's, and the king of Egypt finally relented. After the people of Israel left Egypt, Pharaoh changed his mind. He took his army, including six hundred chariots, and pursued the Israelites.

The Israelites panicked, but not Moses, who said, "Fear not, stand firm, and see the salvation of the Lord, which he will work for you today" (14:13).

And God came through. The people of Israel crossed through the Red Sea "on dry ground, the waters being a wall to them on their right hand and on their left" (v. 22). When Pharaoh's army tried to cross, the walls of water collapsed, and every man in the army drowned.

On the other side of the Red Sea, Moses and the people of Israel praised God for saving them from the Egyptian army. We can praise God every day for saving us from an even worse fate.

Passage: Verse in Context — Exodus 14:26–29; 15:1–2, 4–7

Then the LORD said to Moses, "Stretch out your hand over the sea, that the water may come back upon the Egyptians, upon their chariots, and upon their horsemen." So Moses stretched out his hand over the sea, and the sea returned to its normal course when the morning appeared. And as the Egyptians fled into it, the LORD threw the Egyptians into the midst of the sea. The waters returned and covered the chariots and the horsemen; of all the host of Pharaoh that had followed them into the sea, not one of them remained. But the people of Israel walked on dry ground through the sea, the waters being a wall to them on their right hand and on their left. …

Then Moses and the people of Israel sang this song to the LORD, saying, "I will sing to the LORD, for he has triumphed gloriously; the horse and his rider he has thrown into the sea. The LORD is my strength and my song, and he has become my salvation; this is my God, and I will praise him, my father's God, and I will exalt him. …

"Pharaoh's chariots and his host he cast into the sea, and his chosen officers were sunk in the Red Sea. The floods covered them; they went down into the depths like a stone. Your right hand, O LORD, glorious in power, your right hand, O LORD, shatters the enemy. In the greatness of your majesty you overthrow your adversaries; you send out your fury; it consumes them like stubble."

Questions for Reflection and Application

- In what situations do you allow God to be your strength? When do you grab the steering wheel yourself?
- What does it mean for God to be your song, outside of singing songs and hymns in a Sunday worship service?
- In chapter 6 of Romans, Paul says that we're either slaves to sin or slaves to obedience. Bob Dylan's song "Gotta Serve Somebody" has a similar theme. Do you agree with this idea?
- What does it mean for Jesus to be your salvation? How do you live it out?

Almighty God, you freed the Israelites from bondage in Egypt, and you have freed me from bondage to sin. I praise you! Amen.

SMASHING TABLETS

The Lord said to Moses, "Cut for yourself two tablets
of stone like the first, and I will write on the tablets the words
that were on the first tablets, which you broke."

—*Exodus 34:1*

God was really angry with the Israelites. So was Moses.

After God miraculously freed his people from slavery in Egypt, the Israelites responded by complaining. Endlessly. Some even said that they longed to go back to Egypt because, while they were slaves there, the food was really top-notch.

When they reached Mount Sinai, and Moses went up on the mountain to talk to God, the Israelites decided to make a new god to take the place of the one who hadn't done much for them lately.

God gave the Law to Moses, including "two tablets of the testimony, tablets of stone, written with the finger of God" (31:18). Then God told Moses that the Israelites had corrupted themselves by worshiping a golden calf and needed to feel God's wrath. Moses begged God to reconsider and God agreed. But when Moses saw for himself what was going on in the camp, "his anger burned hot" (32:19). He burned the calf, ground it to powder, put the powder in water, and made the people drink it. Moses commanded the sons of Levi to kill anyone who was not on God's side, and 3,000 men died.

But first Moses broke the stone tablets—the ones written with the finger of God.

Anger can make you do things that you regret, and anger can lead to sin. But anger is not bad, in and of itself. Even Jesus got angry. In Ephesians 4:26, Paul writes, "Be angry and do not sin; do not let the sun go down on your anger." The first two words are a command: Be angry! Just don't sin in your anger.

God didn't want Moses to break the tablets. But God understood why Moses was angry. So God made Moses and the people of Israel new tablets.

When you sin in anger, repent. God will take care of the rest.

Passage: Verse in Context — Exodus 32:15–20; 34:1; 6–7

Then Moses turned and went down from the mountain with the two tablets of the testimony in his hand, tablets that were written on both sides; on the front and on the back they were written. The tablets were the work of God, and the writing was the writing of God, engraved on the tablets. When Joshua heard the noise of the people as they shouted, he said to Moses, "There is a noise of war in the camp." But he said, "It is not the sound of shouting for victory, or the sound of the cry of defeat, but the sound of singing that I hear." And as soon as he came near the camp and saw the calf and the dancing, Moses' anger burned hot, and he threw the tablets out of his hands and broke them at the foot of the mountain. He took the calf that they had made and burned it with fire and ground it to powder and scattered it on the water and made the people of Israel drink it. …

The LORD said to Moses, "Cut for yourself two tablets of stone like the first, and I will write on the tablets the words that were on the first tablets, which you broke. … The LORD passed before him and proclaimed, "The LORD, the LORD, a God merciful and gracious, slow to anger, and abounding in steadfast love and faithfulness, keeping steadfast love for thousands, forgiving iniquity and transgression and sin, but who will by no means clear the guilty, visiting the iniquity of the fathers on the children and the children's children, to the third and the fourth generation."

Questions for Reflection and Application

- What do you do when you are angry? Explode? Try to cover it? Does it depend on who's there? What do you wish that you did when you are angry?
- What makes God angry?
- Think about the last few times you got angry. Was it because of something that would make God angry? If not, then why were you angry?
- Anger is considered a "secondary" emotion because the real issue is something else. Have you ever explored why you get angry? If not, what would cause you to explore that?

Father, I admit that my anger has caused me to sin. Forgive me and heal those whom I have hurt. Amen.

MAGIC IN YOUR TOUCH

He shall lay his hand on the head of the burnt offering,
and it shall be accepted for him to make atonement for him.
—*Leviticus 1:4*

There is power in touch.

Burnt offerings were a big deal to the Israelites because they were a big deal to God. If you wanted to offer a bull, then you had to bring one without blemish to the meeting tent, and the priest would follow specific steps in sacrificing that bull. Before he did, however, you had to lay your hand on the head of the bull. If you didn't, then the offering would not atone for your sins.

We don't offer burnt offerings anymore, but we still recognize the power of laying hands on others. In 1985, the alternative-rock band Thompson Twins scored a hit with the song "Lay Your Hands on Me." The song speaks of chasing dreams that never materialize, running out of inspiration, and feeling that everything is pointless until you feel the magic in another person's touch and are inspired to try again.

Song cowriter Tom Bailey, who was in a church choir as a youth, said that the writing team was influenced by healing festivals and other religious rituals that involve the laying of hands. "I've always been very fond of the kind of layered metaphor where the song can be about one thing but also about another … That's part of a really ancient and noble tradition of religious writing of music. Typically, people talk about their love for God in a religious song, but what they're also saying is that they love someone human. It's a way of evoking that immense emotional weight into a song."[3]

Most people will never feel the direct touch of God on this earth. That's where we come in. As Paul explains in 1 Corinthians 12, each of us is part of the body of Christ. We can be the hands of Jesus to someone in need, and others can return the favor when we are in need.

Oh, lay your hands.

Passage: Verse in Context — Leviticus 1:1–9

The LORD called Moses and spoke to him from the tent of meeting, saying, "Speak to the people of Israel and say to them, When any one of you brings an offering to the LORD, you shall bring your offering of livestock from the herd or from the flock.

"If his offering is a burnt offering from the herd, he shall offer a male without blemish. He shall bring it to the entrance of the tent of meeting, that he may be accepted before the LORD. He shall lay his hand on the head of the burnt offering, and it shall be accepted for him to make atonement for him. Then he shall kill the bull before the LORD, and Aaron's sons the priests shall bring the blood and throw the blood against the sides of the altar that is at the entrance of the tent of meeting. Then he shall flay the burnt offering and cut it into pieces, and the sons of Aaron the priest shall put fire on the altar and arrange wood on the fire. And Aaron's sons the priests shall arrange the pieces, the head, and the fat, on the wood that is on the fire on the altar; but its entrails and its legs he shall wash with water. And the priest shall burn all of it on the altar, as a burnt offering, a food offering with a pleasing aroma to the LORD."

Related Passage — Hosea 6:6

"For I desire steadfast love and not sacrifice, the knowledge of God rather than burnt offerings."

Questions for Reflection and Application

- If close friends were to pray for you, would you want them to lay hands on you? Why or why not? What do you think your friends would prefer if you were praying for them?
- When you were growing up, did your dad show you affection through touch— hugs, arm around shoulder, back-slaps, and so on? How has your relationship with your dad affected your relationship with your heavenly Father?
- Jesus healed people in many different ways. Sometimes he simply spoke; other times, he touched them to heal them. Why do you think he varied his healing approaches?

Father, you touch my life in so many ways. May I touch those around me as I serve as the hands and feet of Christ. Amen.

SIBLING RIVALRY

"You shall not take vengeance or bear a grudge against the sons of your own people, but you shall love your neighbor as yourself: I am the Lord."

—*Leviticus 19:18*

Fights between siblings have been going on since Adam and Eve's first son killed their second. Not a great start.

A 2006 article in *Time* explores the role of siblings in shaping how we think and act:

From the time they are born, our brothers and sisters are our collaborators and co-conspirators, our role models and cautionary tales. …

"In general," says psychologist Daniel Shaw of the University of Pittsburgh, "parents serve the same big-picture role as doctors on grand rounds. Siblings are like the nurses on the ward. They're there every day." All that proximity breeds an awful lot of intimacy—and an awful lot of friction … sibs between 3 and 7 years old engage in some kind of conflict 3.5 times an hour. Kids in the 2-to-4 age group top out at 6.3—or more than one clash every 10 minutes, according to a Canadian study. "Getting along with a sister or brother," Kramer says dryly, "can be a frustrating experience."

But as much as all the fighting can set parents' hair on end, there's a lot of learning going on too, specifically about how conflicts, once begun, can be settled. … "Siblings have a socializing effect on one another," Shaw says. … "Unlike a relationship with friends, you're stuck with your sibs. You learn to negotiate things day to day."[4]

Brothers and sisters emulate each other, and learning flows up and down the age ladder. How we interact with our siblings affects how we treat our spouses, our friends, and our coworkers. Perhaps that's why Leviticus 19:17 virtually equates *brother* with *neighbor*—"You shall not hate your brother in your heart, but you shall reason frankly with your neighbor, lest you incur sin because of him."

Loving your neighbor can be tough. But most of us have had plenty of practice.

Passage: Verse in Context — Leviticus 19:13–18

"You shall not oppress your neighbor or rob him. The wages of a hired worker shall not remain with you all night until the morning. You shall not curse the deaf or put a stumbling block before the blind, but you shall fear your God: I am the Lord.

"You shall do no injustice in court. You shall not be partial to the poor or defer to the great, but in righteousness shall you judge your neighbor. You shall not go around as a slanderer among your people, and you shall not stand up against the life of your neighbor: I am the Lord.

"You shall not hate your brother in your heart, but you shall reason frankly with your neighbor, lest you incur sin because of him. You shall not take vengeance or bear a grudge against the sons of your own people, but you shall love your neighbor as yourself: I am the Lord."

Related Passage — Hebrews 11:4

By faith Abel offered to God a more acceptable sacrifice than Cain, through which he was commended as righteous, God commending him by accepting his gifts. And through his faith, though he died, he still speaks.

Questions for Reflection and Application

- When you were growing up, how were your relationships with your siblings, parents, and other family members? How are those relationships today? How have the relationships in your family shaped your relationships outside your family?
- When you were growing up, how well did you know your neighbors? How well do you know them today? Why?
- In today's Leviticus passage, how does God instruct you to treat your brother? Your neighbor? A deaf or blind person? The poor? Why do you think that God concludes each section in Leviticus 19:13–18 with "I am the Lord"?

Lord, give me the patience to love my neighbor as I would, and should, love my brother and sister. Amen.

DEMANDING A BENEDICTION

The LORD bless you and keep you; the LORD
make his face to shine upon you and be gracious to you; the LORD
lift up his countenance upon you and give you peace.
—*Numbers 6:24–26*

A benediction is a blessing. God gave this benediction to bless the people of Israel. Here are two other biblical benedictions that, like the one from Numbers, are often said in church today:

And the peace of God, which surpasses all understanding, will guard your hearts and your minds in Christ Jesus. (Philippians 4:7)

The grace of the Lord Jesus Christ and the love of God and the fellowship of the Holy Spirit be with you all. (2 Corinthians 13:14)

It is always wonderful to receive a blessing from God. But when do you need such a blessing the most? Isn't it when you are at a crossroads, facing a big decision about your future? You want to walk in the path that is pleasing to God. You want his blessing. You need it.

This idea is captured in the song "Benediction," written by Wayne Kirkpatrick and Billy Simon. The singer longs to do the will of God and to follow a course that will be pleasing to God while other Christians are expressing concerns that the singer is on the wrong path. Facing doubts and even reproach, the singer asks God for a benediction, a confirmation that the chosen path is the right one.

Jacob went a step further, demanding a blessing from God. Genesis 32 recounts how Jacob spent an entire night wresting with a "man" who was more than a man. At daybreak, when the man saw that he could not prevail against Jacob, he touched Jacob's hip socket and put Jacob's hip out of joint. Jacob still refused to yield and said, "I will not let you go unless you bless me" (v. 26). The man not only blessed Jacob but gave him a new name, Israel, which means "he strives with God."

God knows that we need his benediction. And he offers it … when we truly seek it.

Passage: Verse in Context — Numbers 6:22–27

The LORD spoke to Moses, saying, "Speak to Aaron and his sons, saying, Thus you shall bless the people of Israel: you shall say to them, 'The LORD bless you and keep you; the LORD make his face to shine upon you and be gracious to you; the LORD lift up his countenance upon you and give you peace.' So shall they put my name upon the people of Israel, and I will bless them."

Related Passage — Hebrews 13:20–21

Now may the God of peace who brought again from the dead our Lord Jesus, the great shepherd of the sheep, by the blood of the eternal covenant, equip you with everything good that you may do his will, working in us that which is pleasing in his sight, through Jesus Christ, to whom be glory forever and ever. Amen.

Related Passage — Jude 24–25

Now to him who is able to keep you from stumbling and to present you blameless before the presence of his glory with great joy, to the only God, our Savior, through Jesus Christ our Lord, be glory, majesty, dominion, and authority, before all time and now and forever. Amen.

Questions for Reflection and Application

- How do you make big decisions in life? What role does God play in your decision-making?
- Do you recognize God's blessing when you receive it or only later in time? Why?
- When is the last time that you felt—no, you *knew*—that God had given you peace? Think about that time. How did it happen? Do you wish that you had that experience more often?
- Why does Jude describe God as the one "who is able to keep you from stumbling"?

God, when I approach hard decisions in life, help me to follow your voice to receive your benediction. Amen.

OUR MIGHTY RESOURCES

"Hear, O Israel: The Lord our God, the Lord is one. You shall love the Lord your God with all your heart and with all your soul and with all your might."
—*Deuteronomy 6:4–5*

We, like the people of Israel, are called to love God with all our heart, soul, and might. Our heart includes not just our emotions but our intellect too, so loving God with all our heart means loving God with all that we have "inside." The Hebrew word translated as "soul" is *nephesh*, which means "living being" or "life." So loving God with all our soul means loving God with everything we have.

Why does God command us to love him with all our might? Don't heart and soul already cover the bases?

Elsewhere in the Old Testament, the word here translated as the noun "might" is used as an adverb meaning "very" or "much." The Greek translation of this word as a noun is "power," and the Aramaic translation is "wealth." Both of these encompass our resources, or what we have at our disposal.

Our resources certainly include our wealth and our physical resources, such as our home and our possessions. We also have less tangible resources such as gifts, talents, education, training, and experiences. The more we develop our resources, the more impact they can have when we use them to love and honor God.

Goliath was a giant who had killed many men in hand-to-hand combat. His coat of mail weighed 125 pounds, and the head of his spear weighed over fifteen pounds. When he challenged the army of Israel to send one man to face him, no one dared, except a young shepherd named David.

Goliath expected David to fight him with his sword and spear, but David employed other resources: a sling, a stone, and a wealth of experience in using both.

God has given us everything, including our resources. Let's use them to love and serve him in every way we can.

Passage: Verse in Context — Deuteronomy 6:1–2, 4–6

"Now this is the commandment—the statutes and the rules—that the LORD your God commanded me to teach you, that you may do them in the land to which you are going over, to possess it, that you may fear the LORD your God, you and your son and your son's son, by keeping all his statutes and his commandments, which I command you, all the days of your life, and that your days may be long. … Hear, O Israel: The LORD our God, the LORD is one. You shall love the LORD your God with all your heart and with all your soul and with all your might. And these words that I command you today shall be on your heart."

Related Passage — Mark 12:28–31

And one of the scribes came up and heard them disputing with one another, and seeing that he answered them well, asked him, "Which commandment is the most important of all?" Jesus answered, "The most important is, 'Hear, O Israel: The Lord our God, the Lord is one. And you shall love the Lord your God with all your heart and with all your soul and with all your mind and with all your strength.' The second is this: 'You shall love your neighbor as yourself.' There is no other commandment greater than these."

Questions for Reflection and Application

- Take a few minutes and do a self-assessment. What are your primary resources? What are your greatest strengths?
- Why do you think God has blessed you with what you have?
- What are some practical ways that you can love God with everything you have? Which of those ways are you doing already? Are you doing them as well and as often as you can? Which things are you not doing or not doing enough, and why?

Lord, you are a God of unlimited resources, and you have seen fit to bless me with a rich set of those resources. Guide my use of these gifts, that they may honor you. Amen.

WHO'S YOUR DADDY?

"But it is because the LORD loves you and is keeping the oath
that he swore to your fathers, that the LORD has brought you out with
a mighty hand and redeemed you."
—*Deuteronomy 7:8a*

We don't know our ancestors very well, but we'd like to know them better.

In 2012, a market research firm estimated the global market for genealogical products and services would rise to $4.3 billion by 2018.[5] Ancestry.com alone grossed over $2 billion in three years (2014–2016) and has spawned more than a half-dozen competitors, all promising to help customers discover more about themselves by finding out about their ancestors:

- With Ancestry.com, you can "trace your family story with a family tree" and use your DNA to "discover what makes you uniquely you" by finding your ethnic mix, distant relatives, and ancestors.
- 23andMe.com uses your DNA to "tell you more about your family history," and offers "two easy ways to discover you."
- Other competing services promise that you can "uncover your heritage," "find out where you really come from," and "find new relatives."

The people of Israel didn't need genealogical products and services. They knew their ancestors well. Unbelievably well. The Gospel of Luke traces the genealogy of Jesus for 76 generations—76 generations!—from his mother, Mary, all the way back to Adam. Clearly, who was in your family tree was of immense importance to the people of Israel. But what was even more important was that all of them were descendants of Abraham, because God had made a covenant with Abraham "to be God to you and to your offspring after you" (Genesis 17:7).

In Deuteronomy 7, God reminds the Israelites that he chose them not because of any qualities they possess but simply because they are descendants of Jacob (Israel), the grandson of Abraham. Because God is faithful, he keeps his covenants.

That's good news for all of us … even those whose family trees have some rotten branches.

Passage: Verse in Context — Deuteronomy 7:6–14a

"For you are a people holy to the LORD your God. The LORD your God has chosen you to be a people for his treasured possession, out of all the peoples who are on the face of the earth. It was not because you were more in number than any other people that the LORD set his love on you and chose you, for you were the fewest of all peoples, but it is because the LORD loves you and is keeping the oath that he swore to your fathers, that the LORD has brought you out with a mighty hand and redeemed you from the house of slavery, from the hand of Pharaoh king of Egypt. Know therefore that the LORD your God is God, the faithful God who keeps covenant and steadfast love with those who love him and keep his commandments, to a thousand generations, and repays to their face those who hate him, by destroying them. He will not be slack with one who hates him. He will repay him to his face. You shall therefore be careful to do the commandment and the statutes and the rules that I command you today.

"And because you listen to these rules and keep and do them, the LORD your God will keep with you the covenant and the steadfast love that he swore to your fathers. He will love you, bless you, and multiply you. He will also bless the fruit of your womb and the fruit of your ground, your grain and your wine and your oil, the increase of your herds and the young of your flock, in the land that he swore to your fathers to give you. You shall be blessed above all peoples."

Questions for Reflection and Application

- Why did God choose the nation of Israel to be his people? Why has God chosen you to be a part of his family?
- For the Jews of the Old Testament, your family history often determined your position in society. How would you feel if that were the case today?
- How much does your family history affect the way that you feel about yourself? How much does your upbringing affect the way you live your life today?

Father, I thank you that, no matter what my biological family looks like, I'm a part of your family. Amen.

GOD'S "SILENCE"

"… for the LORD your God is he who goes with you to fight for you
against your enemies, to give you the victory."
—*Deuteronomy 20:4*

The people of Israel didn't have to look too far to spot their enemies. Those enemies were all around, and Israel battled regularly against them. Chapter 20 of Deuteronomy begins with this: "When you go out to war against your enemies …"

Unless you are serving in the military, you probably will not be going to war anytime soon, right? Wrong. You already are at war. You're fighting a battle against your enemies every day. And just as God was with the Israelites, God goes with you to fight for you against your enemies.

In chapter 10 of the book of Daniel, Daniel has a troubling vision. It's so troubling that Daniel prays to God for understanding and begins to mourn, refusing to anoint himself, eat meat or other choice food, or drink wine. Three weeks later, an angel finally appears and explains the vision.

What took so long? The angel explains that God dispatched him as soon as Daniel prayed, but the angel was ambushed by a "prince of the kingdom of Persia" (v. 13). That prince, or demon, was so strong and the battle was so fierce that after three weeks the angel and the demon were still deadlocked. The archangel Michael had to join the fray and battle the demon so that the angel could go and meet with Daniel.

When we pray, God hears us, and God responds, often immediately. But our requests are coming from the frontlines of a fierce war that has been raging since the dawn of time, and our enemies are doing everything they can to prevent God's response from getting through.

God and his angel armies are with us and fighting for us against our enemies. Sometimes when God seems silent it's because his troops have their hands full.

Hang in there.

Passage: Verse in Context — Deuteronomy 20:1–4

"When you go out to war against your enemies, and see horses and chariots and an army larger than your own, you shall not be afraid of them, for the LORD your God is with you, who brought you up out of the land of Egypt. And when you draw near to the battle, the priest shall come forward and speak to the people and shall say to them, 'Hear, O Israel, today you are drawing near for battle against your enemies: let not your heart faint. Do not fear or panic or be in dread of them, for the LORD your God is he who goes with you to fight for you against your enemies, to give you the victory.' "

Related Passage — Daniel 10:10–14

And behold, a hand touched me and set me trembling on my hands and knees. And he said to me, "O Daniel, man greatly loved, understand the words that I speak to you, and stand upright, for now I have been sent to you." And when he had spoken this word to me, I stood up trembling. Then he said to me, "Fear not, Daniel, for from the first day that you set your heart to understand and humbled yourself before your God, your words have been heard, and I have come because of your words. The prince of the kingdom of Persia withstood me twenty-one days, but Michael, one of the chief princes, came to help me, for I was left there with the kings of Persia, and came to make you understand what is to happen to your people in the latter days. For the vision is for days yet to come."

Questions for Reflection and Application

- How often do you get a quick answer to prayer? How often does it seem like you get no answer?
- How do you feel when you read that there is a war raging in the spiritual realm? Does it feel real? Have you ever witnessed anything that persuaded you that the war is real?
- Where are you most vulnerable? Where is the devil most likely to strike you? What should you do about it?

God, I thank you that you and your angel armies fight for me in battles that I can't see and have trouble imagining. Please give me patience when my prayers seem to go unanswered. Amen.

COURAGE BEGINS AT EIGHTY

"Be strong and courageous. Do not fear or be in dread of them, for it is the
LORD your God who goes with you. He will not leave you or forsake you."
—*Deuteronomy 31:6*

Confronting Pharaoh took a great deal of courage, especially for a man who had demonstrated little courage for the first eighty years of his life.

A Hebrew who was adopted by Pharaoh's daughter, Moses led a privileged life until he was forty years old, when in a fit of rage he killed an Egyptian for beating a Hebrew. Moses fled to Midian, where he became a shepherd, married, and raised a family.

After forty quiet years, God spoke to Moses from a burning bush and told him that he was to lead the Hebrews from slavery to freedom. Moses objected, so God replied that he would be with Moses every step of the way and that Moses would succeed.

But Moses needed more convincing. He asked for God's name, in case people asked him. God gave it to him and told Moses exactly how to respond to convince people that God had called him. Moses insisted that people would not believe him, so God gave him three signs to use to convince others—and to convince Moses—that Moses was chosen by God. Next, Moses objected that he was "not eloquent" but "slow of speech and of tongue" (4:10). When God said that he would give Moses the right words to say, Moses said, "Send someone else" (v. 13). God, getting a little frustrated at this point, agreed to have Aaron accompany his brother Moses as God's spokesman.

Out of objections, Moses agreed to do what God asked. And the rest, as they say, is history.

At the end of his life, when he was 120 years old, Moses looked back on forty years of leading the people of Israel. He had seen God at work every step of the way, and he instructed his people to "be strong and courageous" and trust in God.

Just as he had started to do—reluctantly—when he was eighty.

Passage: Verse in Context — Deuteronomy 31:1–3, 6

So Moses continued to speak these words to all Israel. And he said to them, "I am 120 years old today. I am no longer able to go out and come in. The LORD has said to me, 'You shall not go over this Jordan.' The LORD your God himself will go over before you. He will destroy these nations before you, so that you shall dispossess them, and Joshua will go over at your head, as the LORD has spoken. ... "Be strong and courageous. Do not fear or be in dread of them, for it is the LORD your God who goes with you. He will not leave you or forsake you."

Related Passage — Exodus 4:10–15

But Moses said to the LORD, "Oh, my LORD, I am not eloquent, either in the past or since you have spoken to your servant, but I am slow of speech and of tongue." Then the LORD said to him, "Who has made man's mouth? Who makes him mute, or deaf, or seeing, or blind? Is it not I, the LORD? Now therefore go, and I will be with your mouth and teach you what you shall speak." But he said, "Oh, my LORD, please send someone else." Then the anger of the LORD was kindled against Moses and he said, "Is there not Aaron, your brother, the Levite? I know that he can speak well. Behold, he is coming out to meet you, and when he sees you, he will be glad in his heart. You shall speak to him and put the words in his mouth, and I will be with your mouth and with his mouth and will teach you both what to do."

Questions for Reflection and Application

- Why do most men get "set in their ways" as they get older? Are you more risk-averse than you were when you were younger? Why or why not? Is risk-aversion a sign of maturity or a mask for fear of failing?
- What does God want you doing now? Are you using your abilities/experiences to their fullest, or are you holding back because, like Moses, you're "not the right man for the job?"

Father, the life of Moses truly began when he was an old man. Help me to have courage no matter what my age or what has happened in my past. Amen.

FOUR PROMISES

"It is the LORD who goes before you. He will be with you;
he will not leave you or forsake you. Do not fear or be dismayed."
—*Deuteronomy 31:8*

Moses has led his people to the edge of the Promised Land, but he will not enter it. God has chosen Joshua to lead the Israelites now.

Speaking to Joshua in front of all the people, Moses tells him that God will (1) go before you, (2) be with you, (3) not leave you, and (4) not forsake you. All four promises are important, not just to Joshua but to all the people of Israel.

Going before: The inhabitants of the Promised Land do not want company. The Israelites will have to fight entrenched residents and strong walled cities. But God will lead the way, just as he did when they escaped Egypt.

Going with: Joshua is a new leader being asked to fill the shoes of a giant—Moses—who has led the Israelites for forty years. Moses has succeeded because God has been with him every step of the way, instructing him and guiding him. Now God will go with Joshua, empowering him to lead and giving him, and his people, success.

Not leaving: At the first hint of trouble, the Israelites feared that God has abandoned them. But God has come through every time, and he reminds them that he will always be there for them.

Not forsaking: The Israelites have a hard time staying faithful to God. At Mount Sinai, even after God invited the Israelites to be his treasured people forever and showed them his power and glory, they told Aaron to make them new gods because "we do not know what has become of [Moses]" (Exodus 32:1). But even when they are unfaithful, God does not forsake them in return.

God will go before you. He will go with you. He will not leave you. He will not forsake you.

Passage: Verse in Context — Deuteronomy 31:7–8

Then Moses summoned Joshua and said to him in the sight of all Israel, "Be strong and courageous, for you shall go with this people into the land that the LORD has sworn to their fathers to give them, and you shall put them in possession of it. It is the LORD who goes before you. He will be with you; he will not leave you or forsake you. Do not fear or be dismayed."

Related Passage — Joshua 1:1–5

After the death of Moses the servant of the LORD, the LORD said to Joshua the son of Nun, Moses' assistant, "Moses my servant is dead. Now therefore arise, go over this Jordan, you and all this people, into the land that I am giving to them, to the people of Israel. Every place that the sole of your foot will tread upon I have given to you, just as I promised to Moses. From the wilderness and this Lebanon as far as the great river, the river Euphrates, all the land of the Hittites to the Great Sea toward the going down of the sun shall be your territory. No man shall be able to stand before you all the days of your life. Just as I was with Moses, so I will be with you. I will not leave you or forsake you."

Questions for Reflection and Application

- What promises has God made to you? How and when did he make them?
- How has God gone before you? How has God gone with you?
- Have you had a time in your life where it felt like God had abandoned you? Did he? If not, then why did it feel that way? What did you learn from that experience?
- Do you feel closer to God now than you did five years ago, or do you feel further away? Why?

Almighty God, you go before and with me. You never leave or forsake me. Amen.

THE ROCK

"The Rock, his work is perfect, for all his ways are justice.
A God of faithfulness and without iniquity, just and upright is he."
—*Deuteronomy 32:4*

What is the first thing you think of when you hear the word "rock"? If you were a Jew at the time of Jesus, then you might answer: "foundation." Jesus certainly associated "rock" with "foundation." Here are two examples:

- When Jesus renamed Simon, son of Jonah, he gave him the name Peter, which means "rock," and said, "on this rock I will build my church" (Matthew 16:18).
- In the parable of the wise and foolish builders, the wise man builds his house on a rock, and the foolish man builds his house on sand (7:24–27).

In the Middle East during and before the time of Jesus, houses were built in the dry summer, when the clay soil is extremely hard. An unwise builder might get tired of digging for rock and just use the rock-hard soil as his foundation. But when winter arrived, so did steady rain, and that rain could give the formerly hard soil the consistency of chocolate pudding.[6]

When the Israelites of the Old Testament referred to God as a rock or "the Rock," however, they saw much more than a solid foundation. In Deuteronomy 32:4, "the Rock" is described as perfect, just, faithful, sinless, and upright. Here are some other references to God as "the Rock":

- "The Rock that bore you … the God who gave you birth." (Deuteronomy 32:18)
- "The LORD lives, and blessed be my rock … the rock of my salvation." (2 Samuel 22:47)
- "They remembered that God was their rock … their redeemer." (Psalm 78:35)
- "You have forgotten the God of your salvation … the Rock of your refuge." (Isaiah 17:10)

God offered the people of Israel and us life, salvation, redemption, strength, refuge … everything we need. The Rock. Why build on anything else?

Passage: Verse in Context — Deuteronomy 32:1, 3–4

"Give ear, O heavens, and I will speak, and let the earth hear the words of my mouth. ... For I will proclaim the name of the LORD; ascribe greatness to our God! The Rock, his work is perfect, for all his ways are justice. A God of faithfulness and without iniquity, just and upright is he."

Related Passage — Matthew 16:13–19

Now when Jesus came into the district of Caesarea Philippi, he asked his disciples, "Who do people say that the Son of Man is?" And they said, "Some say John the Baptist, others say Elijah, and others Jeremiah or one of the prophets." He said to them, "But who do you say that I am?" Simon Peter replied, "You are the Christ, the Son of the living God." And Jesus answered him, "Blessed are you, Simon Bar-Jonah! For flesh and blood has not revealed this to you, but my Father who is in heaven. And I tell you, you are Peter, and on this rock I will build my church, and the gates of hell shall not prevail against it. I will give you the keys of the kingdom of heaven, and whatever you bind on earth shall be bound in heaven, and whatever you loose on earth shall be loosed in heaven."

Questions for Reflection and Application

- How do you think that Simon, son of Jonah, felt when Jesus gave him the name that means "rock"? How would you feel?
- Has God given you a name? If so, what is it? If not, what would you like it to be?
- What areas of your life have you built on the foundation of God, the Rock? What areas of your life are built on something else?
- How would you describe the task of moving a part of your life from the wrong foundation to the Rock? How can you do it? Who can help?

Lord, as I struggle through difficult circumstances, keep me grounded on the Rock and not a clay substitute. Amen.

A PREGAME PEP TALK

"Have I not commanded you? Be strong and courageous. Do not be frightened,
and do not be dismayed, for the LORD your God is with you wherever you go."
—*Joshua 1:9*

Moses is dead. God has anointed his long-time assistant, Joshua, as the leader. God commands Joshua to lead his people across the Jordan and into the land that he has promised to give them.

Joshua's head must be swimming. He is replacing the only leader he and the rest of his people had ever known. He will have to coordinate the movements of thousands and thousands of people, ensure that these people and their possessions are protected, ensure that everyone has adequate food and water, and, most importantly, lead the Israelite army into battle against entrenched, unknown enemies. The future of every Israelite is dependent on his performance as a leader.

Like a coach before a big game that is sure to be pressure-packed, God gives a speech that reassures Joshua through repetition. Three times God tells Joshua to be strong and courageous:

- "Be strong and courageous, for you shall cause this people to inherit the land that I swore to their fathers to give them." (v. 6)
- "Be strong and very courageous, being careful to do according to all the law that Moses my servant commanded you. Do not turn from it to the right hand or to the left, that you may have good success wherever you go." (v. 7)
- "Have I not commanded you? Be strong and courageous. Do not be frightened, and do not be dismayed, for the LORD your God is with you wherever you go." (v. 9)

At the end of the speech, Joshua is ready to lead.

What challenges will you face today? Tomorrow? Next week? You may not be sure, but God knows. Are you prepared? Are you ready? Do you have what it takes? If you rely on God, then the answer to each of these questions is "yes." He has commanded you to be strong and courageous, because he is with you wherever you go.

Passage: Verse in Context — Joshua 1:5–11, 16–17a

"No man shall be able to stand before you all the days of your life. Just as I was with Moses, so I will be with you. I will not leave you or forsake you. Be strong and courageous, for you shall cause this people to inherit the land that I swore to their fathers to give them. Only be strong and very courageous, being careful to do according to all the law that Moses my servant commanded you. Do not turn from it to the right hand or to the left, that you may have good success wherever you go. This Book of the Law shall not depart from your mouth, but you shall meditate on it day and night, so that you may be careful to do according to all that is written in it. For then you will make your way prosperous, and then you will have good success. Have I not commanded you? Be strong and courageous. Do not be frightened, and do not be dismayed, for the LORD your God is with you wherever you go."

And Joshua commanded the officers of the people, "Pass through the midst of the camp and command the people, 'Prepare your provisions, for within three days you are to pass over this Jordan to go in to take possession of the land that the LORD your God is giving you to possess.' " …

And they answered Joshua, "All that you have commanded us we will do, and wherever you send us we will go. Just as we obeyed Moses in all things, so we will obey you."

Questions for Reflection and Application

- What did you do to prepare the last time you faced a challenge that you weren't sure you could handle? Did anyone offer you guidance or encouragement? How well did you handle the challenge? Should you have done anything differently?
- What challenges loom on the horizon for you? Do you feel ready for them? What role is God playing in your facing these challenges? How can you rely more on God?
- How did Moses prepare Joshua for taking command? Is there anyone in your life whom you should be preparing for a leadership role? If so, how should you be preparing that person?

Father, help me to tackle today like a well-trained athlete prepared for your plan. Amen.

FEAR OF LEADING

*"That the leaders took the lead in Israel, that the people
offered themselves willingly, bless the LORD!"*
—Judges 5:2

A few generations after Joshua, the people of Israel abandoned God and "did what was evil in the sight of the LORD" (2:11). As a result, Israel began to be overwhelmed by its enemies. God raised up judges to lead the Israelites but, whenever a judge died, the people reverted to corrupt ways and lost whatever ground they had gained.

When the prophetess Deborah became judge, the Israelites were being oppressed by the Canaanites. God told an Israelite named Barak that if he took 10,000 men to battle the Canaanite army, led by a general named Sisera, then the Israelites would win. But Barak was afraid, so he told Deborah, "If you will go with me, I will go, but if you will not go with me, I will not go" (4:8). Deborah agreed but advised Barak that he would not get the glory and "the LORD will sell Sisera into the hand of a woman" (v. 9).

Barak's army was victorious against Sisera's. Fleeing on foot, Sisera ended up at the tent of Jael, the wife of Heber the Kenite. As Sisera slept, Jael took a tent peg and drove it into his temple, killing him. The Israelites continued to battle the Canaanite forces until they destroyed Jabin, king of Canaan.

The song of victory sung by Barak and Deborah begins with the assertion that "the leaders took the lead" (5:2). Deborah certainly did, but Barak had refused to lead unless Deborah went with him and, as a result, all the glory for the victory went to the women—Deborah and Jael—and to God. Barak was okay with that. So were the people of Israel, even centuries later. The "Faith Hall of Fame" in Hebrews chapter 11 lists Barak among those who were faithful.

Feel like you can't do what God wants you to do? Find a trusted friend to go with you. You may not get the glory, but you're not in it for the glory anyway.

Passage: Verse in Context — Judges 4:12–16, 5:1–5

When Sisera was told that Barak the son of Abinoam had gone up to Mount Tabor, Sisera called out all his chariots, 900 chariots of iron, and all the men who were with him, from Harosheth-hagoyim to the river Kishon. And Deborah said to Barak, "Up! For this is the day in which the LORD has given Sisera into your hand. Does not the LORD go out before you?" So Barak went down from Mount Tabor with 10,000 men following him. And the LORD routed Sisera and all his chariots and all his army before Barak by the edge of the sword. And Sisera got down from his chariot and fled away on foot. And Barak pursued the chariots and the army to Harosheth-hagoyim, and all the army of Sisera fell by the edge of the sword; not a man was left. ...

Then sang Deborah and Barak the son of Abinoam on that day: "That the leaders took the lead in Israel, that the people offered themselves willingly, bless the LORD! Hear, O kings; give ear, O princes; to the LORD I will sing; I will make melody to the LORD, the God of Israel. LORD, when you went out from Seir, when you marched from the region of Edom, the earth trembled and the heavens dropped, yes, the clouds dropped water. The mountains quaked before the LORD, even Sinai before the LORD, the God of Israel."

Questions for Reflection and Application

- Why do you think that Barak insisted that Deborah go with him? Do you think that Barak considered Deborah "closer" to God because she was the judge over Israel?
- What are some situations in your life where you let others take the lead when you should be leading? Why do you do that?
- God challenges us to step out of our comfort zones in his service. How is God challenging you to do that right now? How will you respond to the challenge?
- Do you have a trusted friend who can help you be obedient to God's calling? If not, then what is your plan to address that?

Lord, grant me the courage to lead, and surround me with trusted friends who will help me lead as you want. Amen.

TESTING GOD'S PATIENCE

> Then Gideon said to God, "Let not your anger burn against me;
> let me speak just once more. Please let me test just once more with the fleece.
> Please let it be dry on the fleece only, and on all the ground let there be dew."
> And God did so that night; and it was dry on the fleece only,
> and on all the ground there was dew.
> —*Judges 6:39–40*

Today's understatement: God is very patient.

An angel appears to Gideon and says that God is with him. Gideon's response is that, if the LORD is with him, then why does it appear that God has forsaken Israel? Undaunted, the angel states that God has chosen Gideon to save Israel from its enemy, Midian. Gideon replies that his clan is the weakest, and he is the least in his clan. God will help you, says the angel. I need a sign, replies Gideon. So the angel gives him a sign, and Gideon realizes that he is speaking with an angel of God.

God gives Gideon a task: tear down an altar to Baal and replace it with an altar to God. Gideon does it—at night, to avoid being seen. The men of the town figure out that he was the culprit anyway. Gideon's father deftly prevents them from killing Gideon, but the avoided skirmish mushrooms into a looming war. The Midianites and their allies amass across the Jordan River, ready for battle against the people of Israel and their fearless leader, Gideon.

Except Gideon is not so fearless. "I need another sign," he tells God. "I will lay a fleece of wool on the threshing floor. If there is dew on the wool and not the floor, then I'll know that you have chosen me to lead Israel." He gets the sign, and so … he asks for another. This time the fleece must be dry and the floor wet. God gives him that sign too.

And Gideon leads Israel to victory.

God is patient with all his children. He is extraordinarily patient.

Passage: Verse in Context — Judges 6:12–15, 36–40

And the angel of the LORD appeared to him and said to him, "The LORD is with you, O mighty man of valor." And Gideon said to him, "Please, my lord, if the LORD is with us, why then has all this happened to us? And where are all his wonderful deeds that our fathers recounted to us, saying, 'Did not the LORD bring us up from Egypt?' But now the LORD has forsaken us and given us into the hand of Midian." And the LORD turned to him and said, "Go in this might of yours and save Israel from the hand of Midian; do not I send you?" And he said to him, "Please, LORD, how can I save Israel? Behold, my clan is the weakest in Manasseh, and I am the least in my father's house." ...

Then Gideon said to God, "If you will save Israel by my hand, as you have said, behold, I am laying a fleece of wool on the threshing floor. If there is dew on the fleece alone, and it is dry on all the ground, then I shall know that you will save Israel by my hand, as you have said." And it was so. When he rose early next morning and squeezed the fleece, he wrung enough dew from the fleece to fill a bowl with water. Then Gideon said to God, "Let not your anger burn against me; let me speak just once more. Please let me test just once more with the fleece. Please let it be dry on the fleece only, and on all the ground let there be dew." And God did so that night; and it was dry on the fleece only, and on all the ground there was dew.

Questions for Reflection and Application

- Why did the angel call Gideon "a mighty man of valor"?
- Why did Gideon ask for a second sign? Why did God oblige?
- What is God calling you to do that takes you outside your comfort zone? How have you responded to this call?
- Do you feel that God is patient with you? Why do you feel that way?
- Do you test God's patience? How?

Father, your extraordinary patience astounds me beyond measure—even after I act like Gideon, tentative and trying. Amen.

WITH GREAT POWER ...

But the hair of his head began to grow again after it had been shaved.
—Judges 16:22

Bitten by an experimental spider, Peter Parker has acquired some of the abilities of the spider, as well as its proportional strength. After using that strength to win a fight with Flash Thompson, Peter is confronted by his Uncle Ben in a scene from the film *Spider-Man*. "Remember," says Ben, "with great power comes great responsibility."

Peter ignores the advice. When he has the opportunity to stop a man who just committed a robbery, Peter lets the man go. That man ends up shooting and killing Uncle Ben.

Samson also had great power, because his mother followed an angel's directive and raised Samson as a Nazirite (one separated and consecrated to God), so that he could "begin to save Israel from the hand of the Philistines" (13:5). Samson took his great power for granted and led a sinful life, expecting God to bail him out again and again. When Samson told Delilah that the secret of his strength was his long hair, Delilah had a man shave off Samson's hair. God allowed the Philistines to overpower Samson, gouge out his eyes, and take him as a prisoner.

But God also allowed Samson to live long enough for his hair to grow back, which was enough time for Samson to understand that his strength had come from God, not his hair. When Samson was brought out to "entertain" three thousand Philistines, he called out to God and asked for strength one more time. And God granted his request. Pushing against the two pillars that supported the roof, Samson literally brought the house down, killing everyone inside.

You may not have the strength of Samson, but God has blessed you in many ways. How will you use those blessings? When you choose to use them to honor God, other people are blessed ... and so are you.

Passage: Verse in Context — Judges 16:18–22, 28–30

When Delilah saw that he had told her all his heart, she sent and called the lords of the Philistines, saying, "Come up again, for he has told me all his heart." Then the lords of the Philistines came up to her and brought the money in their hands. She made him sleep on her knees. And she called a man and had him shave off the seven locks of his head. Then she began to torment him, and his strength left him. And she said, "The Philistines are upon you, Samson!" And he awoke from his sleep and said, "I will go out as at other times and shake myself free." But he did not know that the LORD had left him. And the Philistines seized him and gouged out his eyes and brought him down to Gaza and bound him with bronze shackles. And he ground at the mill in the prison. But the hair of his head began to grow again after it had been shaved. …

Then Samson called to the LORD and said, "O LORD God, please remember me and please strengthen me only this once, O God, that I may be avenged on the Philistines for my two eyes." And Samson grasped the two middle pillars on which the house rested, and he leaned his weight against them, his right hand on the one and his left hand on the other. And Samson said, "Let me die with the Philistines." Then he bowed with all his strength, and the house fell upon the lords and upon all the people who were in it. So the dead whom he killed at his death were more than those whom he had killed during his life.

Questions for Reflection and Application

- What are the primary abilities with which God has blessed you? How often do you thank God for them? Do you use them to honor God and bless others? As often as you should?
- How did Samson respond to losing his strength? How have you responded to losing something important to your identity?
- Why did God give Samson one more chance? How many chances has God given you? Why?

Father, remind me that my strength does not come from economic success or other accomplishments, my family, or even myself, but every good and perfect gift comes from you. Amen.

LEAVING HOME

But Ruth said, "Do not urge me to leave you or to return from following you. For where you go I will go, and where you lodge I will lodge. Your people shall be my people, and your God my God."
—Ruth 1:16

"I'll be home for Christmas." – Bing Crosby

"Home is where the heart is." — Pliny the Elder

"There's no place like home." — Dorothy, *The Wizard of Oz*

"Wherever I lay my hat, that's my home." — Marvin Gaye

"Home is where you feel at home and are treated well." — Dalai Lama

What do you consider your home? For Ruth, it was the land of Moab. She had lived there all her life. Her friends and family were there. Her people, the Moabites, were there. She had met and married her husband, a son of Naomi from Bethlehem in Judah, there.

Moab was not Naomi's home. She, her husband, and her sons had arrived ten years before because of a famine in Judah. During their time in Moab, Naomi's husband and both of her sons had died. Now that the famine was over, Naomi would return to her home, Judah.

"Go, return each of you to her mother's house," Naomi told Ruth and Orpah, her daughters-in-law. "May the Lord deal kindly with you, as you have dealt with the dead and with me. The Lord grant that you may find rest, each of you in the house of her husband!" (vv. 8–9).

Orpah kissed Naomi and left, but Ruth insisted that she journey with Naomi to Judah and make her home with her.

Imagine the courage needed to leave the only home you had ever known; to leave your parents, sisters and brothers, other relatives, and friends. To journey to a strange land where you know one person, a childless widow who has been away for ten years.

Ruth knew about God from her former husband and Naomi. Now Ruth would trust in God for everything.

And God would come through, as he always does.

Passage: Verse in Context — Ruth 1:11–19a, 22

But Naomi said, "Turn back, my daughters; why will you go with me? Have I yet sons in my womb that they may become your husbands? Turn back, my daughters; go your way, for I am too old to have a husband. If I should say I have hope, even if I should have a husband this night and should bear sons, would you therefore wait till they were grown? Would you therefore refrain from marrying? No, my daughters, for it is exceedingly bitter to me for your sake that the hand of the LORD has gone out against me." Then they lifted up their voices and wept again. And Orpah kissed her mother-in-law, but Ruth clung to her.

And she said, "See, your sister-in-law has gone back to her people and to her gods; return after your sister-in-law." But Ruth said, "Do not urge me to leave you or to return from following you. For where you go I will go, and where you lodge I will lodge. Your people shall be my people, and your God my God. Where you die I will die, and there will I be buried. May the LORD do so to me and more also if anything but death parts me from you." And when Naomi saw that she was determined to go with her, she said no more.

So the two of them went on until they came to Bethlehem … So Naomi returned, and Ruth the Moabite her daughter-in-law with her, who returned from the country of Moab. And they came to Bethlehem at the beginning of barley harvest.

Questions for Reflection and Application

- What do you consider your home? How strong is your affinity for home?
- Have you ever decided to move to a location with which you were completely unfamiliar? Why did you move there? What were the biggest challenges you faced in adjusting?
- Think of a time when you had to be as courageous as Ruth when she decided to leave her homeland. What was the source of your courage? How did it help you?

Father, wherever my heart is … there my home will be. Remind me who lives inside my heart and where my home truly lies. Amen.

LANCE'S RISE AND FALL

The LORD makes poor and makes rich;
he brings low and he exalts.
—*1 Samuel 2:7*

In 1996, Lance Armstrong was as feeble as they come. An aggressive form of testicular cancer had metastasized into his lymph nodes, lungs, and brain. The life of the world's top-rated cyclist was in danger. He was just twenty-five.

After two surgeries and four rounds of chemotherapy, Armstrong was cancer-free. His experience caused him to appreciate his life "in a completely new and better way." He formed the Lance Armstrong Foundation to raise money for testicular cancer research. And he began to train again for cycling.[7]

Ten years later, Armstrong was on top of the world. His autobiography, *It's Not About the Bike: My Journey Back to Life*, had been an inspiring bestseller. He had won the Tour de France, cycling's most prestigious event, seven times in a row. By selling LIVESTRONG-branded wristbands, the Lance Armstrong Foundation was raising over $30 million per year for cancer research.[8] His name had become synonymous with overcoming adversity and success—not just in sports, but also in life.

And then it all came crashing down. A year after Armstrong retired from cycling, the United States Anti-Doping Agency formally charged him with doping and trafficking performance-enhancing drugs. He was stripped of his seven Tour de France wins and lost all his corporate sponsorships. His public reputation ruined, he stepped down from the board of his foundation, which changed its name to the Livestrong Foundation.[9]

Armstrong's biggest regret is not the doping but the fact that, while other cyclists doped, "None of them attacked another human being. None of them sued another human being. And I did all those things."[10] In the end, it *was* about the bike, and the fame and glory that came with success on the bike.

When the mighty forget their dependence on God, their bows are broken. When the feeble depend on God, they get all the strength they need from the source of unending strength.

Passage: Verse in Context — 1 Samuel 1:10–11, 2:1–7

[Hannah] was deeply distressed and prayed to the LORD and wept bitterly. And she vowed a vow and said, "O LORD of hosts, if you will indeed look on the affliction of your servant and remember me and not forget your servant, but will give to your servant a son, then I will give him to the LORD all the days of his life, and no razor shall touch his head." ...

And Hannah prayed and said, "My heart exults in the LORD; my horn is exalted in the LORD. My mouth derides my enemies, because I rejoice in your salvation. There is none holy like the LORD: for there is none besides you; there is no rock like our God. Talk no more so very proudly, let not arrogance come from your mouth; for the LORD is a God of knowledge, and by him actions are weighed.

The bows of the mighty are broken, but the feeble bind on strength. Those who were full have hired themselves out for bread, but those who were hungry have ceased to hunger. The barren has borne seven, but she who has many children is forlorn. The LORD kills and brings to life; he brings down to Sheol and raises up. The LORD makes poor and makes rich; he brings low and he exalts."

Questions for Reflection and Application

- Do you agree with Hannah that the bows of the mighty are broken but the feeble bind on strength? When have you witnessed that?
- Do you think that when he overcame cancer, Lance Armstrong really appreciated his life in a completely new and better way? If so, then what went wrong for him?
- If God were to rate your appreciation or gratitude on a scale of one to ten, how would he score you?
- How much do you rely on God for strength? In what situations are you willing to admit that you cannot "win" on your own?

God, help me to remember that while some people appear to be strong on their own, true and lasting strength comes only from you. Amen.

AN ESSAY FOR MR. VERNON

"For the LORD sees not as man sees: man looks on the outward appearance,
but the LORD looks on the heart."
—*1 Samuel 16:7b*

Israel desperately wanted a king. Saul looked like the perfect man for the job—he was rich, tall, strong, handsome, and even humble. On the battlefield, he was a fierce warrior and strong leader.

But Saul couldn't follow God faithfully. Ultimately, God had to replace him as king.

In the film *The Breakfast Club,* five students must spend an entire Saturday serving detention in their high school's library. As they gather at 7 a.m., they see each other as their classmates and teachers see them: "as a brain, an athlete, a basket case, a princess, and a criminal." Their interactions during the first few hours are dictated by the preconceived notions that they have of each other, notions that are reinforced by each person's outward appearance.

As the five begin to reveal more about themselves, they realize that they have a great deal in common: experiences, dreams, fears, and feelings of isolation. By the end of the day, the five have become friends and united against a common enemy: the vice principal, who required each of them to write an essay. One student, the "brain", writes the essay for all of them:

Dear Mr. Vernon,

We accept the fact that we had to sacrifice a whole Saturday in detention for whatever it was we did wrong. But we think you're crazy to make us write an essay telling you who we think we are. You see us as you want to see us—in the simplest terms, in the most convenient definitions. But what we found out is that each one of us is a brain, and an athlete, and a basket case, a princess, and a criminal. Does that answer your question?

Sincerely yours,
The Breakfast Club

The Mr. Vernons of the world look only at your outward appearance. God knows your heart.

Passage: Verse in Context — 1 Samuel 16:4–13a

Samuel did what the LORD commanded and came to Bethlehem. The elders of the city came to meet him trembling and said, "Do you come peaceably?" And he said, "Peaceably; I have come to sacrifice to the LORD. Consecrate yourselves, and come with me to the sacrifice." And he consecrated Jesse and his sons and invited them to the sacrifice.

When they came, he looked on Eliab and thought, "Surely the LORD's anointed is before him." But the LORD said to Samuel, "Do not look on his appearance or on the height of his stature, because I have rejected him. For the LORD sees not as man sees: man looks on the outward appearance, but the LORD looks on the heart." Then Jesse called Abinadab and made him pass before Samuel. And he said, "Neither has the LORD CHOSEN THIS ONE." Then Jesse made Shammah pass by. And he said, "Neither has the LORD CHOSEN THIS ONE." And Jesse made seven of his sons pass before Samuel. And Samuel said to Jesse, "The LORD has not chosen these." Then Samuel said to Jesse, "Are all your sons here?" And he said, "There remains yet the youngest, but behold, he is keeping the sheep." And Samuel said to Jesse, "Send and get him, for we will not sit down till he comes here." And he sent and brought him in. Now he was ruddy and had beautiful eyes and was handsome. And the LORD said, "Arise, anoint him, for this is he." Then Samuel took the horn of oil and anointed him in the midst of his brothers. And the Spirit of the LORD rushed upon David from that day forward.

Questions for Reflection and Application

- How did others see you in high school? How do people see you now?
- Do you think that others see you through the lens of your accomplishments (or failures)? As a role that you play at work or in your family? As someone you used to be?
- How does God see you? Why?
- Why did God choose David?
- For what has God chosen you? Why did God choose you for that?

Father, help me to look past outward appearances, just as you urged Samuel to anoint a small shepherd boy as the future king of Israel. Amen.

SACRIFICIAL LOVE

And David said to him, "Do not fear, for I will show you kindness
for the sake of your father Jonathan, and I will restore to you all
the land of Saul your father, and you shall eat at my table always."
—2 Samuel 9:7

Jonathan was the rightful heir to the throne of his father, Saul. But from the moment he met David, who was much younger than he, Jonathan treated David like his brother.

David's success made Saul insanely jealous, and the king tried to kill David several times. Jonathan became David's protector, warning him of Saul's plots to kill David. Jonathan also defended David to Saul. Jonathan and David swore an oath to each other that God would be between them, and between their offspring, forever.

A few years later, Saul and Jonathan were killed in the same battle. When the nurse of Jonathan's five-year-old son heard the news, she picked up the child, Mephibosheth, and started to flee, but in her haste, she dropped him. He injured his feet so badly that he was permanently disabled. No one told David of Mephibosheth.

David became king of Judah, unified Judah and Israel, and ruled the combined kingdom. He led the army to many victories and "administered justice and equity to all his people" (8:15). And he remembered his oath with Jonathan. "Is there still anyone left of the house of Saul, that I may show him kindness for Jonathan's sake?" he asked (9:1). After learning that Jonathan's son Mephibosheth was alive and crippled, David ensured that Mephibosheth would be treated as if he were David's own son.

David showed compassion on Mephibosheth not only because he was Jonathan's son, but also because he was Saul's grandson. David honored Saul, even though Saul had hated him and tried to kill him. Why? Because Saul's son, Jonathan, was willing to sacrifice everything, including his right to the throne and his relationship with his father, for David.

Jonathan was a terrific model of sacrificial love. A thousand years later, we'd have an even better one.

Passage: Verse in Context — 2 Samuel 9:1–10

And David said, "Is there still anyone left of the house of Saul, that I may show him kindness for Jonathan's sake?" Now there was a servant of the house of Saul whose name was Ziba, and they called him to David. And the king said to him, "Are you Ziba?" And he said, "I am your servant." And the king said, "Is there not still someone of the house of Saul, that I may show the kindness of God to him?" Ziba said to the king, "There is still a son of Jonathan; he is crippled in his feet." The king said to him, "Where is he?" And Ziba said to the king, "He is in the house of Machir the son of Ammiel, at Lo-debar." Then King David sent and brought him from the house of Machir the son of Ammiel, at Lo-debar. And Mephibosheth the son of Jonathan, son of Saul, came to David and fell on his face and paid homage. And David said, "Mephibosheth!" And he answered, "Behold, I am your servant." And David said to him, "Do not fear, for I will show you kindness for the sake of your father Jonathan, and I will restore to you all the land of Saul your father, and you shall eat at my table always." And he paid homage and said, "What is your servant, that you should show regard for a dead dog such as I?"

Then the king called Ziba, Saul's servant, and said to him, "All that belonged to Saul and to all his house I have given to your master's grandson. And you and your sons and your servants shall till the land for him and shall bring in the produce, that your master's grandson may have bread to eat. But Mephibosheth your master's grandson shall always eat at my table." Now Ziba had fifteen sons and twenty servants.

Questions for Reflection and Application

- Jonathan was raised in a culture where a son was to show his father absolute respect, and his father was the king. So why did Jonathan choose David over his father, protecting David against Saul and defending David before Saul?
- Have you ever had a friend as steadfast and true as Jonathan was to David? Have you ever been such a friend to someone?
- What have you sacrificed for another? What would you be willing to sacrifice and for whom?
- Why did David honor Saul by caring for Saul's grandson?

Lord, you sacrificed everything for a spiritually crippled person—me. Amen.

A PART OF THE PLAN

"The Lord is my rock and my fortress and my deliverer, my God, my rock, in whom I take refuge, my shield, and the horn of my salvation, my stronghold and my refuge, my savior."
—*2 Samuel 22:2b–3a*

David was too old to face Philistine giants.

As a teenager, he had killed Goliath by slinging a rock into his forehead. Now David was in his sixties and had served as Israel's king for over thirty years. Israel was still at war with the Philistines, and in four successive battles the Philistines had a giant on their side.

In the first, the giant saw that David had grown weary and raced to kill him. Leaping to the aid of his king, Abishai attacked and killed the Philistine. Concerned about their king's safety, David's men put him on the sidelines and proceeded to win the next three battles, killing a giant in each.

After the battles were won, David sang the song recorded in 2 Samuel 22. In the song's opening, David called God his rock, fortress, deliverer, source of refuge, shield, salvation's horn, stronghold, and savior. But it was David's men who saved the life of their king, by coming to his aid on the battlefield and then persuading him to let them handle the fighting. All during David's reign there were many individuals who came to the aid of their king, in every area of David's life. Was David ignoring their efforts by directing all his praise to God?

No. God had chosen David as Israel's king. By protecting and helping David, the people were serving and honoring God. They were doing God's will. When David praised God, he also praised those who served God along the way.

God is your rock, fortress, and deliverer. Sometimes he helps you through the efforts of those who obey him, and sometimes you get to be a part of his helping others.

Passage: Verse in Context — 2 Samuel 22:1–7, 17–20

And David spoke to the LORD the words of this song on the day when the LORD delivered him from the hand of all his enemies, and from the hand of Saul. He said, "The LORD is my rock and my fortress and my deliverer, my God, my rock, in whom I take refuge, my shield, and the horn of my salvation, my stronghold and my refuge, my savior; you save me from violence. I call upon the LORD, who is worthy to be praised, and I am saved from my enemies.

"For the waves of death encompassed me, the torrents of destruction assailed me; the cords of Sheol entangled me; the snares of death confronted me. In my distress I called upon the LORD; to my God I called. From his temple he heard my voice, and my cry came to his ears. …

"He sent from on high, he took me; he drew me out of many waters. He rescued me from my strong enemy, from those who hated me, for they were too mighty for me. They confronted me in the day of my calamity, but the LORD was my support. He brought me out into a broad place; he rescued me, because he delighted in me."

Questions for Reflection and Application

- What motivates you to help others? Are there times when it is to reciprocate as a favor done for you? Or in the hopes of getting some recognition or praise? Or to build up some "equity" with another person?
- Do you believe that God rewards people who do his will, either in this life or the next? Or do you think that God expects his followers to be obedient, regardless of whether or not they receive a reward for their good work?
- When is the last time that you saw someone doing something good and praised God for it? Why do we tend to do that so rarely?

Father, even though I will fight many battles in this life, help me to remember to whom the glory goes for winning the good fight. Amen.

DOUBTING GOD

This God—his way is perfect; the word of the LORD proves true;
he is a shield for all those who take refuge in him.
—*2 Samuel 22:31*

In a song of remembrance of his three decades as king, David recalls how God has delivered him, time and time again, from his enemies. In the middle of this song, David describes God's way as perfect.

When you look back on your life, it's easy to see how God has worked in your life and to recognize that his way, indeed, has been perfect. But in the midst of the struggles, disappointments, heartaches, and pain of today, seeing God's perfect plan can be difficult. That's why David added this: The LORD's word is flawless; he shields all those who take refuge in him.

God knows that when times get tough, we are likely to doubt him. Consider the behavior of the Israelites recorded in Exodus after God delivered them from Egypt, where they were slaves for centuries:

Problem	People's Reaction	God's Response
The Egyptian army is bearing down on the people at the Red Sea.	We'll die here!	God parts the Red Sea, and then closes it on the Egyptians.
Food begins to run out.	We'll starve!	God provides manna every day.
They camp where there is no water.	We'll die of thirst!	Moses strikes a rock; water!
They get tired of eating only manna.	God doesn't care!	God provides quail.
Moses is on Mount Sinai for forty days.	Make a golden calf!	Moses returns; God forgives them.

Even when the Israelites doubted, God came through for them. So why did they doubt God, again and again? Why do we? It's because, in the stress of the moment, we forget how God has helped us in the past, and we forget God's promises, which he always keeps. We need to trust in God. After all, his way is perfect, his word is flawless, and, if we take refuge in him, then he will shield us.

Every time.

Passage: Verse in Context — 2 Samuel 22:26–33, 47–51

"With the merciful you show yourself merciful; with the blameless man you show yourself blameless; with the purified you deal purely, and with the crooked you make yourself seem tortuous. You save a humble people, but your eyes are on the haughty to bring them down. For you are my lamp, O LORD, and my God lightens my darkness. For by you I can run against a troop, and by my God I can leap over a wall. This God—his way is perfect; the word of the LORD proves true; he is a shield for all those who take refuge in him.

"For who is God, but the LORD? And who is a rock, except our God? This God is my strong refuge and has made my way blameless. …

"The LORD lives, and blessed be my rock, and exalted be my God, the rock of my salvation, the God who gave me vengeance and brought down peoples under me, who brought me out from my enemies; you exalted me above those who rose against me; you delivered me from men of violence. For this I will praise you, O LORD, among the nations, and sing praises to your name. Great salvation he brings to his king, and shows steadfast love to his anointed, to David and his offspring forever."

Questions for Reflection and Application

- Are you going through a tough stretch right now? If so, how has it affected your faith in God? How do life's challenges affect how you interact with God? How much do you rely on God?
- When is the last time you doubted God? How quickly did God come through for you? If you had to wait for a while, then what was that like?
- Have you ever looked back on the challenges in your life and recorded how God helped you through those challenges? If not, take some time to do that now. When you look back on your life (with the benefit of hindsight), do you see any patterns in how God works?

God, as I look back upon my life, I see you respond to my struggles time and time again. Remind me of your goodness in periods of hardship. Amen.

NOT A PERFECT PROPHET

The LORD listened to the voice of Elijah. And the life of the child
came into him again, and he revived.
—1 Kings 17:22

Elijah had a flair for the dramatic.

In his first act as a prophet of God, Elijah announced to Ahab, "As the LORD, the God of Israel, lives, before whom I stand, there shall be neither dew nor rain these years, except by my word" (v. 1). To demonstrate that Baal was a false god, Elijah challenged 450 prophets of Baal to a public duel of divine altar lighting. The prophets of Baal went first, and Elijah mocked them and Baal the entire time. When it was Elijah's turn, he insisted that his altar be saturated with water before he called to God to light it on fire.

Elijah also was a bit of a whiner.

Shortly after Elijah announced the drought, God sent him to live with a widow, promising her that her supply of flour and oil would not run out, and it didn't. When the widow's son became ill and died, however, she accused Elijah of causing the son's death, and Elijah passed the buck to God. God responded to Elijah's cries by bringing the son back to life.

After God demonstrated his power in the duel with Baal's prophets, and Elijah killed the prophets, Jezebel threatened to kill Elijah. God's mighty prophet ran for his life. After a day of running, he asked God that he might die. God responded by sending angels to feed Elijah. Then Elijah ran again, ending up living in a cave, and complained to God that he was the only faithful person left in Israel. God responded that there were 7,000 others in Israel who had never worshiped Baal.

Despite his penchant for being dramatic and whining, Elijah was revered as one of the greatest prophets, if not the greatest prophet, in Israel's history.

All of us, even Elijah, have personality traits that are, well, less than perfect. When God calls us, he doesn't expect perfection. He simply wants us to heed the call.

Passage: Verse in Context — 1 Kings 17:17–22

After this the son of the woman, the mistress of the house, became ill. And his illness was so severe that there was no breath left in him. And she said to Elijah, "What have you against me, O man of God? You have come to me to bring my sin to remembrance and to cause the death of my son!" And he said to her, "Give me your son." And he took him from her arms and carried him up into the upper chamber where he lodged, and laid him on his own bed. And he cried to the LORD, "O LORD my God, have you brought calamity even upon the widow with whom I sojourn, by killing her son?" Then he stretched himself upon the child three times and cried to the LORD, "O LORD my God, let this child's life come into him again." And the LORD listened to the voice of Elijah. And the life of the child came into him again, and he revived.

Related Passage — 1 Kings 19:1–4

Ahab told Jezebel all that Elijah had done, and how he had killed all the prophets with the sword. Then Jezebel sent a messenger to Elijah, saying, "So may the gods do to me and more also, if I do not make your life as the life of one of them by this time tomorrow." Then he was afraid, and he arose and ran for his life and came to Beersheba, which belongs to Judah, and left his servant there. But he himself went a day's journey into the wilderness and came and sat down under a broom tree. And he asked that he might die, saying, "It is enough; now, O LORD, take away my life, for I am no better than my fathers."

Questions for Reflection and Application

- Why is Elijah considered one of the greatest prophets in the Bible? When the life of Elijah is reviewed, what stands out: his weaknesses or what he accomplished by following God's direction?
- How do you think God saw Elijah? How does God see you?
- To what has God called you in the past? How did you respond?
- To what is God calling you right now? How will you respond?

Lord, like Elijah, I am fraught with flaws. Use me as a vessel to do your work anyway. Amen.

HAVING A CATCH

> Then he went to the spring of water and threw salt in it and said,
> "Thus says the LORD, I have healed this water; from now on neither death
> nor miscarriage shall come from it."
> —2 Kings 2:21

If God can heal a spring of water with a bit of salt, then God can heal your heart with anything. Even with a few minutes from a film.

In the movie *Field of Dreams*, Ray Kinsella recounts how his father "never made it as a ball player, so he tried to get his son to make it for him." But Ray refused to pursue his father's dream and even refused to "have a catch" with his father. Ray left home at seventeen and never returned, until his father's funeral.

At the end of the film, Ray's father, John, appears on the field of dreams that Ray had built on his Iowa cornfield. Ray introduces his dad to his wife and daughter. As John begins to walk away, Ray asks, "Hey … Dad … you wanna have a catch?" John turns around and answers, "I'd like that." They toss the ball back and forth as the film ends.

The 1989 film has never ended for Dwier Brown, who played John. "For people who had a difficult relationship with their dad," he says, "that scene got tattooed on the back of their retina." Everywhere he goes strangers approach him to talk about their dads. "Some people come up and literally cry on my shoulder."

An attorney once confessed to Brown that "tears were pouring down" his cheeks during the pivotal scene. The man realized that he had made himself miserable trying to please his father; the film prompted major changes in his life.

If you have trouble connecting with your father, Brown suggests having a catch with him. "You have this wonderful back-and-forth. Playing catch is just enough of a distraction, especially for men. They might start talking about things they wouldn't normally talk about. When you're playing catch, the words just kind of come out of your mouth."[11]

Have a catch and let the healing begin.

Passage: Verse in Context — 2 Kings 2:19–22

Now the men of the city said to Elisha, "Behold, the situation of this city is pleasant, as my lord sees, but the water is bad, and the land is unfruitful." He said, "Bring me a new bowl, and put salt in it." So they brought it to him. Then he went to the spring of water and threw salt in it and said, "Thus says the LORD, I have healed this water; from now on neither death nor miscarriage shall come from it." So the water has been healed to this day, according to the word that Elisha spoke.

Related Passage — Matthew 5:13

"You are the salt of the earth, but if salt has lost its taste, how shall its saltiness be restored? It is no longer good for anything except to be thrown out and trampled under people's feet."

Related Passage — Colossians 4:2–6

Continue steadfastly in prayer, being watchful in it with thanksgiving. At the same time, pray also for us, that God may open to us a door for the word, to declare the mystery of Christ, on account of which I am in prison—that I may make it clear, which is how I ought to speak. Walk in wisdom toward outsiders, making the best use of the time. Let your speech always be gracious, seasoned with salt, so that you may know how you ought to answer each person.

Questions for Reflection and Application

- When you were growing up, what challenges did you face in connecting with your father? Did the relationship get better or worse as you got older? Why?
- If your father still is alive, what can you do to improve your relationship with him? If you have sons, how can you develop a strong relationship with them?
- What other family relationships do you have that could be improved, and what are you prepared to do to improve those relationships?

Almighty God, just as you can heal poisonous water with salt, you can heal anything—even deep hurts from my past—with anything. I ask for your healing in whatever way you choose to deliver it. Amen.

GOD IS GOOD

Oh give thanks to the LORD, for he is good;
for his steadfast love endures forever!
—*1 Chronicles 16:34*

If God is good and loving, then why is there pain and suffering in the world? Why do bad things happen to good people? Why does hell exist, and why do some people end up there?

Questioning the goodness of God has led many people away from faith in God, including Charles Templeton. Once a well-known evangelist and close friend of Billy Graham, Templeton ended his life a staunch agnostic who was bitterly opposed to Christianity.

In the introduction to his book *The Case for Faith*, Lee Strobel interviews Templeton and asks him if there was one thing in particular that caused Templeton to lose his faith in God. Templeton responds that it was a *Life* magazine photograph of an African woman holding her baby, who had died of thirst in a drought. Templeton's summary: "Who else but a fiend could destroy a baby and virtually kill its mother with agony—when all that was needed was *rain*?"

Strobel spends the rest of the book responding to objections about God posed by Templeton and others: those who have left the Christian faith and those who remain Christians but still have doubts.

God knows that even his most faithful followers sometimes will have doubts. Consider David, whose song of praise to God is recorded in 1 Chronicles 16. Psalm 13 opens with this: "How long, O LORD? Will you forget me forever? How long will you hide your face from me? How long must I take counsel in my soul and have sorrow in my heart all the day? How long shall my enemy be exalted over me?" (vv. 1–2).

While David's psalms open with expressions of doubt about God, they close with reminders that God is faithful and God is good.

All of us need to remind ourselves of God's goodness and love. And then praise him for it.

Passage: Verse in Context — 1 Chronicles 16:7, 28–34

Then on that day David first appointed that thanksgiving be sung to the LORD by Asaph and his brothers. … Ascribe to the LORD, O families of the peoples, ascribe to the LORD glory and strength! Ascribe to the LORD the glory due his name; bring an offering and come before him! Worship the LORD in the splendor of holiness; tremble before him, all the earth; yes, the world is established; it shall never be moved. Let the heavens be glad, and let the earth rejoice, and let them say among the nations, "The LORD reigns!" Let the sea roar, and all that fills it; let the field exult, and everything in it! Then shall the trees of the forest sing for joy before the LORD, for he comes to judge the earth. Oh give thanks to the LORD, for he is good; for his steadfast love endures forever!

Related Passage — Psalm 13:1–6

How long, O LORD? Will you forget me forever? How long will you hide your face from me? How long must I take counsel in my soul and have sorrow in my heart all the day? How long shall my enemy be exalted over me?

Consider and answer me, O LORD my God; light up my eyes, lest I sleep the sleep of death, lest my enemy say, "I have prevailed over him," lest my foes rejoice because I am shaken.

But I have trusted in your steadfast love; my heart shall rejoice in your salvation. I will sing to the LORD, because he has dealt bountifully with me.

Questions for Reflection and Application

- What are your biggest doubts about God? If God could answer three questions for you, then what would they be?
- How do you think God felt when David levied charges that God was forgetting him, hiding his face, and letting David's enemies win? How do you think God feels when you lodge similar complaints against him?
- What things help you remember that God is faithful and God is good?

Father, remind me that the bad in the world does not detract from your goodness. Amen.

STEP BY STEP

"If my people who are called by my name humble themselves, and pray and seek my face and turn from their wicked ways, then I will hear from heaven and will forgive their sin and heal their land."

—2 Chronicles 7:14

We all want forgiveness. We all want healing. God tells us repeatedly in the Bible that forgiveness and healing are available to us. But first we must do some things that can be, well, really difficult sometimes.

Humble ourselves: Humility is the opposite of pride, which, as C. S. Lewis writes, is "the essential vice, the utmost evil. … Pride leads to every other vice: it is the complete anti-God state of mind."[12] Humbling ourselves, or overcoming our pride, enables us to receive God's forgiveness.

Pray: It may seem obvious, but if we want forgiveness then we must ask God for it. Before we can ask God to forgive something that we have done, we must admit to God and to ourselves that we have done something wrong that requires forgiveness.

Seek God's face: When you look closely at a friend's face, you can read his or her emotions and feelings. If we want God's forgiveness, then we first must seek to understand what pain our sin has caused him. Understanding comes from studying his Word and listening for his promptings.

Turn from our wicked ways: Repentance is more than just admitting that you did something wrong, saying that you're sorry, and asking for forgiveness. God wants us to turn away from what we have done and follow a new path of righteous behavior.

The good news is that God stands ready to hear us, forgive our sins, and heal us. The ~~bad~~ better news is that we must take some steps to receive God's forgiveness. God requires those steps because they make us value and appreciate his forgiveness even more. They move us closer to him. So the next time you have to take those steps, there will be fewer of them to take.

Passage: Verse in Context — 2 Chronicles 7:11b–20

All that Solomon had planned to do in the house of the Lord and in his own house he successfully accomplished. Then the Lord appeared to Solomon in the night and said to him: "I have heard your prayer and have chosen this place for myself as a house of sacrifice. When I shut up the heavens so that there is no rain, or command the locust to devour the land, or send pestilence among my people, if my people who are called by my name humble themselves, and pray and seek my face and turn from their wicked ways, then I will hear from heaven and will forgive their sin and heal their land. Now my eyes will be open and my ears attentive to the prayer that is made in this place. For now I have chosen and consecrated this house that my name may be there forever. My eyes and my heart will be there for all time. And as for you, if you will walk before me as David your father walked, doing according to all that I have commanded you and keeping my statutes and my rules, then I will establish your royal throne, as I covenanted with David your father, saying, 'You shall not lack a man to rule Israel.'

"But if you turn aside and forsake my statutes and my commandments that I have set before you, and go and serve other gods and worship them, then I will pluck you up from my land that I have given you, and this house that I have consecrated for my name, I will cast out of my sight, and I will make it a proverb and a byword among all peoples."

Questions for Reflection and Application

- How much do you struggle with pride? What can you do to humble yourself before God?
- What is your prayer life like? Is it better or worse than it was six months or a year ago? What can you do to improve it?
- How often do you study the Bible? How often do you listen for promptings from God?
- What sins have you committed for which you have never fully repented? What is needed for full repentance?

Father, whether I need to walk one hundred steps or one hundred thousand, lead me away from the wicked path and walk with me toward the path of righteousness. Amen.

WHEN YOU'RE AWAKE

For the eyes of the LORD range throughout the earth to strengthen
those whose hearts are fully committed to him.
—*2 Chronicles 16:9a NIV*

"He sees you when you're sleeping, he knows when you're awake. He knows if you've been bad or good, so be good, for goodness sake!"

Every year around Christmastime, various pieces on the physics of Santa Claus make the rounds on social media. Here are some of the highlights:[13]

- Santa visits an estimated 500 million households worldwide on Christmas Eve.
- He has about thirty-one hours—from the first sundown just west of the International Date Line to just before dawn a little east of there— to make his deliveries.
- The average distance between households targeted by Santa is about two-tenths of a mile.
- He has to reach 10,000 households every 2.23 seconds.
- Even if Santa can make each delivery instantaneously, he still needs to travel at 6,400 miles per hour.

What about Santa having to determine if children are good or bad? If he has to monitor 500 million children worldwide and can make a valid judgment with a check of only thirty seconds per child each year—a pretty tall order—he would have to watch 475 children simultaneously. Every second.

God, of course, doesn't just check in periodically on a subset of the world's children. His eyes range throughout the earth to watch everyone, everywhere, all the time. He knows much more than who did something good or bad at last check. His eyes see not just actions but motives. He sees the heart.

Why does God watch us constantly? It is not to catch us being bad so that he can give us a lump of coal in our Christmas stocking. God watches us because he loves us and wants a deep and lasting relationship with us. By knowing every facet of our lives, God knows just how to help when we are struggling. He is ready to strengthen us when we rely on him completely.

Passage: Verse in Context — 2 Chronicles 16:7–9

At that time Hanani the seer came to Asa king of Judah and said to him, "Because you relied on the king of Syria, and did not rely on the LORD your God, the army of the king of Syria has escaped you. Were not the Ethiopians and the Libyans a huge army with very many chariots and horsemen? Yet because you relied on the LORD, he gave them into your hand. For the eyes of the LORD run to and fro throughout the whole earth, to give strong support to those whose heart is blameless toward him. You have done foolishly in this, for from now on you will have wars."

Related Passage — Psalm 34:11–19

Come, O children, listen to me; I will teach you the fear of the LORD. What man is there who desires life and loves many days, that he may see good? Keep your tongue from evil and your lips from speaking deceit. Turn away from evil and do good; seek peace and pursue it.

The eyes of the LORD are toward the righteous and his ears toward their cry. The face of the LORD is against those who do evil, to cut off the memory of them from the earth. When the righteous cry for help, the LORD hears and delivers them out of all their troubles. The LORD is near to the brokenhearted and saves the crushed in spirit. Many are the afflictions of the righteous, but the LORD delivers him out of them all.

Questions for Reflection and Application

- How often do you consider the fact that God is with you and watching you at all times? Does that thought give you comfort or make you uneasy? Why?
- When you think about God watching you, what image or images come to mind? (For example: loving father or joyless taskmaster.) Why do you have those images?
- What things does God see in how you live your life that makes him proud of you? What things does God want to chat with you about?

God, you watch me because you care for me. Keep your eyes on my steps and strengthen me. Amen.

FIVE FEET NOTHING

Thus says the LORD to you, "Do not be afraid and do not be dismayed
at this great horde, for the battle is not yours but God's."
—*2 Chronicles 20:15b*

"You're five feet nothing. A hundred and nothing. And you've got hardly a speck of athletic ability." So says Fortune to the title character in the film *Rudy*, which tells the true story of how Daniel "Rudy" Ruettiger overcame overwhelming odds to achieve his dream of playing football for the University of Notre Dame.

When Rudy's best friend is killed in an explosion at their hometown steel mill, Rudy heads to South Bend, home of Notre Dame, and enrolls at Holy Cross College. Fortune, a Notre Dame stadium groundskeeper, gives Rudy a job and lets him sleep on a cot in his office. After two years at Holy Cross, Rudy is admitted to Notre Dame and promptly tries out for the football team, landing a spot on the practice squad. For the next two years, Rudy dreams of appearing in uniform on the sidelines for one home game.

When Rudy sees that he is not on the dress list for the final home game of his senior year, he quits the team. Fortune spots him at the stadium and chastises the "five feet nothing" Rudy for quitting. When Rudy rejoins the team, the other players persuade the head coach to let Rudy dress. With his family members watching from the stands, Rudy gets in the game, makes a tackle, and is carried off the field at the game's end. (No player has been carried off the Notre Dame field by his teammates since.)

We love stories of people succeeding in the face of overwhelming odds, primarily because they happen so rarely in our world. Why, then, is the Bible full of such stories, including little-known stories such as the one in 2 Chronicles 20? It's God's way of reminding us that when he is on our side, the odds don't matter. So don't be afraid. Don't be dismayed. Nothing overwhelms God.

Passage: Verse in Context — 2 Chronicles 20:1–4, 14–17

After this the Moabites and Ammonites, and with them some of the Meunites, came against Jehoshaphat for battle. Some men came and told Jehoshaphat, "A great multitude is coming against you from Edom, from beyond the sea; and, behold, they are in Hazazon-tamar" (that is, Engedi). Then Jehoshaphat was afraid and set his face to seek the LORD, and proclaimed a fast throughout all Judah. And Judah assembled to seek help from the LORD; from all the cities of Judah they came to seek the LORD. …

And the Spirit of the LORD came upon Jahaziel the son of Zechariah, son of Benaiah, son of Jeiel, son of Mattaniah, a Levite of the sons of Asaph, in the midst of the assembly. And he said, "Listen, all Judah and inhabitants of Jerusalem and King Jehoshaphat: Thus says the LORD to you, 'Do not be afraid and do not be dismayed at this great horde, for the battle is not yours but God's. Tomorrow go down against them. Behold, they will come up by the ascent of Ziz. You will find them at the end of the valley, east of the wilderness of Jeruel. You will not need to fight in this battle. Stand firm, hold your position, and see the salvation of the LORD on your behalf, O Judah and Jerusalem.' Do not be afraid and do not be dismayed. Tomorrow go out against them, and the LORD will be with you."

Questions for Reflection and Application

- What's your favorite underdog story? Why is it your favorite?
- If our favorite athlete or team is not playing, then many of us cheer for the underdog. Do you? Why or why not?
- In what situations have you been the underdog? What happened?
- What is God teaching you through the underdog stories you have seen and your experiences of being the underdog?

God, thank you for taking five feet nothings and turning them into five feet somethings when they follow your plan. Amen.

COMMANDING RESPECT

And the king granted him all that he asked, for the hand
of the LORD his God was on him.

—Ezra 7:6

Stand-up comedian Rodney Dangerfield was famous for his catch-phrase, "I get no respect." Many Jews in Babylon felt the same way.

Nearly six hundred years before the birth of Jesus, the Chaldeans conquered Jerusalem, destroyed the Temple, and forced ten thousand of the best and brightest young Jews (such as Daniel) to relocate to Babylon, the capital of the Chaldean empire. Blaming their disastrous circumstances on betraying God and allowing their religious practices to become corrupt, the exiled Jews looked forward to a day when they would be purified and gathered together once more in a re-established unified kingdom.

Seventy years later, the Persians overthrew the Chaldeans, and the Persian king Cyrus announced that God had instructed him to allow Jews to return Jerusalem and rebuild "the house of the LORD" (1:3). Led by Zerubbabel, a group of about fifty thousand returned to their homeland, and they rebuilt the Temple in Jerusalem. Sixty years later, Ezra, a descendant of Moses' brother Aaron and "a scribe skilled in the Law of Moses" (7:6), led a second group of exiles to Israel. Ezra brought the Torah with him, and because he led the people of Israel to study the Torah, he is known as the "Father of Judaism."[14]

Before Ezra left Persia, King Artaxerxes decreed that anyone who wanted to return to Jerusalem with Ezra could do so because the Law of the God of Israel was in Ezra's hands. Artaxerxes gave Ezra silver and gold and instructed him to use it however he pleased, "according to the will of your God" (7:18). He told Ezra to appoint magistrates and judges to judge the people of Israel. None of this went to Ezra's head, because he knew who had the real power: God.

Because he was obedient to God, Ezra commanded respect. If Rodney Dangerfield had taken tips from Ezra, then he finally would have had respect ... but not much of a stand-up act.

Passage: Verse in Context — Ezra 7:6, 10–13, 25–28

Ezra went up from Babylonia. He was a scribe skilled in the Law of Moses that the LORD, the God of Israel, had given, and the king granted him all that he asked, for the hand of the LORD his God was on him. ... For Ezra had set his heart to study the Law of the LORD, and to do it and to teach his statutes and rules in Israel. This is a copy of the letter that King Artaxerxes gave to Ezra the priest, the scribe, a man learned in matters of the commandments of the LORD and his statutes for Israel:

"Artaxerxes, king of kings, to Ezra the priest, the scribe of the Law of the God of heaven. Peace. And now I make a decree that anyone of the people of Israel or their priests or Levites in my kingdom, who freely offers to go to Jerusalem, may go with you. ... And you, Ezra, according to the wisdom of your God that is in your hand, appoint magistrates and judges who may judge all the people in the province Beyond the River, all such as know the laws of your God. And those who do not know them, you shall teach. Whoever will not obey the law of your God and the law of the king, let judgment be strictly executed on him, whether for death or for banishment or for confiscation of his goods or for imprisonment."

Blessed be the LORD, the God of our fathers, who put such a thing as this into the heart of the king, to beautify the house of the LORD that is in Jerusalem, and who extended to me his steadfast love before the king and his counselors, and before all the king's mighty officers. I took courage, for the hand of the LORD my God was on me, and I gathered leading men from Israel to go up with me.

Questions for Reflection and Application

- Who have you encountered in life that commanded respect from everyone? Why did he or she command respect?
- Who do you expect to receive respect from? What happens when you don't get it?
- What qualities of Ezra would you like to emulate? How can you do that?

Father, when I approach you and your Word with respect, then I will command respect, because your hand will be on me. Amen.

TRAINING TO WIN

And they said, "Let us rise up and build."
So they strengthened their hands for the good work.
—*Nehemiah 2:18b*

Thirty years after Mark Spitz shocked the sports world by winning seven gold medals in a single Olympic Games, a young swimmer named Michael Phelps set his sights on winning eight. Phelps had the perfect build for swimming, but physique alone would not enable him to defeat the world's elite swimmers. So Phelps focused on an incredibly rigorous training regime. Six days a week he swam 8.5 miles a day, doing intervals at a brisk tempo with very short breaks in between, thereby extending his aerobic range to handle more distance and speed without going into oxygen debt. The training enabled Phelps to tap fewer lactic acids—producing greater anaerobic energy reserves than his competitors did.[15][16] Phelps won six gold and two bronze medals in the 2004 Games and then eight gold medals in the 2008 Games.

When Nehemiah traveled from Babylon to Jerusalem, he found a city that still was in ruins 150 years after being conquered by the Chaldeans. The wall around the city was broken down; the gates had been burned to the ground. The people of Jerusalem suffered derision by those who lived nearby and, with no wall to protect it, the city was under constant threat of attack. Nehemiah had a simple solution. "Come, let us build the wall of Jerusalem," he said (v. 17).

Rebuilding a wall that had been in ruins for 150 years was an enormous task. But God had charged the people of Jerusalem with doing it, so they agreed. And then they "strengthened their hands for the good work." In other words, they went into training. Once they were trained and ready, they began to work around the clock. Fifty-two days later, they were done.

When God gives you a task, especially a tough one, he expects you to train for it, and to train the right way for it. After all, you're not going for gold medals at the Olympics … you're going for something much more valuable.

Passage: Verse in Context — Nehemiah 2:13–15, 17–18

I went out by night by the Valley Gate to the Dragon Spring and to the Dung Gate, and I inspected the walls of Jerusalem that were broken down and its gates that had been destroyed by fire. Then I went on to the Fountain Gate and to the King's Pool, but there was no room for the animal that was under me to pass. Then I went up in the night by the valley and inspected the wall, and I turned back and entered by the Valley Gate, and so returned. …

Then I said to them, "You see the trouble we are in, how Jerusalem lies in ruins with its gates burned. Come, let us build the wall of Jerusalem, that we may no longer suffer derision." And I told them of the hand of my God that had been upon me for good, and also of the words that the king had spoken to me. And they said, "Let us rise up and build." So they strengthened their hands for the good work.

Related Passage — 1 Corinthians 9:24–27

Do you not know that in a race all the runners run, but only one receives the prize? So run that you may obtain it. Every athlete exercises self-control in all things. They do it to receive a perishable wreath, but we an imperishable. So I do not run aimlessly; I do not box as one beating the air. But I discipline my body and keep it under control, lest after preaching to others I myself should be disqualified.

Questions for Reflection and Application

- For what tasks have you undertaken extensive training? What was that like? Was it worth it?
- Do you gravitate toward things for which you have experience, or do you welcome the challenge of learning something new? Why?
- What tasks does God have for you in the near future that will require training? How do you feel about those tasks?

Father, if I want to earn something worth more than a gold medal, then I must train more diligently than an Olympic athlete. Help me to do this. Amen.

UNLOCKING JOY

"...the joy of the LORD is your strength."
—Nehemiah 8:10b

Twila Paris' song, "The Joy of the Lord," is based on today's verse and repeats that verse as the chorus. That song, and the message behind it, helped Twila and her husband, Jack Wright, get through a major disruption in their lives.

As Twila was establishing her career as a Christian singer, Jack traveled with her on all her tours and acted as her manager. Then Jack was stricken with an autoimmune condition known as chronic fatigue syndrome. For a while, he tried to continue touring with his wife, but eventually he was forced to pursue "aggressive rest" by staying in their home under the care of a doctor, while Twila continued to travel from city to city.

Dealing with his illness forced him to delegate some things to people who did a better job than he had. "As far as my relationship with the Lord," he said, "I was caught up with the day-to-day problems that come up. This has forced me to re-evaluate, with a lot more quiet time to spend with the Lord. I see the overall thing as a blessing."

"I know of several people who have prayed specifically for me for joy," added Twila. "Once I made the choice not to say, 'Lord, my joy has to come from this source in this way at this time,' He has brought joy in the most unexpected ways from the most unexpected places. And I have to tell you honestly, I have been, for the most part, a happy person for the past year."[17]

The joy of the Lord is the joy that God gives you. It is the joy about which Jesus spoke in John 15, after stating that he is the vine and we are the branches. To receive his joy, we must abide in him and keep his commandments, especially the command to love each other.

The joy of the Lord is your strength. The key to unlocking that joy is to love God and love others.

Passage: Verse in Context — Nehemiah 8:9–12

And Nehemiah, who was the governor, and Ezra the priest and scribe, and the Levites who taught the people said to all the people, "This day is holy to the LORD your God; do not mourn or weep." For all the people wept as they heard the words of the Law. Then he said to them, "Go your way. Eat the fat and drink sweet wine and send portions to anyone who has nothing ready, for this day is holy to our LORD. And do not be grieved, for the joy of the LORD is your strength." So the Levites calmed all the people, saying, "Be quiet, for this day is holy; do not be grieved." And all the people went their way to eat and drink and to send portions and to make great rejoicing, because they had understood the words that were declared to them.

Related Passage — James 1:2–4, 12–13, 17

Count it all joy, my brothers, when you meet trials of various kinds, for you know that the testing of your faith produces steadfastness. And let steadfastness have its full effect, that you may be perfect and complete, lacking in nothing. … Blessed is the man who remains steadfast under trial, for when he has stood the test he will receive the crown of life, which God has promised to those who love him. Let no one say when he is tempted, "I am being tempted by God," for God cannot be tempted with evil, and he himself tempts no one. … Every good gift and every perfect gift is from above, coming down from the Father of lights, with whom there is no variation or shadow due to change.

Questions for Reflection and Application

- We hear a lot about happiness but not a lot about joy. What's the difference? Which would you rather have and why?
- In the last few months, have you experienced the joy of the Lord? Why or why not?
- How much do your situations in life affect how you feel about your life and about God? What can you do to make your joy less dependent on your circumstances?

God, your steadfast love brings me joy, even when I am going through tough times. Help me to find that joy today. Amen.

ESTHER'S COURAGE

And who knows whether you have not come
to the kingdom for such a time as this?
—*Esther 4:14b*

King Ahasuerus loved his wife, Esther, and owed his life to her cousin, Mordecai, who had warned the king through Esther of a plot to kill the king. But Ahasuerus did not know that Esther and Mordecai were Jews.

Haman, the king's lead official, knew that Mordecai was a Jew. When Mordecai refused to bow down or pay homage to him, Haman decided to rid the kingdom not just of Mordecai but of all Mordecai's people. Haman persuaded Ahasuerus to issue a decree to completely rid the Persian kingdom of the Jews.

Mordecai told Esther about the decree and told her to go to the king and "plead with him on behalf of her people" (v. 8). Esther told Mordecai that approaching the king violated a law, and had the penalty of death. Mordecai responded that now was Esther's appointed time with destiny. Esther agreed and said, "If I perish, I perish" (v. 16).

When the king saw Esther standing in his inner court, he told her that he would give her whatever she wanted. She asked for a banquet with him and Haman. At that banquet, she asked for an identical banquet the following evening. The night after the first banquet, the king remembered how Mordecai had saved his life and was told that Mordecai had not been honored for his deed. The king summoned Mordecai and had Haman bestow honors on Mordecai. At the banquet the next evening, Esther revealed that she was a Jew and that her people were in peril because of Haman. The king had Haman hanged—on the same gallows that Haman had prepared for Mordecai—and rescinded the order to have the Jews killed.

Esther realized that God made her queen so she could save her people. God always has a plan, but we usually don't know what it is until after the fact. We must trust God, and that takes courage. A lot of courage. But it's worth it.

Passage: Verse in Context — Esther 4:9–17

And Hathach went and told Esther what Mordecai had said. Then Esther spoke to Hathach and commanded him to go to Mordecai and say, "All the king's servants and the people of the king's provinces know that if any man or woman goes to the king inside the inner court without being called, there is but one law—to be put to death, except the one to whom the king holds out the golden scepter so that he may live. But as for me, I have not been called to come in to the king these thirty days."

And they told Mordecai what Esther had said. Then Mordecai told them to reply to Esther, "Do not think to yourself that in the king's palace you will escape any more than all the other Jews. For if you keep silent at this time, relief and deliverance will rise for the Jews from another place, but you and your father's house will perish. And who knows whether you have not come to the kingdom for such a time as this?" Then Esther told them to reply to Mordecai, "Go, gather all the Jews to be found in Susa, and hold a fast on my behalf, and do not eat or drink for three days, night or day. I and my young women will also fast as you do. Then I will go to the king, though it is against the law, and if I perish, I perish." Mordecai then went away and did everything as Esther had ordered him.

Questions for Reflection and Application

- Esther was bold, but she was savvy too. Once she made the decision to approach the king, she devised a plan for how to do it. Would people describe you as bold? Savvy? Both? Or neither?
- How has your approach to taking bold action changed as you have aged? Are you more or less bold? More or less savvy?
- Mordecai recognized that Esther's becoming queen was a part of God's plan. What is God's plan for the next few years of your life? How do you know, or how can you find out?

Lord God, courage comes in taking the next step in your plan. Give me the courage to do what you have created me to do. Amen.

TWO IMPOSTERS

> And he said, "Naked I came from my mother's womb,
> and naked shall I return. The LORD gave, and the LORD has taken away;
> blessed be the name of the LORD."
> —Job 1:21

If you can meet with Triumph and Disaster
And treat those two impostors just the same.

Those words, from Rudyard Kipling's inspirational poem "If", are inscribed above the players' entrance to Centre Court at the All-England Lawn Tennis Club at Wimbledon, site of the world's most prestigious tennis tournament. Every year, 128 men enter the men's singles draw, and 128 women enter the women's singles draw. At the end of the tournament, 254 elite athletes go home a loser.

Job went through a lot more than a heartbreaking defeat in tennis. Few of us will ever endure anything close to the calamities that befell him. But even if our hardships don't seem like much to others, they can be devastating to us. Kipling's poem speaks of many of the challenges that we face and, for each, how a true man should respond:

If you can keep your head when all about you
Are losing theirs and blaming it on you;
If you can trust yourself when all men doubt you,
But make allowance for their doubting too:
If you can wait and not be tired by waiting,
Or, being lied about, don't deal in lies,
Or being hated don't give way to hating,
And yet don't look too good, nor talk too wise ...[18]

Kipling's poem asks the impossible. But Job's response after his incredible hardships was impossible too. How did Job do the impossible? He submitted completely to God, recognizing that everything that he ever had or ever would have comes from God.

Triumph and disaster are imposters. The only real deal is God.

Passage: Verse in Context — Job 1:13–22

Now there was a day when his sons and daughters were eating and drinking wine in their oldest brother's house, and there came a messenger to Job and said, "The oxen were plowing and the donkeys feeding beside them, and the Sabeans fell upon them and took them and struck down the servants with the edge of the sword, and I alone have escaped to tell you." While he was yet speaking, there came another and said, "The fire of God fell from heaven and burned up the sheep and the servants and consumed them, and I alone have escaped to tell you." While he was yet speaking, there came another and said, "The Chaldeans formed three groups and made a raid on the camels and took them and struck down the servants with the edge of the sword, and I alone have escaped to tell you." While he was yet speaking, there came another and said, "Your sons and daughters were eating and drinking wine in their oldest brother's house, and behold, a great wind came across the wilderness and struck the four corners of the house, and it fell upon the young people, and they are dead, and I alone have escaped to tell you."

Then Job arose and tore his robe and shaved his head and fell on the ground and worshiped. And he said, "Naked I came from my mother's womb, and naked shall I return. The LORD gave, and the LORD has taken away; blessed be the name of the LORD."

In all this Job did not sin or charge God with wrong.

Questions for Reflection and Application

- Why does Kipling refer to triumph and disaster as imposters?
- Find Kipling's entire poem online and read it. What elements in it seem impossible for you to do, at least consistently? What things in your life seem next to impossible? Which of those things does God want you to pursue anyway? Why?
- When in your life did you face calamity and respond as Job did? What enabled you to do that? If you haven't done it, then what would it take for you to do that?

Father, triumph is a fair-weather friend, and disaster can strike at any time. Give me the strength to praise you when either comes knocking at my door. Amen.

A SOPRANO'S SWEET SONG

For I know that my Redeemer lives, and at the last he will stand upon the earth.
And after my skin has been thus destroyed, yet in my flesh I shall see God.
—*Job 19:25–26*

Because performing all of Handel's masterful oratorio *Messiah* takes about three hours, most groups do just Part I, which covers the prophesies about and the birth of Jesus, and then they add the boisterous and popular "Hallelujah Chorus" at the end. That chorus, however, is not the final piece in *Messiah* but simply the end of Part II. The final part of the oratorio opens with a slow and quiet soprano solo, "I Know That My Redeemer Liveth," which includes Job 19:25–26.

Job, who likely lived at least hundreds of years before Moses, was a "blameless and upright" man who "feared God and turned away from evil" (1:1). God had blessed him with ten children and enough property, possessions, and servants to make him "the greatest of all the people of the east (v. 3). When Satan told God that Job was faithful only because God had blessed and protected Job, God allowed Satan to take away all of Job's blessings: his children, property, possessions, and even his good health. Yet Job continued to worship God.

Much of the book of Job is a long conversation between Job and three friends who believe that Job's suffering is a punishment for sin. When Bildad the Shuhite reiterates that God punishes only the wicked, implying that Job is wicked, Job responds that he will be vindicated—or redeemed—after he dies.

Job did not know exactly how this would happen. But Handel did. That's why, after singing the passage from Job, the soprano soloist sings this line from 1 Corinthians 15:20: "For now is Christ risen from the dead, the first fruits of them that sleep."

We can join her song with confidence. Our Redeemer lives and, in the end, he will stand upon the earth. We will join him in our resurrected bodies and gaze upon the face of God.

Passage: Verse in Context — Job 19:23–27

"Oh that my words were written! Oh that they were inscribed in a book! Oh that with an iron pen and lead they were engraved in the rock forever! For I know that my Redeemer lives, and at the last he will stand upon the earth. And after my skin has been thus destroyed, yet in my flesh I shall see God, whom I shall see for myself, and my eyes shall behold, and not another. My heart faints within me!"

Related Passage — 1 Corinthians 15:12–22

Now if Christ is proclaimed as raised from the dead, how can some of you say that there is no resurrection of the dead? But if there is no resurrection of the dead, then not even Christ has been raised. And if Christ has not been raised, then our preaching is in vain and your faith is in vain. We are even found to be misrepresenting God, because we testified about God that he raised Christ, whom he did not raise if it is true that the dead are not raised. For if the dead are not raised, not even Christ has been raised. And if Christ has not been raised, your faith is futile and you are still in your sins. Then those also who have fallen asleep in Christ have perished. If in Christ we have hope in this life only, we are of all people most to be pitied. But in fact Christ has been raised from the dead, the firstfruits of those who have fallen asleep. For as by a man came death, by a man has come also the resurrection of the dead. For as in Adam all die, so also in Christ shall all be made alive.

Questions for Reflection and Application

- Why does God allow you to go through tough times?
- When you are going through a tough time, how much comfort do you take from knowing that you have a Redeemer and that you will "win in the end"? Do you tend to view your challenges from an eternal perspective, or do you complain about them and ask God to "fix" them? Why?
- When you see your Redeemer face-to-face, what will you ask him?

Father, when everything around me seems to perish—friendships, family relations, dreams for the future—remind me that my Redeemer lives. Amen.

A VOICE FROM A WHIRLWIND

"I know that you can do all things,
and that no purpose of yours can be thwarted."
—*Job 42:2*

The book of Job begins with an exchange between God and Satan in which Satan claims that, if Job were to lose everything then he would curse God. Then a series of calamities befall Job. His many animals are stolen or killed. Almost all his servants, and all ten of his children, are killed. Job is struck with "loathsome sores" (2:7) that disfigure him. His wife says, "Curse God and die" (v. 9). But Job refuses to sin against God.

Job's friends arrive to "show him sympathy and comfort him" (v. 11). Seeing his suffering, they sit with him for seven days and nights without saying a word. When they speak, it is to persuade Job that his suffering is due to his sin. For thirty-four chapters(!) his friends and he talk, with Job occasionally stating that he would like to argue his case before God in a courtroom.

Finally, God speaks from a whirlwind. God does not explain why Job suffered or give Job the opportunity to argue his case. Instead, God contrasts his abilities with those of Job and every other human. Humbled, Job meekly responds that he had no right to question the purpose of an all-powerful God.

Why not? When we suffer, isn't it fair to ask God why we are suffering? Why do bad things happen to godly people? Where is God in suffering? The book of Job provides no easy answers to these and other tough questions about suffering.

But the Book does make one thing very clear: God does not cause us to suffer to punish us for our sins. He wants us to repent of our sins and follow him, but he does not manipulate us to make that happen. Instead, God allows us to use our free will to decide how we will respond to blessings, suffering, or anything in between.

God wants an eternal relationship with you. And no purpose of his can be thwarted.

Passage: Verse in Context — Job 38:1–9, 42:1–6

Then the LORD answered Job out of the whirlwind and said: "Who is this that darkens counsel by words without knowledge? Dress for action like a man; I will question you, and you make it known to me.

"Where were you when I laid the foundation of the earth? Tell me, if you have understanding. Who determined its measurements—surely you know! Or who stretched the line upon it? On what were its bases sunk, or who laid its cornerstone, when the morning stars sang together and all the sons of God shouted for joy?" …

Then Job answered the LORD and said: "I know that you can do all things, and that no purpose of yours can be thwarted. 'Who is this that hides counsel without knowledge?' Therefore I have uttered what I did not understand, things too wonderful for me, which I did not know. 'Hear, and I will speak; I will question you, and you make it known to me.'

I had heard of you by the hearing of the ear, but now my eye sees you; therefore I despise myself, and repent in dust and ashes."

Questions for Reflection and Application

- Why does God allow his followers to suffer?
- With Elijah, God was silent in a mighty wind, an earthquake, and a fire, and then spoke in a whisper. Why did God speak to Job from a whirlwind?
- Why didn't God explain why Job suffered or give Job the opportunity to argue his case? Was God angry at Job for asking why he had suffered? Why or why not?
- When you suffer, how does that change your relationship with God?

Father, whatever circumstance I am placed in, may I praise and not curse you. May I follow and not flee from you. Amen.

WITH FRIENDS LIKE THESE ...

And the LORD restored the fortunes of Job,
when he had prayed for his friends.
—*Job 42:10a*

With friends like these, Job didn't need enemies.

Oh, sure, Job's friends meant well. As soon as they heard about Job's devastating calamities—the loss of his vast property and possessions, the deaths of his ten children, his disfiguring and debilitating skin condition—they rushed to his side to comfort him. Seeing his suffering, they said nothing for a week.

But when they finally spoke to Job, they were almost relentless in their attempts to persuade him that his suffering was the result of his sin. Eliphaz stated that Job must confess the sins for which he is being punished. Bildad maintained that God rejected Job because Job refused to accept God's fair and just punishment. Zophar accused Job of being wicked, proud, and too ignorant to understand God's ways. Under the weight of the accusations of his three friends, Job began to question the fairness and justice of God. And seeing God as silent, Job asked to plead his case in God's court.

Then a true friend, Elihu, arrived to give Job good counsel. Elihu explained that God is not silent but speaks to us in dreams and visions. More importantly, Elihu said that suffering is not punishment for sin but designed to draw us closer to our just and caring God. As soon as Elihu finished, God spoke to Job from a whirlwind. When God finished, Job repented for questioning God's goodness. But when God turned to Eliphaz, Bildad, and Zophar, he defended Job and expressed his anger against the three for misrepresenting him. God told Job to pray for his three friends and once Job did that God restored Job's fortunes.

We all have friends who, though they mean well, can lead us away from God instead of toward him. Rather than following them, we need to pray that God leads them, and us, on the right path. And we need to look for, and listen to, true friends such as Elihu.

Passage: Verse in Context — Job 42:7–13, 16–17

After the LORD had spoken these words to Job, the LORD said to Eliphaz the Temanite: "My anger burns against you and against your two friends, for you have not spoken of me what is right, as my servant Job has. Now therefore take seven bulls and seven rams and go to my servant Job and offer up a burnt offering for yourselves. And my servant Job shall pray for you, for I will accept his prayer not to deal with you according to your folly. For you have not spoken of me what is right, as my servant Job has." So Eliphaz the Temanite and Bildad the Shuhite and Zophar the Naamathite went and did what the LORD had told them, and the LORD accepted Job's prayer.

And the LORD restored the fortunes of Job, when he had prayed for his friends. And the LORD gave Job twice as much as he had before. Then came to him all his brothers and sisters and all who had known him before, and ate bread with him in his house. And they showed him sympathy and comforted him for all the evil that the LORD had brought upon him. And each of them gave him a piece of money and a ring of gold.

And the LORD blessed the latter days of Job more than his beginning. And he had 14,000 sheep, 6,000 camels, 1,000 yoke of oxen, and 1,000 female donkeys. He had also seven sons and three daughters. … And after this Job lived 140 years, and saw his sons, and his sons' sons, four generations. And Job died, an old man, and full of days.

Questions for Reflection and Application

- Do you have any friends like Eliphaz, Bildad, or Zophar? Why do you have these friends?
- Do you have any friends like Elihu? How did you become friends with them? When do you lean on them? When do they lean on you?
- What steps can you take to cultivate friendships with men who will strengthen your relationship with God?

Lord, help me to recognize the friends who try to help but hurt instead. Give me discernment in friendships. Amen.

HAPPY AND BLESSED

Blessed is the man who walks not in the counsel of the wicked,
nor stands in the way of sinners, nor sits in the seat of scoffers; but his delight
is in the law of the LORD, and on his law he meditates day and night.

—*Psalm 1:1–2*

Some scholars believe that Psalm 1 was one of David's favorite psalms because it opens with the Hebrew word *esher*, which can be translated as "happy" or "blessed." What does it mean to be *esher*? Here are some other times that the word appears in the Psalms, with a description of who is happy or blessed (and why):

- the one whose sins are forgiven and covered by the LORD (32:1–2)
- the nation whose God is the LORD (33:12)
- those who take refuge in our good God (2:12, 34:8, 40:4, 84:12)
- the one who considers the poor and weak (41:1)
- those who are chosen to dwell with God (65:4)
- those whose strength is the LORD and who have his ways in their heart (84:5)
- those who walk in the light of God's face (89:15)
- the one who is taught and disciplined by God (94:12)
- those who observe justice and do righteousness at all times (106:3)
- those who fear the LORD and delight in his commandments (112:1, 128:1)
- those whose way is blameless and walk in the Law of the LORD (119:1)
- those who seek the LORD with all their heart (119:2)

In Psalm 1, David writes that we will be happy and blessed if we seek out a relationship with God and avoid listening to the wicked, emulating the behavior of sinners, and hanging out with scoffers. For David and others of his time, the primary way to have a close relationship with God was to delight in God's Law, learn it, meditate on it, and practice it.

As we learn in Matthew 5:17–20, Jesus is the fulfillment of that Law, which even the best of us cannot keep perfectly. Happy and blessed is the one who follows him.

Passage: Verse in Context — Psalm 1:1–6

Blessed is the man who walks not in the counsel of the wicked, nor stands in the way of sinners, nor sits in the seat of scoffers; but his delight is in the law of the LORD, and on his law he meditates day and night. He is like a tree planted by streams of water that yields its fruit in its season, and its leaf does not wither. In all that he does, he prospers. The wicked are not so, but are like chaff that the wind drives away. Therefore the wicked will not stand in the judgment, nor sinners in the congregation of the righteous; for the LORD knows the way of the righteous, but the way of the wicked will perish.

Related Passage — Psalm 119:1–8

Blessed are those whose way is blameless, who walk in the law of the LORD! Blessed are those who keep his testimonies, who seek him with their whole heart, who also do no wrong, but walk in his ways! You have commanded your precepts to be kept diligently. Oh that my ways may be steadfast in keeping your statutes! Then I shall not be put to shame, having my eyes fixed on all your commandments. I will praise you with an upright heart, when I learn your righteous rules. I will keep your statutes; do not utterly forsake me!

Questions for Reflection and Application

- Around Thanksgiving, it is common to "count your blessings." Do that now. Take a minute to write down some of the ways that God has blessed you. Which of these blessings stand out, and why?
- What people in your life tend to drag you down or draw you away from God? What people tend to reinforce your desire to follow God's Law?
- What are two things that you can do today to begin to plant your roots deep, draw strength from, and find happiness with God?

Father, remind me that happiness—happiness that lasts—comes from following your Son. Amen.

A SHIELD ABOUT ME

But you, O LORD, are a shield about me, my glory,
and the lifter of my head.
—*Psalm 3:3*

In the time of David, a shield was a vital piece of military equipment. Nearly every soldier had a shield to protect his body from his enemy's weapons, including spears, swords, and arrows. The larger a shield, the more it protected, but the heavier and less maneuverable it was. So shield-makers experimented with different sizes, shapes, and materials. Shapes included rectangular, circular, triangular, and figure-eight. Some shields were flat; others were convex. Materials included wood, leather, plaited twigs or reeds, and metal.

The vast majority of shields were personal shields, carried by the fighter himself. But a few soldiers, such as archers, used a very large, wall-like shield that was carried by a second person, the shield-bearer. His job was to accompany the archer or other warrior and ensure that the shield was positioned to protect that warrior. The Philistine giant Goliath, for example, had a shield-bearer so that he could use both his hands for his spear and sword.

In Psalm 3, David says that he has a shield that is all around him. No warrior in Israel's army, or any other, had a shield that could protect a soldier's entire body from any attack, coming from any direction. If David had such a shield in his arsenal, then he certainly couldn't carry it or use it. He would be dependent on a very strong shield-bearer to use such a shield to protect him. But no one had to handle the shield that David mentions, because God was that shield.

Often, we want to protect ourselves and we ask God for shields and weapons to enable us do that. David took a different approach—he was completely dependent on God for his protection. God protected David, revealed his glory to David, and reassured David during a time of great danger.

Let's follow David's example and turn to God during challenging times.

Passage: Verse in Context — Psalm 3:1–8

O LORD, how many are my foes! Many are rising against me; many are saying of my soul, "There is no salvation for him in God."

But you, O LORD, are a shield about me, my glory, and the lifter of my head. I cried aloud to the LORD, and he answered me from his holy hill.

I lay down and slept; I woke again, for the LORD sustained me. I will not be afraid of many thousands of people who have set themselves against me all around.

Arise, O LORD! Save me, O my God! For you strike all my enemies on the cheek; you break the teeth of the wicked.

Salvation belongs to the LORD; your blessing be on your people!

Related Passage — Ephesians 6:13–18a

Therefore take up the whole armor of God, that you may be able to withstand in the evil day, and having done all, to stand firm. Stand therefore, having fastened on the belt of truth, and having put on the breastplate of righteousness, and, as shoes for your feet, having put on the readiness given by the gospel of peace. In all circumstances take up the shield of faith, with which you can extinguish all the flaming darts of the evil one; and take the helmet of salvation, and the sword of the Spirit, which is the word of God, praying at all times in the Spirit, with all prayer and supplication.

Questions for Reflection and Application

- A shield is not a weapon of offense but something used for protection. Why does David refer to God as his shield? How can a shield bring you glory and lift your head?
- Why does Paul refer to faith as a shield? How does faith protect us from attacks by the evil one?
- How can you strengthen your faith and thereby enlarge the protection that God provides?

God, let me turn to you during spiritual battles. While virtues can give a false sense of protection, full reliance on you shields me from Satan's arrows. Amen.

RICHEST MAN IN TOWN

The LORD has heard my plea; the LORD accepts my prayer.
—*Psalm 6:9*

Two-thirds of the way through the film *It's a Wonderful Life*, when George Bailey is at his lowest point, he says this prayer of desperation: "God ... God, dear Father in heaven, I'm not a praying man, but if you're up there and you can hear me, show me the way. I'm at the end of my rope. Show me the way, God."

Thirty seconds later, George is punched in the jaw by the husband of a teacher George had insulted earlier that evening. "That's what I get for praying," George says.

What he doesn't know is that God is responding to his prayer, and the prayers of others for him. Not with a punch in the mouth, but with someone who can do exactly what George requested: show him the way.

The prayers for George begin before his prayer for himself. Troubled by George's behavior before he leaves home in confusion and fear, his wife, Mary, asks her children to pray for their dad. When she learns that George's fear is over his Uncle Billy's misplacing $8,000 from the family business, Mary begins to call everyone in town to ask for help for George. Many people respond to Mary's request by praying for George (as was shown at the very beginning of the film).

Hearing these prayers in heaven, angel Joseph and his (unnamed) superior send second-class angel Clarence Oddbody, who arrives just as George prepares to end his life by jumping off a bridge into the freezing river below. Clarence proceeds to show George what the world would be like if George had never been born. At the film's end, George's problem hasn't changed—his business still owes the bank $8,000 and he doesn't have the money—but he doesn't care. He asked God to show him the way, and God did exactly that.

God hears our petitions. God accepts our prayers. And God responds with just what we need.

Passage: Verse in Context — Psalm 6:1–10

O LORD, rebuke me not in your anger, nor discipline me in your wrath. Be gracious to me, O LORD, for I am languishing; heal me, O LORD, for my bones are troubled. My soul also is greatly troubled. But you, O LORD—how long?

Turn, O LORD, deliver my life; save me for the sake of your steadfast love. For in death there is no remembrance of you; in Sheol who will give you praise?

I am weary with my moaning; every night I flood my bed with tears; I drench my couch with my weeping. My eye wastes away because of grief; it grows weak because of all my foes.

Depart from me, all you workers of evil, for the LORD has heard the sound of my weeping. The LORD has heard my plea; the LORD accepts my prayer. All my enemies shall be ashamed and greatly troubled; they shall turn back and be put to shame in a moment.

Related Passage — 1 Thessalonians 5:16–19

Rejoice always, pray without ceasing, give thanks in all circumstances; for this is the will of God in Christ Jesus for you. Do not quench the Spirit.

Questions for Reflection and Application

- Are you more comfortable with short, pithy prayers or long, eloquent prayers? Which do you think God prefers from you? Why?
- How often do you pray for other people? For which people do you pray? How can you become a more consistent and more effective prayer warrior?
- What does Paul mean by "pray without ceasing"? What would enable you to rejoice and give thanks, even when your life is a complete mess?

Father, thank you that you hear my every plea, prayer, and petition, and you respond by showing me the way. Amen.

PRAISING GOD IN UNCERTAINTY

O Lord , our Lord, how majestic is your name in all the earth!
You have set your glory above the heavens.
—Psalm 8:1

Michael W. Smith grew up in the small town of Kenova, West Virginia. The son of an oil refinery worker and a caterer, Michael became a Christian at the age of ten. During his teen years, he was surrounded with a solid support group of fellow believers who gathered frequently to play music. After a semester at nearby Marshall University, he dropped out of college and moved over three hundred miles away to Nashville to pursue a career in music. When his attempt to get a record deal failed, he began to experiment with drugs and alcohol and had an emotional breakdown.

In October 1979, just before his twenty-second birthday, Michael rededicated his life to Christ, and good things began to happen. He met and fell in love with Debbie Davis and married her in late 1981. Earlier that same year, he was signed by Meadowgreen Music and began writing gospel hits for other artists. After touring as a keyboardist for Amy Grant and becoming her opening act, he recorded his first solo album, which was nominated for a Grammy. That album included "Friends," the first of many hit songs for Michael which he cowrote with Debbie.

"How Majestic Is Your Name," one of the songs that Michael wrote for Sandi Patti in 1981, has simple lyrics repeating the first sentence of Psalm 8:1 and then lauding the name and power of God. The song became a hit, even resulting in publication in many church hymnals and songbooks.

When Michael wrote the song, he had no idea that he would become one of the most successful Christian performing artists in history, selling over eighteen million albums. He was a poor, young, unproven songwriter living in a big city far from his small hometown. But he praised God with everything that he had.

We can do the same.

Passage: Verse in Context — Psalm 8:1–3, 9

O Lord, our Lord, how majestic is your name in all the earth! You have set your glory above the heavens. Out of the mouth of babies and infants, you have established strength because of your foes, to still the enemy and the avenger. …

O Lord, our Lord, how majestic is your name in all the earth!

Related Passage — 2 Peter 1:16–21

For we did not follow cleverly devised myths when we made known to you the power and coming of our Lord Jesus Christ, but we were eyewitnesses of his majesty. For when he received honor and glory from God the Father, and the voice was borne to him by the Majestic Glory, "This is my beloved Son, with whom I am well pleased," we ourselves heard this very voice borne from heaven, for we were with him on the holy mountain. And we have the prophetic word more fully confirmed, to which you will do well to pay attention as to a lamp shining in a dark place, until the day dawns and the morning star rises in your hearts, knowing this first of all, that no prophecy of Scripture comes from someone's own interpretation. For no prophecy was ever produced by the will of man, but men spoke from God as they were carried along by the Holy Spirit.

Questions for Reflection and Application

- Michael W. Smith's first success came not the way he wanted—as a performer—but as a songwriter for other performers. What experience do you have with operating in the background and helping others succeed? How do you feel in that role?
- How well and often do you praise God during a time of uncertainty? What can you do to be more consistent in praising God?
- What are three things for which you can—and really should—praise God today?

Father, even when it seems like I have very little, I know that you have given me everything I need … and so much more. I praise you for that. Amen.

A LITTLE LOWER

*What is man that you are mindful of him, and the son of man
that you care for him? Yet you have made him a little lower than
the heavenly beings and crowned him with glory and honor.*

—Psalm 8:4–5

What does the Bible tell us about angels? For starters, we have some things in common with them. God created them (Daniel 7:10). They are not to be worshiped (Colossians 2:18, Revelation 19:10). They are not infallible (Job 4:18). They have different ranks (Daniel 10:13). God created angels with a free will, and some angels were tempted and fell with the devil (Matthew 25:41, Revelation 12:7–9).

In other ways however, angels are very different than humans and superior to us. Angels live forever (Luke 20:36). They possess superhuman power (2 Thessalonians 1:7, Psalm 103:20). They are called "holy" (Luke 9:26) and "elect" (1 Timothy 5:21). They are spirits (Hebrews 1:14) but, when they appear to people, angels can adopt a human form (Genesis 18:2, Hebrews 13:2). We can be "equal to angels" only when we are resurrected and in heaven (Luke 20:36).

Angels serve God in many ways. Amazingly, their service often is on behalf of us. In Daniel 10, the archangel Michael must relieve an angel in battle with a demon so that the angel can meet with Daniel. In Luke 2, God sends thousands of angels to announce the birth of Jesus to a group of lowly shepherds in a field near Bethlehem. At the end of the parable of the lost coin, Jesus says, "Just so, I tell you, there is joy before the angels of God over one sinner who repents" (Luke 15:10).

Who am I, God, that you are mindful of me and care for me? Yet you have made me only a little lower than your amazing servants, the angels. And those angels care for me, because you command them to.

Passage: Verse in Context — Psalm 8:3–8

When I look at your heavens, the work of your fingers, the moon and the stars, which you have set in place, what is man that you are mindful of him, and the son of man that you care for him? Yet you have made him a little lower than the heavenly beings and crowned him with glory and honor. You have given him dominion over the works of your hands; you have put all things under his feet, all sheep and oxen, and also the beasts of the field, the birds of the heavens, and the fish of the sea, whatever passes along the paths of the seas.

Related Passage — Hebrews 1:1–6

Long ago, at many times and in many ways, God spoke to our fathers by the prophets, but in these last days he has spoken to us by his Son, whom he appointed the heir of all things, through whom also he created the world. He is the radiance of the glory of God and the exact imprint of his nature, and he upholds the universe by the word of his power. After making purification for sins, he sat down at the right hand of the Majesty on high, having become as much superior to angels as the name he has inherited is more excellent than theirs. For to which of the angels did God ever say, "You are my Son, today I have begotten you"? Or again, "I will be to him a father, and he shall be to me a son"? And again, when he brings the firstborn into the world, he says, "Let all God's angels worship him."

Questions for Reflection and Application

- Take some time to read the verses and passages on angels referenced in yesterday's devotion. How does the biblical view of angels compare to your previous view of them?
- Why do angels help people?
- God created both angels and people. Angels are incredible beings. So why does God care so much for people? Why does God care so much for you?

Father, I marvel in the fact you created me just a little lower than angels, who are amazing, holy beings. Amen.

A STRONGHOLD IN EGYPT

The LORD is a stronghold for the oppressed,
a stronghold in times of trouble.

—*Psalm 9:9*

For several generations after the twelve sons of Jacob (renamed Israel) and their families moved there, Egypt was a wonderful place for the Israelites to live. But then an Egyptian king who feared the Israelites came to power and enslaved them, and the Israelites remained slaves for several hundred years. They cried out to God for help, and God selected Moses to lead them out of slavery.

But it wouldn't be easy. God explained to Moses and Aaron that Pharaoh, the leader of Egypt, would not be persuaded by their words or by the "signs and wonders" that God promised to demonstrate. God even told them that he would harden Pharaoh's heart against them. Moses, Aaron, and the Israelites would have to rely on God as their stronghold. And God promised to deliver them from Egypt.

At their first meeting with Pharaoh, Moses and Aaron gave a demonstration of God's power—turning a staff into a serpent—but it had no impact on Pharaoh. God then brought nine plagues upon Egypt: turning water (the Nile River) into blood; swarms of frogs, gnats, and flies; death of livestock; boils, hail, locusts, and darkness. Pharaoh still refused to free the Israelites, so God resorted to a final plague: the death of every firstborn son in Egypt.

God instructed the people of Israel to protect their sons by sacrificing lambs and putting lamb's blood on the doorposts of every Israelite home. God said, "And when I see the blood, I will pass over you" (Exodus 12:13). God passed over the Israelite homes but killed the firstborn son in every Egyptian home, including Pharaoh's. Only then did Pharaoh let the Israelites go.

Every year the people of Israel celebrate Passover to remember their deliverance by God, who is a stronghold for the oppressed.

Passage: Verse in Context — Psalm 9:7–14

But the LORD sits enthroned forever; he has established his throne for justice, and he judges the world with righteousness; he judges the peoples with uprightness. The LORD is a stronghold for the oppressed, a stronghold in times of trouble. And those who know your name put their trust in you, for you, O LORD, have not forsaken those who seek you.

Sing praises to the LORD, who sits enthroned in Zion! Tell among the peoples his deeds! For he who avenges blood is mindful of them; he does not forget the cry of the afflicted. Be gracious to me, O LORD! See my affliction from those who hate me, O you who lift me up from the gates of death, that I may recount all your praises, that in the gates of the daughter of Zion I may rejoice in your salvation.

Related Passage — Exodus 15:1–3

Then Moses and the people of Israel sang this song to the LORD, saying, "I will sing to the LORD, for he has triumphed gloriously; the horse and his rider he has thrown into the sea. The LORD is my strength and my song, and he has become my salvation; this is my God, and I will praise him, my father's God, and I will exalt him. The LORD is a man of war; the LORD is his name."

Questions for Reflection and Application

- One of the definitions for *oppressed* is to feel distressed, anxious, or uncomfortable, usually because of the actions of another person. What people or situations are causing you to feel distressed, anxious, or uncomfortable?
- How do you respond to feeling distressed or anxious? Do you ask God for help? How does God respond?
- The Israelites cried out to God for generations before God responded. Why? How do you feel when God does not respond quickly to your requests for help?

Lord God, just as the Israelites were slaves to the Egyptians, I was a slave to sin. I praise you that you have delivered me from my oppressor and given me new life. Amen.

A LIFE NAVIGATION APP

You make known to me the path of life; in your presence
there is fullness of joy; at your right hand are pleasures forevermore.
—*Psalm 16:11*

A good navigation app uses GPS to determine your position, maps to plot potential routes, and live information sources to determine current speeds along each route. But the app won't start functioning until you supply your target destination. If it tried, then you might have an exchange like that between Alice and the Cheshire Cat:

> "Would you tell me, please, which way I ought to go from here?"
> "That depends a good deal on where you want to get to," said the Cat.
> "I don't much care where—" said Alice.
> "Then it doesn't matter which way you go," said the Cat.
> "—so long as I get SOMEWHERE," Alice added as an explanation.
> "Oh, you're sure to do that," said the Cat, "if you only walk long enough."[19]

God, of course, is the world's best life navigation app. He can supply you with not only the optimal path to your target destination, but the destination itself. Jesus identifies that target destination in John 10:10b: "I came that they may have life and have it abundantly."

Your target destination is abundant life. Not just forgiveness of your sins. Not just eternal life in heaven after you die. Not just salvation and an ongoing relationship with a loving God. Abundant life. Right now.

As David expressed in Psalm 16, God can reveal to you the route that leads to abundant life. For God to do this, you need to be in regular communication with him; not just talking but listening intently. You need to do whatever you can to spend time with God, because in so doing you will receive not only the path of life, but also fullness of joy and pleasures forevermore.

It's a good deal.

Passage: Verse in Context — Psalm 16:1–11

Preserve me, O God, for in you I take refuge. I say to the LORD, "You are my LORD; I have no good apart from you."

As for the saints in the land, they are the excellent ones, in whom is all my delight. The sorrows of those who run after another god shall multiply; their drink offerings of blood I will not pour out or take their names on my lips.

The LORD is my chosen portion and my cup; you hold my lot. The lines have fallen for me in pleasant places; indeed, I have a beautiful inheritance.

I bless the LORD who gives me counsel; in the night also my heart instructs me, I have set the LORD always before me; because he is at my right hand, I shall not be shaken.

Therefore my heart is glad, and my whole being rejoices; my flesh also dwells secure. For you will not abandon my soul to Sheol, or let your holy one see corruption.

You make known to me the path of life; in your presence there is fullness of joy; at your right hand are pleasures forevermore.

Questions for Reflection and Application

- Let's say you are programming a destination in your life navigation app. Where do you want to be next week? Next month? Next year? What path is going to take you to each of those destinations?
- What do you think Jesus meant by having an abundant life? What is your reaction to the proposal that you can have an abundant life right now? What steps have you taken already toward that destination? What additional steps do you need to take?
- How do you spend time with God? How can you spend more time with him?

Father, wherever I am, and wherever I am to go, lead me. Amen.

THE APPLE OF HIS EYE

Keep me as the apple of your eye;
hide me in the shadow of your wings.
—*Psalm 17:8*

No one is sure where the expression "the apple of your eye" originated. Many believe that the apple is the pupil. The Hebrew phrase for the apple of your eye can be translated as "the daughter of your eye" or "the little man of your eye." If you look closely at the pupil of someone's eye, then you will see your reflection in the pupil.

The meaning of the expression today is similar to what it was in biblical times. If you are the apple of God's eye, then God is extremely fond of you, proud of you, and cherishes you. And you are in very good company.

There are two other Old Testament passages that refer to one or more people being the apple of God's eye:

- "But the LORD's portion is his people, Jacob his allotted heritage. He found him in a desert land, and in the howling waste of the wilderness; he encircled him, he cared for him, he kept him as the apple of his eye." (Deuteronomy 32:9–10)
- "For thus said the LORD of hosts, after his glory sent me to the nations who plundered you, for he who touches you touches the apple of his eye." (Zechariah 2:8)

The Deuteronomy passage refers to Jacob, whom God renamed Israel. Even though Jacob was a schemer who made plenty of mistakes, God selected him as the patriarch of God's chosen people, the nation of Israel. The Zechariah passage is part of a prophecy about God's chosen people, who have been spread abroad "as the four winds of the heavens" (v. 6) but are called to escape from the wicked people around them and return to Zion.

Throughout history, those who follow God have been precious to him. Each of them has been the apple of his eye.

And you are one of them.

Passage: Verse in Context — Psalm 17:1–9, 15

Hear a just cause, O LORD; attend to my cry! Give ear to my prayer from lips free of deceit! From your presence let my vindication come! Let your eyes behold the right!

You have tried my heart, you have visited me by night, you have tested me, and you will find nothing; I have purposed that my mouth will not transgress. With regard to the works of man, by the word of your lips I have avoided the ways of the violent. My steps have held fast to your paths; my feet have not slipped.

I call upon you, for you will answer me, O God; incline your ear to me; hear my words. Wondrously show your steadfast love, O Savior of those who seek refuge from their adversaries at your right hand.

Keep me as the apple of your eye; hide me in the shadow of your wings, from the wicked who do me violence, my deadly enemies who surround me. …

As for me, I shall behold your face in righteousness; when I awake, I shall be satisfied with your likeness.

Questions for Reflection and Application

- The name Israel means, "He strives with God." Why did God give Jacob that name? (See Genesis 32:22–32.) Why do you think God chose Jacob, who had major flaws, to be the patriarch of his chosen people? What does that tell you about God?
- Why are you the apple of God's eye?
- How do you keep God's teachings and commandments before you, so that you follow them?

Father, I praise you because you consider me the apple of your eye. May I be the apple that doesn't fall too far from your tree. Amen.

HEROIC RESTRAINT

It is God who arms me with strength and keeps my way secure.
—*Psalm 18:32 (NIV)*

Some Christians were heroic because they fought back against evil. Jackie Robinson was heroic because he had the courage not to fight back.

In August 1945, Robinson was called into the office of Brooklyn Dodgers general manager Branch Rickey, who informed Robinson that if he did well with the Dodgers minor league affiliate (Montreal), he would promote him to be the first black player in Major League Baseball. Rickey knew that Robinson's challenge would be to control his temper when subjected to the vicious bigotry that was sure to come. So during their initial conversation, Rickey acted out how some white hotel managers, restaurant waiters, and ballplayers would attack Robinson with racial epithets and even physical violence. He challenged Robinson to see how he would respond.

Knowing that Robinson shared his Christian faith, Rickey pulled out a copy of the book *Life of Christ* by Giovanni Papini and flipped to a passage on the Sermon on the Mount. There Rickey referred to Jesus' call to "turn the other cheek" as "the most stupefying of [Jesus'] revolutionary teachings." Robinson would have to learn how to follow that call.

After a year in the minors, Robinson got his chance to play with the Dodgers, becoming the team's starting first baseman on opening day in 1947. That season, Robinson's terrific performance on the field—including a .297 batting average and a league-leading twenty-nine stolen bases—earned him the inaugural MLB Rookie of the Year Award. And as Rickey had predicted, Robinson endured horrible bigotry almost every day. Every night Robinson asked God for the strength he needed to endure the hatred without fighting back. God, of course, came through, and Robinson was able to act heroically with love and restraint.[20]

God gifted Jackie Robinson with talent and armed him with strength on and off the field.

Passage: Verse in Context — Psalm 18:1–6, 25–32

I love you, O LORD, my strength. The LORD is my rock and my fortress and my deliverer, my God, my rock, in whom I take refuge, my shield, and the horn of my salvation, my stronghold. I call upon the LORD, who is worthy to be praised, and I am saved from my enemies. The cords of death encompassed me; the torrents of destruction assailed me; the cords of Sheol entangled me; the snares of death confronted me. In my distress I called upon the LORD; to my God I cried for help. From his temple he heard my voice, and my cry to him reached his ears. …

With the merciful you show yourself merciful; with the blameless man you show yourself blameless; with the purified you show yourself pure; and with the crooked you make yourself seem tortuous. For you save a humble people, but the haughty eyes you bring down. For it is you who light my lamp; the LORD my God lightens my darkness. For by you I can run against a troop, and by my God I can leap over a wall. This God—his way is perfect; the word of the LORD proves true; he is a shield for all those who take refuge in him.

For who is God, but the LORD? And who is a rock, except our God?—the God who equipped me with strength and made my way blameless.

Questions for Reflection and Application

- Branch Rickey was a key mentor for Jackie Robinson. What men have been mentors for you? What did these men teach you? Whom have you mentored?
- When someone verbally attacks you or belittles you—including on social media—how do you typically respond? Do you fight back or turn the other cheek? How does it feel to say nothing in response to an unfair attack?
- How can you ensure the next time someone provokes you, that you rely on God for the strength you need to respond in a Christ-like fashion?

God, sometimes the greatest feat of strength is letting you handle the battle. Give me the discernment to know when to fight. Amen.

NOTHING BUT BLUE SKIES

The heavens declare the glory of God,
and the sky above proclaims his handiwork.
—*Psalm 19:1*

How does the sky proclaim the handiwork of God? Clouds can bring needed rain, but clouds rarely brighten someone's day. Blue skies, on the other hand, are a day-brightener. They also are a terrific demonstration of God's handiwork.

Sunlight that reaches the earth is scattered in all directions by molecules of air in the earth's atmosphere. That sunlight consists of all colors; the blue portion of the light spectrum is scattered more than the other colors because it travels as shorter waves. The greater scattering of blue light makes the sky appear to be blue most of the time.

Most other planets in our solar system—including earth's closest neighbors, Mars and Venus—have atmospheres, but none have blue skies. Mars has a "thin" and dusty atmosphere, and the Martian sky has a light brown or orange-red color when seen from the surface. The atmosphere on Venus is composed almost entirely of carbon dioxide, and the atmospheric pressure is so high that landers on the surface are crushed within a few hours. No blue skies there; just a heavy cloud cover, literally!

The most important attribute of earth's atmosphere is not that it yields blue skies but that it contains oxygen, which people and animals breathe. That oxygen is supplied by plants in their process of photosynthesis. Plants use light energy to convert carbon dioxide and water into carbohydrates, giving off oxygen as a by-product. That oxygen forms almost 21 percent of earth's atmosphere, whereas carbon dioxide is only 0.04 percent.

Earth's atmosphere also manages radiation and heat from the sun. The atmosphere filters out harmful ultraviolet radiation while storing and redistributing solar energy. Water vapor and carbon dioxide in the air trap heat from the sun via the greenhouse effect, thereby keeping the earth's surface warm, especially at night. And winds circulate warm air from hotter areas to colder areas.

Truly the sky proclaims God's handiwork and demonstrates how much he loves us.

Passage: Verse in Context — Psalm 19:1–14

The heavens declare the glory of God, and the sky above proclaims his handiwork. Day to day pours out speech, and night to night reveals knowledge. There is no speech, nor are there words, whose voice is not heard. Their voice goes out through all the earth, and their words to the end of the world. In them he has set a tent for the sun, which comes out like a bridegroom leaving his chamber, and, like a strong man, runs its course with joy. Its rising is from the end of the heavens, and its circuit to the end of them, and there is nothing hidden from its heat.

The law of the LORD is perfect, reviving the soul; the testimony of the LORD is sure, making wise the simple; the precepts of the LORD are right, rejoicing the heart; the commandment of the LORD is pure, enlightening the eyes; the fear of the LORD is clean, enduring forever; the rules of the LORD are true, and righteous altogether. More to be desired are they than gold, even much fine gold; sweeter also than honey and drippings of the honeycomb. Moreover, by them is your servant warned; in keeping them there is great reward.

Who can discern his errors? Declare me innocent from hidden faults. Keep back your servant also from presumptuous sins; let them not have dominion over me! Then I shall be blameless, and innocent of great transgression. Let the words of my mouth and the meditation of my heart be acceptable in your sight, O LORD, my rock and my redeemer.

Questions for Reflection and Application

- If you are like most people, then you probably take the earth's atmosphere for granted and rarely consider how wondrous it is. What are some other things you take for granted? How can you stop doing that?
- Psalm 19 praises the law, testimony, precepts, commandment, fear, and rules of the Lord. Which of these is the most important to you? Which one or ones do you rarely consider?
- We don't talk much about keeping God's Law. What role does the Law play in your everyday life? What role should it play?

God, every breath that I take is a reminder of how much you love me. Amen.

MOVING TO A NEW PASTURE

The LORD is my shepherd; I shall not want.
—Psalm 23:1

As a former shepherd in a society where sheep were prized for their wool and a source of food, David knew a lot about sheep. He knew that without a shepherd, sheep wander off on their own, become scattered and lost, and are easy prey for predators, such as wolves and lions.

He and other biblical writers also knew that people have the same tendencies as sheep. That's why many passages in the Bible liken people to sheep.

- We wander off on our own and become scattered and lost. (1 Kings 22:17, Isaiah 53:6, Zechariah 13:7, Luke 15:4–7, 1 Peter 2:25)
- We cannot defend ourselves against our primary predator, the devil. (Matthew 9:36, John 10:12, 1 Peter 5:18)

A good shepherd must do more than prevent the sheep from wandering off and protect the sheep from predators. He also must prevent overgrazing of a good area, because overgrazing can ruin land for future grazing by destroying edible plants and preventing them from growing back. To prevent overgrazing, a shepherd must move the sheep to new pasture. But that is a challenge. The sheep don't want to move, and once they start moving they tend to wander, which exposes them to a variety of threats. Protecting a moving flock is much more difficult than protecting a stationary flock.

We can be like sheep in our spiritual lives: content to stay where we are, even when our spiritual life is stagnant because we have "overgrazed" that area. We may not even recognize that we are beginning to starve. We need to trust our Good Shepherd when he tells us that it is time to move to a new pasture, even if the journey there will be difficult. He'll guide us and protect us, making sure we get there safely. If we follow his voice, then we shall not want.

Passage: Verse in Context — Psalm 23:1–3

The LORD is my shepherd; I shall not want. He makes me lie down in green pastures. He leads me beside still waters. He restores my soul. He leads me in paths of righteousness for his name's sake.

Related Passage — John 10:11–18

"I am the good shepherd. The good shepherd lays down his life for the sheep. He who is a hired hand and not a shepherd, who does not own the sheep, sees the wolf coming and leaves the sheep and flees, and the wolf snatches them and scatters them. He flees because he is a hired hand and cares nothing for the sheep. I am the good shepherd. I know my own and my own know me, just as the Father knows me and I know the Father; and I lay down my life for the sheep. And I have other sheep that are not of this fold. I must bring them also, and they will listen to my voice. So there will be one flock, one shepherd. For this reason the Father loves me, because I lay down my life that I may take it up again. No one takes it from me, but I lay it down of my own accord. I have authority to lay it down, and I have authority to take it up again. This charge I have received from my Father."

Questions for Reflection and Application

- How vibrant is your spiritual life? What areas are becoming stagnant or overgrazed?
- To what new pasture is God calling you? What are the characteristics of that pasture? Are you hesitant or reluctant to move there? If so, why?
- Finding a new pasture often does *not* mean finding a new church. What are some ways that you can bring a new pasture or fresh grass to your existing church and to the men with whom you interact today? Which of these men are most in need of a refresh to their spiritual lives?

Father, wherever you want me to move, let me be willing to follow. Amen.

ROD AND STAFF

Even though I walk through the valley of the shadow of death, I will fear no evil, for you are with me; your rod and your staff, they comfort me.
—*Psalm 23:4*

As they travel through a strange valley on their way to a new pasture, sheep are in a figurative shadow of potential harm and even death. They must rely on their shepherd to protect them and, when necessary, rescue them.

A shepherd in David's day would rely on his rod and staff. A rod was a club that resembled a walking stick, used to protect the sheep from predators and robbers. A staff was a longer piece of wood with a hook at one end and a spoon-shaped shovel at the other. The shepherd would use the hook to correct and re-direct sheep and, when necessary, to pull a sheep out of a hole, pit, or crevice. The shepherd would use the shovel to flick dirt or mud on a wandering sheep to guide it back to the rest of the flock.

Sheep were comforted by the rod and staff because they knew that their shepherd would use those tools to guide and protect them. Our Good Shepherd, Jesus, has much greater tools, as explained in the hymn "Come, Thou Fount of Every Blessing" by Robert Robinson:

> Jesus sought me when a stranger, Wandering from the fold of God;
> He, to rescue me from danger, Bought me with his precious blood …
> … Oh, to grace how great a debtor Daily I'm constrained to be!
> Let Thy goodness, like a fetter, Bind my wandering heart to Thee:
> Prone to wander, Lord, I feel it, Prone to leave the God I love;
> Here's my heart, O take and seal it; Seal it for Thy courts above.

Whatever valleys you travel through in life, whatever threats and dangers you face, God is ready to guide and protect you. Just ask, and he'll be there, with a staff in his hand and a rod on his belt. He knows how to use them.

Passage: Verse in Context — Psalm 23:1–4

The LORD is my shepherd; I shall not want. He makes me lie down in green pastures. He leads me beside still waters. He restores my soul. He leads me in paths of righteousness for his name's sake. Even though I walk through the valley of the shadow of death, I will fear no evil, for you are with me; your rod and your staff, they comfort me.

Related Passage — 1 Samuel 17:32–37

And David said to Saul, "Let no man's heart fail because of him. Your servant will go and fight with this Philistine." And Saul said to David, "You are not able to go against this Philistine to fight with him, for you are but a youth, and he has been a man of war from his youth." But David said to Saul, "Your servant used to keep sheep for his father. And when there came a lion, or a bear, and took a lamb from the flock, I went after him and struck him and delivered it out of his mouth. And if he arose against me, I caught him by his beard and struck him and killed him. Your servant has struck down both lions and bears, and this uncircumcised Philistine shall be like one of them, for he has defied the armies of the living God." And David said, "The LORD who delivered me from the paw of the lion and from the paw of the bear will deliver me from the hand of this Philistine." And Saul said to David, "Go, and the LORD be with you!"

Questions for Reflection and Application

- David recognized that even though he had many enemies on earth, his worst enemies were in the spiritual realm. He relied on God as his protector against his spiritual enemies. How much do you rely on God for protection from the forces of evil? How do you enlist God's help?
- From what has Jesus saved you already?
- What guidance and protection do you need from God today? This week?

God, guide me and protect me with your rod and staff. When I stray, get me back. When I face danger from the enemy, come to my aid. Amen.

THE PURSUIT OF SINNERS

Surely goodness and mercy shall follow me all the days of my life,
and I shall dwell in the house of the LORD forever.

—Psalm 23:6

What does it mean for God's goodness and mercy to follow you? The answer probably is better than you have imagined.

The Hebrew word that is translated as "follow" is *radaph*, which means, "pursue." God's goodness and mercy are not dependent on our actions. Certainly, God wants us to follow him with all that we have. When we don't do so, however, God pursues us.

Jesus made this clear in the three "lost" parables: the lost sheep, the lost coin, and the lost (or prodigal) son. First, Jesus explained that if anyone had one hundred sheep but lost one, he would leave the ninety-nine and pursue the one that is lost. Next, Jesus described a woman with ten silver coins who loses one and searches diligently until she finds it. Jesus likened finding the lost sheep, or the lost coin, to a sinner repenting.

Jesus saved the best, and most shocking, story for last. The younger of two sons essentially tells his father, "I wish you were dead so that I could have my inheritance." The father gives the son what he wants, and the son proceeds to squander it all in a foreign land. Completely destitute, the son decides to beg his father to take him back as a servant.

A good Jewish father had every right to refuse the son's request. But the father in Jesus' story does the unthinkable: every day he scans the horizon for his son and, when he spots him, the father debases himself, *runs* to the son, and embraces him. When the son repents, the father accepts him not as a servant but as a son.

God doesn't wait for us to get our act together. He doesn't make us jump through hoops before we can get a bit of his goodness and mercy. He *pursues* us. And when we repent, he and the angels rejoice in heaven.

Passage: Verse in Context — Psalm 23:5–6

You prepare a table before me in the presence of my enemies; you anoint my head with oil; my cup overflows. Surely goodness and mercy shall follow me all the days of my life, and I shall dwell in the house of the LORD forever.

Related Passage — Luke 15:1–7

Now the tax collectors and sinners were all drawing near to hear him. And the Pharisees and the scribes grumbled, saying, "This man receives sinners and eats with them."

So he told them this parable: "What man of you, having a hundred sheep, if he has lost one of them, does not leave the ninety-nine in the open country, and go after the one that is lost, until he finds it? And when he has found it, he lays it on his shoulders, rejoicing. And when he comes home, he calls together his friends and his neighbors, saying to them, 'Rejoice with me, for I have found my sheep that was lost.' Just so, I tell you, there will be more joy in heaven over one sinner who repents than over ninety-nine righteous persons who need no repentance."

Questions for Reflection and Application

- Why did Jesus start with a story of one lost sheep out of one hundred, then tell of one lost coin out of ten, and then tell of one lost son out of two?
- What is consistent about each of the "lost" parables?
- How is God pursuing you with his love and mercy? How are you responding?
- Do you ever find yourself acting like a Pharisee and getting mad at God for pursuing people who seem unredeemable? What should you do when you feel that way?

Father, when I run away from you, you pursue me. You never give up. Amen.

THE LORD OF HOSTS

Lift up your heads, O gates! And lift them up, O ancient doors,
that the King of glory may come in. Who is this King of glory?
The LORD of hosts, he is the King of glory!

—Psalm 24:9–10

Psalm 24:7–10 is the text for a choral piece in Part II of Handel's *Messiah*. The first half of the piece is unique in the oratorio because it has two soprano parts instead of one, and the choir divides into two groups to sing sections of the psalm passage back and forth. When the entire choir sings together for the first time, it is to repeat the phrase "The Lord of hosts."

Why did Handel emphasize "The Lord of hosts" in this piece? What does the expression mean?

In *Waking the Dead*, author John Eldredge recounts how his Bible version translated the expression as "the Lord Almighty," which sounded too religious and "churchy" to Eldredge. He discovered that the original Hebrew means "the God of angel armies" or "the God of the armies who fight for his people." Eldredge writes:

> *The God who is at war.* Does "Lord Almighty" convey "the God who is at war"? Not to me, it doesn't. Not to anyone I've asked. It sounds like "the god who is out there but still in charge." Powerful, in control. The God of angel armies sounds like the one who would roll up his sleeves, take up sword and shield to break down gates of bronze, and cut through bars of iron to rescue me. Compare "Joe is a good man who is in control" to "Joe is a Navy Seal." It changes the way you think about Joe and what he's up to.[21]

Our God is a God of love and compassion, a God of forgiveness and peace. But he also is the God of angel armies. He and his armies are fighting the forces of evil to rescue us so that we may have life, and have it to the full. The Lord of hosts: he is the King of glory!

Passage: Verse in Context — Psalm 24:1–10

The earth is the Lord's and the fullness thereof, the world and those who dwell therein, for he has founded it upon the seas and established it upon the rivers.

Who shall ascend the hill of the Lord? And who shall stand in his holy place? He who has clean hands and a pure heart, who does not lift up his soul to what is false and does not swear deceitfully. He will receive blessing from the Lord and righteousness from the God of his salvation. Such is the generation of those who seek him, who seek the face of the God of Jacob.

Lift up your heads, O gates! And be lifted up, O ancient doors, that the King of glory may come in. Who is this King of glory? The Lord, strong and mighty, the Lord, mighty in battle! Lift up your heads, O gates! And lift them up, O ancient doors, that the King of glory may come in. Who is this King of glory? The Lord of hosts, he is the King of glory!

Questions for Reflection and Application

- Now that you know what "the Lord of hosts" means, what images does it bring to your mind? How do those images compare to the images of God as the God of grace, mercy, forgiveness, love, and compassion?
- How does knowing that God is the Lord of Hosts change your impressions of Jesus?
- How do you feel about the fact that God commands armies of angels to fight on your behalf?
- Can you ascend the hill of the Lord? Do you have "clean hands and a pure heart"? What do you need to do? How can you start today?

Almighty God, I often forget your power. I praise you that you are the Lord of Hosts and that you and your hosts fight for me. Amen.

FEARLESS STEPHEN

The LORD is my light and my salvation; whom shall I fear?
—Psalm 27:1a

Stephen was chosen to "serve tables" (Acts 6:2). But God had much bigger plans for him.

The twelve apostles who headed the early Christian church chose seven men to take care of widows. One of those chosen was Stephen, "a man full of faith and of the Holy Spirit" (v. 5). Stephen began to do "great wonders and signs among the people" (v. 8). This caught the attention of some Jews who were not Christians. These Jews lost every argument with Stephen, so they began to spread lies about him, claiming that he spoke "blasphemous words against Moses and God" (v. 11). Once the lies took hold, the Jews seized Stephen, brought him before the council, and set up false witnesses to testify against him.

When the high priest asked him, "Are these things so?" (7:11), Stephen had a choice. He could operate out of fear of what the council may do to him and simply refute the false witnesses, or he could be fearless and try to persuade people to follow Christ. Because God was his light and his salvation, Stephen chose the latter.

After citing their common faith, Stephen reminded the assembly how the Jews repeatedly had strayed from a right relationship with God, resisting the Holy Spirit and persecuting the prophets. He concluded by stating that they had betrayed and murdered Jesus, whom he called "the Righteous One" (v. 52). The Jews responded by stoning Stephen to death.

What did Stephen's bold approach accomplish, other than getting him killed? A devout Jew named Saul, who had observed the proceedings and approved of Stephen's death, had listened to Stephen. Saul bitterly opposed Stephen and other Christians that day but, after his conversion to Christianity, Saul (who became the apostle Paul) remembered Stephen's arguments and used them as his own.

When God is your light and your salvation, you have nothing to fear, not even death. God will use your words and actions to build his kingdom, even when you are opposed.

Passage: Verse in Context — Psalm 27:1–5

The LORD is my light and my salvation; whom shall I fear? The LORD is the stronghold of my life; of whom shall I be afraid? When evildoers assail me to eat up my flesh, my adversaries and foes, it is they who stumble and fall. Though an army encamp against me, my heart shall not fear; though war arise against me, yet I will be confident. One thing have I asked of the LORD, that will I seek after: that I may dwell in the house of the LORD all the days of my life, to gaze upon the beauty of the LORD and to inquire in his temple. For he will hide me in his shelter in the day of trouble; he will conceal me under the cover of his tent; he will lift me high upon a rock.

Related Passage — Acts 7:54–60

Now when they heard these things they were enraged, and they ground their teeth at him. But he, full of the Holy Spirit, gazed into heaven and saw the glory of God, and Jesus standing at the right hand of God. And he said, "Behold, I see the heavens opened, and the Son of Man standing at the right hand of God." But they cried out with a loud voice and stopped their ears and rushed together at him. Then they cast him out of the city and stoned him. And the witnesses laid down their garments at the feet of a young man named Saul. And as they were stoning Stephen, he called out, "Lord Jesus, receive my spirit." And falling to his knees he cried out with a loud voice, "Lord, do not hold this sin against them." And when he had said this, he fell asleep.

Questions for Reflection and Application

- In Psalm 27, why does David have no fear? What is his only real ambition in life? Why was Stephen so bold, even though he knew that the council had the power to kill him?
- In what situations are you most confident and bold? When do you hold back? Why? What are you most afraid of losing?
- How do you know when God wants you to act boldly?

Father, even when my words and actions seem to produce no results, you use all of me—past, present, and future—to bring others to you. Amen.

A GENTLE REMINDER

Wait for the LORD; be strong, and let your heart take courage;
wait for the LORD!
—*Psalm 27:14*

These days, it's difficult for people to wait for anything. According to the Urban Dictionary, the term "microwave generation" applies to the many people today who expect instant information on their smartphones and instant gratification in almost every aspect of life. We have become so impatient, says the Urban Dictionary, that we stand in front of a microwave, tapping our foot and yelling, "Come on!"

We may have taken impatience to a new level, but being patient was tough even in biblical times. In many of his psalms, David cries out to God with complaints that God has not come through for him and seems distant or even silent. "Answer me when I call, O God of my righteousness!" (4:1). "Why, O LORD, do you stand far away? Why do you hide yourself in times of trouble?" (10:1). "How long, O LORD? Will you forget me forever? How long will you hide your face from me?" (13:1).

In Psalm 27, David makes similar pleas to God: "Hear, O LORD, when I cry aloud; be gracious to me and answer me! ... Hide not your face from me. Turn not your servant away in anger, O you who have been my help. Cast me not off; forsake me not, O God of my salvation!" (vv. 7, 9).

David's pattern in most of the "complaint psalms" is to follow the complaints with reminders of how God always comes through for him. In Psalm 27 however, David simply makes one confident statement: "I believe that I shall look upon the goodness of the LORD in the land of the living!" (v. 13). He then finishes the psalm with today's verse, where he exhorts himself to wait with courage.

When God seems distant, we need to follow David's pattern: cry out to God, remind ourselves of God's help in the past, and exhort ourselves to be strong in God. The result will be reassurance and confidence that enable us to be patient … even when we don't want to.

Passage: Verse in Context — Psalm 27:7–14

Hear, O LORD, when I cry aloud; be gracious to me and answer me! You have said, "Seek my face." My heart says to you, "Your face, LORD, do I seek." Hide not your face from me. Turn not your servant away in anger, O you who have been my help. Cast me not off; forsake me not, O God of my salvation! For my father and my mother have forsaken me, but the LORD will take me in.

Teach me your way, O LORD, and lead me on a level path because of my enemies. Give me not up to the will of my adversaries; for false witnesses have risen against me, and they breathe out violence. I believe that I shall look upon the goodness of the LORD in the land of the living! Wait for the LORD; be strong, and let your heart take courage; wait for the LORD!

Related Passage — Romans 5:3–5

Not only that, but we rejoice in our sufferings, knowing that suffering produces endurance, and endurance produces character, and character produces hope, and hope does not put us to shame, because God's love has been poured into our hearts through the Holy Spirit who has been given to us.

Questions for Reflection and Application

- What is the longest that you have waited for God to answer (or respond to) one of your prayer requests? What was the request? Why do you think God waited so long to respond?
- Take a minute and consider times that God has come through for you. List them. For each, how long did it take for God to respond, and how long did it take for the situation to be resolved? What patterns do you see?
- Why does God want us to wait for him? Think of at least three reasons.

Father, amidst a microwave generation give me the patience to follow David's pattern—even when you seem miles away. Amen.

OFFERING REASSURANCE

The LORD is my strength and my shield; in him my heart trusts,
and I am helped.
—Psalm 28:7a

We know that we need to trust in God and that, when we do, we will be helped. But sometimes we need some reassurance that God hears us and will respond.

For the people of Israel, children were considered a blessing from God. When a woman could not have children, she often felt that, and was treated as if, her barrenness was a curse. Sarah, Rebekah, Rachel, and Samson's mother all were barren for a time, but God answered their prayers, and the prayers of their husbands, for children.

The book of 1 Samuel opens with the story of Hannah, who was "deeply distressed" (1:10) about being barren and often provoked by her husband's other wife, who had borne children. One day when she was near the temple, Hannah, while weeping bitterly, said a silent prayer to God in which she promised that if God gave her a son, she would dedicate him to God's service.

Seeing her lips moving but hearing no sound, Eli the priest confronted Hannah and accused her of being drunk. Hannah answered that she was not drunk but had been pouring out her soul to God, speaking out of her "great anxiety and vexation" (v. 16). Eli believed her. Not knowing her prayer request, he said, "Go in peace, and the God of Israel grant your petition that you have made to him" (v. 17).

The brief exchange with Eli caused Hannah to trust that God heard her prayer and would respond. God had, and God did, giving Hannah a son, whom she named Samuel, which sounds like the Hebrew for "God has heard." Hannah kept her promise and brought Samuel to Eli to serve God all his life.

Sometimes when we're not sure that God hears us, it is good for us to get reassurance from another believer. And sometimes we need to offer that reassurance to someone else.

Passage: Verse in Context — Psalm 28:1–2, 6–9

To you, O LORD, I call; my rock, be not deaf to me, lest, if you be silent to me, I become like those who go down to the pit. Hear the voice of my pleas for mercy, when I cry to you for help, when I lift up my hands toward your most holy sanctuary. … Blessed be the LORD! For he has heard the voice of my pleas for mercy. The LORD is my strength and my shield; in him my heart trusts, and I am helped; my heart exults, and with my song I give thanks to him. The LORD is the strength of his people; he is the saving refuge of his anointed. Oh, save your people and bless your heritage! Be their shepherd and carry them forever.

Related Passage — 1 Samuel 1:12–18

As she continued praying before the LORD, Eli observed her mouth. Hannah was speaking in her heart; only her lips moved, and her voice was not heard. Therefore Eli took her to be a drunken woman. And Eli said to her, "How long will you go on being drunk? Put your wine away from you." But Hannah answered, "No, my lord, I am a woman troubled in spirit. I have drunk neither wine nor strong drink, but I have been pouring out my soul before the LORD. Do not regard your servant as a worthless woman, for all along I have been speaking out of my great anxiety and vexation." Then Eli answered, "Go in peace, and the God of Israel grant your petition that you have made to him." And she said, "Let your servant find favor in your eyes." Then the woman went her way and ate, and her face was no longer sad.

Questions for Reflection and Application

- When you are waiting for a response from God, how much does it help you to be reminded that God is your strength and shield and that God will come through for you eventually?
- Who has reassured you that God has heard you and God is faithful? How much did that reassurance help you?
- When have you reassured another believer of God's faithfulness? Whom can you reassure this week?

God, in the barren moments of my life, send me someone who reassures me. When I sense barrenness in another person, lead me to offer reassurance. Amen.

A PRE-FIGHT BLESSING

The LORD gives strength to his people;
the LORD blesses his people with peace.
—*Psalm 29:11 (NIV)*

In *Rocky II*, Rocky Balboa has spent the past few weeks training at a furious pace. He has become what his trainer Mick wanted: "a greasy, fast Italian monster." He is ready for his rematch with Apollo Creed.

But when it comes time for him to leave his house for the fight, he stalls. He tells his infant son not to worry about anything and tells his wife, Adrian, that he wishes she could be at the fight. As he steps outside, in front of an adoring crowd, he instructs Adrian's brother, Paulie, to take care of the baby, to take care of "everything." When Adrian tells him that he is going to be late for his fight, he responds, unconvincingly, that everything will be fine. He is not at peace.

When he drives away, he doesn't go to the arena but to his church and yells for Father Carmine. The priest opens a window and asks in Italian why Rocky is there when he is supposed to be at the fight. Rocky responds by asking for a favor.

"Well, it's about the fight, you know," begins Rocky. "Now that I've got the family and the baby and all that stuff, I was wondering, you know, if you could throw down a blessing so that, if I get beat up tonight, you know, it won't be too bad, you know. Could you do something like that?"

Father Carmine blesses Rocky, who takes off his hat. After the blessing, Rocky makes the sign of the cross, kisses his cross necklace, and says, "Thanks a lot, Father. I really appreciate it. I've gotta go—I'm so late. I'll see ya in church, I hope. Take care!" He jumps back in his car and peels away, heading for the arena.

His mood has changed completely. He is at peace.

Regardless of what we face in the hours and days ahead, God offers us that kind of peace. We just have to ask.

Passage: Verse in Context — Psalm 29:1–11

Ascribe to the LORD, O heavenly beings, ascribe to the LORD glory and strength. Ascribe to the LORD the glory due his name; worship the LORD in the splendor of holiness.

The voice of the LORD is over the waters; the God of glory thunders, the LORD, over many waters. The voice of the LORD is powerful; the voice of the LORD is full of majesty.

The voice of the LORD breaks the cedars; the LORD breaks the cedars of Lebanon. He makes Lebanon to skip like a calf, and Sirion like a young wild ox.

The voice of the LORD flashes forth flames of fire. The voice of the LORD shakes the wilderness; the LORD shakes the wilderness of Kadesh. The voice of the LORD makes the deer give birth and strips the forests bare, and in his temple all cry, "Glory!"

The LORD sits enthroned over the flood; the LORD sits enthroned as king forever. May the LORD give strength to his people! May the LORD bless his people with peace!

Questions for Reflection and Application

- Are you at peace now? If so, why? If not, how long has it been since you felt at peace? What is keeping you from having peace?
- How often do you ask God for peace? Where does peace rate on your priority scale? What things are more important to you than your heart being at peace?
- What is the relationship between strength and peace? How can you get both? What challenges or obstacles do you face in doing that?

Father, before I face a challenge, big or small, give me peace. Amen.

PLENTY AND FAMINE

Oh, how abundant is your goodness, which you have stored up
for those who fear you and worked for those who take refuge in you,
in the sight of the children of mankind!
—*Psalm 31:19*

For much of Psalm 31, David is in distress and "wasted from grief" (v. 9). But in the depth of his despair, David puts his trust in God. That action changes his mood and outlook, and by the end of the psalm he exudes confidence in God: "Be strong, and let your heart take courage, all you who wait for the LORD!" (v. 24).

When describing God's goodness, David uses an interesting phrase. He says that God stores up goodness for those who fear him. Why does God store up goodness for us?

Storing up something is a good practice when that item is not always readily available. When Joseph recognized that seven years of plenty in Egypt would be followed by seven years of famine, he recommended that Egypt store up one-fifth of the food produced during the years of plenty as a reserve for the seven years of famine. Because Pharaoh heeded Joseph's advice, there was food for everyone in Egypt and surrounding lands, including Joseph's family, during the horrible famine.

There is never a famine for God's goodness, though. God has abundant goodness all the time, enough for everyone. So why does God store it up for those who fear him?

God does this for our own good. If we were showered with blessings all the time, then we probably wouldn't recognize the goodness of God, and we might even feel entitled to all those blessings and more. So God does something similar to what Pharaoh did. Rather than overloading us with blessings during times of plenty, God sets some aside for us. Then during times of famine, when we go to God and ask him for help, he responds by giving us blessings from our storehouse.

God's goodness is abundant. He makes sure that we have all we need, when we need it ... and when we ask.

Passage: Verse in Context — Psalm 31:1–5, 9–10, 19–24

In you, O LORD, do I take refuge; let me never be put to shame; in your righteousness deliver me! Incline your ear to me; rescue me speedily! Be a rock of refuge for me, a strong fortress to save me! For you are my rock and my fortress; and for your name's sake you lead me and guide me; you take me out of the net they have hidden for me, for you are my refuge. Into your hand I commit my spirit; you have redeemed me, O LORD, faithful God. ...

Be gracious to me, O LORD, for I am in distress; my eye is wasted from grief; my soul and my body also. For my life is spent with sorrow, and my years with sighing; my strength fails because of my iniquity, and my bones waste away. ...

Oh, how abundant is your goodness, which you have stored up for those who fear you and worked for those who take refuge in you, in the sight of the children of mankind! In the cover of your presence you hide them from the plots of men; you store them in your shelter from the strife of tongues. Blessed be the LORD, for he has wondrously shown his steadfast love to me when I was in a besieged city. I had said in my alarm, "I am cut off from your sight." But you heard the voice of my pleas for mercy when I cried to you for help. Love the LORD, all you his saints! The LORD preserves the faithful but abundantly repays the one who acts in pride. Be strong, and let your heart take courage, all you who wait for the LORD!

Questions for Reflection and Application

- What are three reasons God stores up goodness for you rather than giving you a steady rain of it all the time? How do you feel about that?
- How do your communications with and prayers to God during difficult or lean times compare with your communications during good times? If they are different, then why? How can your prayers be more consistent?
- What can you do to get God to store up more blessings for you?

God, in famished times of my life, please remind me that you store your goodness and it overflows in abundance for me. Amen.

WEE LITTLE MAN IN JERICHO

I acknowledged my sin to you, and I did not cover my iniquity;
I said, "I will confess my transgressions to the LORD,"
and you forgave the iniquity of my sin.
—*Psalm 32:5*

Tax collectors were extremely unpopular in Jesus' day. Rome ruled the Jewish homeland, and Jews considered the Roman Empire to be an oppressive regime. Tax collectors were Jews working for Rome, so they were seen as traitors by their countrymen. Rather than collecting just what Rome was owed, tax collectors cheated people out of extra money and then kept the extra funds.

Zacchaeus was a chief tax collector who had built a fortune on the backs of others in Jericho. When Jesus visited Jericho, Zacchaeus wanted to see him. But Zacchaeus was short. Really short. With a crowd of people around Jesus wherever he went, Zacchaeus would never get a glimpse of him. The chief tax collector had no choice but to debase himself, run ahead along the path that Jesus was walking, and climb a sycamore tree, just as a child or youth would do.

When Jesus came near the tree he said, "Zacchaeus, hurry and come down, for I must stay at your house today" (Luke 19:5). Zacchaeus couldn't believe it! Practically leaping from the tree, Zacchaeus hit the ground and received Jesus joyfully. Others, however, were not so joyful. They grumbled that Jesus had "gone in to be the guest of a man who is a sinner" (v. 7).

But the call from Jesus had transformed Zacchaeus' life. "Behold, Lord, the half of my goods I give to the poor," he said to Jesus. "And if I have defrauded anyone of anything, I restore it fourfold" (v. 8). Jesus replied that salvation had come to Zacchaeus.

Like Zacchaeus, all of us are sinners. Jesus calls us anyway, because he came "to seek and to save the lost" (v. 10). When we confess our sins to God—not trying to hide them, not making excuses for them, but acknowledging them openly—God forgives the iniquity of our sins.

Passage: Verse in Context — Psalm 32:1–5

Blessed is the one whose transgression is forgiven, whose sin is covered. Blessed is the man against whom the LORD counts no iniquity, and in whose spirit there is no deceit. For when I kept silent, my bones wasted away through my groaning all day long. For day and night your hand was heavy upon me; my strength was dried up as by the heat of summer. I acknowledged my sin to you, and I did not cover my iniquity; I said, "I will confess my transgressions to the LORD," and you forgave the iniquity of my sin.

Related Passage — Luke 19:1–10

[Jesus] entered Jericho and was passing through. And behold, there was a man named Zacchaeus. He was a chief tax collector and was rich. And he was seeking to see who Jesus was, but on account of the crowd he could not, because he was small in stature. So he ran on ahead and climbed up into a sycamore tree to see him, for he was about to pass that way. And when Jesus came to the place, he looked up and said to him, "Zacchaeus, hurry and come down, for I must stay at your house today." So he hurried and came down and received him joyfully. And when they saw it, they all grumbled, "He has gone in to be the guest of a man who is a sinner." And Zacchaeus stood and said to the Lord, "Behold, Lord, the half of my goods I give to the poor. And if I have defrauded anyone of anything, I restore it fourfold." And Jesus said to him, "Today salvation has come to this house, since he also is a son of Abraham. For the Son of Man came to seek and to save the lost."

Questions for Reflection and Application

- What type of person today would be comparable to a tax collector in the time of Jesus? How would you compare to such a person in the eyes of others? In God's eyes?
- When do you find it most difficult to confess your sins to God?
- Which is easier: admitting to someone that you have sinned against him, or admitting that same sin to God? Why?

Creator of the Universe, you saw this wee little man and decided I was worth saving. Thank you! Amen.

GREAT AND GOOD

I sought the LORD, and he answered me
and delivered me from all my fears.
—*Psalm 34:4*

When you were a child, perhaps you said a prayer like this before meals: "God is great; God is good. Let us thank him for our food. By his hands we all are fed. Thank you, Lord, for daily bread. Amen."

Today's verse implies that God is great and God is good. To have the ability to deliver anyone, anywhere, in any situation, from all his or her fears, God must have authority and power over all things. God must be great. To respond to someone—and further, to help someone—even though that person has sinned against others and against him many times, God must be very gracious and loving. God must be good.

Often we are drawn to the "good" qualities of God. It is comforting to know that he loves us, even when we don't feel worthy of his love. It is reassuring to know that God forgives us when we repent, even if find ourselves repenting again, and again, and again. We marvel at the fact that Jesus bore the penalty for our sins on the cross. God truly is good.

The "great" qualities of God can be a little frightening. In the flood, God destroyed every living creature on earth, allowing only the inhabitants of Noah's ark to be saved. When Jesus calmed a violent storm with a stern command, the disciples were "filled with great fear" (Mark 4:41). In the Old Testament, God is known as "God of angel armies" (see April 27–28), and in the book of Revelation Jesus is clothed in a robe dipped in blood, leading the armies of heaven.

If God were great but not good, then he would be the source of our fears. If God were good but not great, then he would lack the power to help us. To be delivered from our fears, we need a God who is great and good.

And that's what we have. Let us thank him for our food … and everything else.

Passage: Verse in Context — Psalm 34:1–7, 15–22

I will bless the LORD at all times; his praise shall continually be in my mouth. My soul makes its boast in the LORD; let the humble hear and be glad. Oh, magnify the LORD with me, and let us exalt his name together! I sought the LORD, and he answered me and delivered me from all my fears. Those who look to him are radiant, and their faces shall never be ashamed. This poor man cried, and the LORD heard him and saved him out of all his troubles. The angel of the LORD encamps around those who fear him, and delivers them. …

The eyes of the LORD are toward the righteous and his ears toward their cry. The face of the LORD is against those who do evil, to cut off the memory of them from the earth. When the righteous cry for help, the LORD hears and delivers them out of all their troubles. The LORD is near to the brokenhearted and saves the crushed in spirit.

Many are the afflictions of the righteous, but the LORD delivers him out of them all. He keeps all his bones; not one of them is broken. Affliction will slay the wicked, and those who hate the righteous will be condemned. The LORD redeems the life of his servants; none of those who take refuge in him will be condemned.

Questions for Reflection and Application

- Are you drawn more to the goodness of God or the greatness of God? Why?
- In the Lord's Prayer, the only thing that you really ask God to give you is your daily bread. Psalm 34, on the other hand, says that God hears the cries of the righteous and "delivers them out of all their troubles" (v. 17). What requests does God want to hear from you? How does God want those requests made to him?
- What fears do you have today from which you want God to deliver you?

God, I want to be delivered from my fears. Only you can do that because you are great and good. Deliver me! Amen.

PERSON TO PERSON

Those who look to him are radiant,
and their faces shall never be ashamed.
—*Psalm 34:5*

Shame is a powerful force. In the acclaimed television series *Mad Men*, shame drives the lead character, Don Draper, to spend most of his life running from his past … and himself.

The illegitimate son of a prostitute who died during childbirth, Don grows up in a brothel, where he receives little love from his father or his father's wife. As a young adult, Don is deployed to Korea. When his lieutenant is killed at an isolated base, Don switches identity tags with the deceased, changing his name, and his identity, from Dick Whitman to Don Draper.

For years Don seems to thrive in his new identity. He marries a model named Betty, and they have three children. He rises in New York City ad agencies, eventually becoming an executive and partner in an agency. But Don never seems satisfied or happy. He cheats on Betty incessantly, leading her to divorce him. He drinks and smokes constantly. He manipulates people in the workplace. And he is haunted by his past. When his younger brother, Adam Whitman, discovers that he is alive and visits him, Don tells him to forget him and his past. Rejected by his brother, Adam hangs himself.

When Don finally begins to face his past, his mask peels away and his world crumbles. He runs away, ending up in California. There, at the end of his rope, he calls his protégé, Peggy, for what Don believes will be their final conversation. Peggy begs him to come home, but Don confesses that he is not the man Peggy thinks he is: "I broke all my vows. I scandalized my child. I took another man's name and made nothing of it."

Don cannot run from his shame. It follows him wherever he goes.

Thanks to God, we don't have to try to run from our shame. When we trust in him and accept his forgiveness, we are radiant, and we shall never be ashamed.

Passage: Verse in Context — Psalm 34:1–7

I will bless the Lord at all times; his praise shall continually be in my mouth. My soul makes its boast in the Lord; let the humble hear and be glad. Oh, magnify the Lord with me, and let us exalt his name together! I sought the Lord, and he answered me and delivered me from all my fears. Those who look to him are radiant, and their faces shall never be ashamed. This poor man cried, and the Lord heard him and saved him out of all his troubles. The angel of the Lord encamps around those who fear him, and delivers them.

Related Passage — 2 Corinthians 3:12–18

Since we have such a hope, we are very bold, not like Moses, who would put a veil over his face so that the Israelites might not gaze at the outcome of what was being brought to an end. But their minds were hardened. For to this day, when they read the old covenant, that same veil remains unlifted, because only through Christ is it taken away. Yes, to this day whenever Moses is read a veil lies over their hearts. But when one turns to the Lord, the veil is removed. Now the Lord is the Spirit, and where the Spirit of the Lord is, there is freedom. And we all, with unveiled face, beholding the glory of the Lord, are being transformed into the same image from one degree of glory to another. For this comes from the Lord who is the Spirit.

Questions for Reflection and Application

- In *Mad Men*, when Don Draper faces his past and tries to stop living a life of lies, his career suffers. What are your biggest fears when it comes to being honest with others about who you really are?
- For what things are you ashamed? How does God feel about those things? How do you know?
- Psalm 34 says that those who look to God will never be ashamed. In 2 Corinthians, Paul says that those who turn to the Lord are being transformed into the image of Christ. How are you looking to God in your day-to-day life? How are you turning to the Lord?

Lord, I never have to hide my face in shame because you allow me to look to you and reflect your glory. Amen.

TASTE AND SEE

Oh, taste and see that the LORD is good!
Blessed is the man who takes refuge in him!
—*Psalm 34:8*

In Psalm 34, David encourages us to use all five of our senses to experience the goodness of God, including our most underused sense: taste. In John chapter 2, Jesus performs a miracle that enables a large group of people to taste the goodness of God.

When we come on the scene, the wine has run out at a wedding in Cana that Jesus and his disciples are attending. This is a catastrophe in the making for the groom's family. In Jesus' day, a wedding celebration could last five to seven days, and often the entire village gathered to celebrate. The groom's family was responsible for ensuring that there was enough food and drink for the entire celebration. To run out of wine was to invite shame and even legal action from the village.

Seeing six stone jars used for washing, each holding twenty to thirty gallons, Jesus instructs the servants to fill the jars with water. By the time the master of the feast appears, he finds the jars filled not with water but with wine. Jesus has saved the day, and in an extravagant fashion. The quality of the wine is so good that it surpasses that of the wine that was served earlier. Rather than being simply sufficient for drunk guests late at night, the wine is perfect for the beginning of the next day's celebration. By creating 120 to 180 gallons of the wine, Jesus has ensured that there is enough wine for the rest of the celebration, regardless of how long it continues.

In Romans 1, Paul says that God's invisible attributes—his eternal power and divine nature—can be perceived by observing the things that God has made. That includes items of food and drink that tickle our taste buds. Taste and see that the Lord is good!

Passage: Verse in Context — Psalm 34:8-14

Oh, taste and see that the LORD is good! Blessed is the man who takes refuge in him! Oh, fear the LORD, you his saints, for those who fear him have no lack! The young lions suffer want and hunger; but those who seek the LORD lack no good thing. Come, O children, listen to me; I will teach you the fear of the LORD. What man is there who desires life and loves many days, that he may see good? Keep your tongue from evil and your lips from speaking deceit. Turn away from evil and do good; seek peace and pursue it.

Related Passage — John 2:6-11

Now there were six stone water jars there for the Jewish rites of purification, each holding twenty or thirty gallons. Jesus said to the servants, "Fill the jars with water." And they filled them up to the brim. And he said to them, "Now draw some out and take it to the master of the feast." So they took it. When the master of the feast tasted the water now become wine, and did not know where it came from (though the servants who had drawn the water knew), the master of the feast called the bridegroom and said to him, "Everyone serves the good wine first, and when people have drunk freely, then the poor wine. But you have kept the good wine until now." This, the first of his signs, Jesus did at Cana in Galilee, and manifested his glory. And his disciples believed in him.

Questions for Reflection and Application

- How did God feel about Jewish marriage celebrations in Jesus' day? What types of celebrations and events do you think God appreciates today? Why?
- Sometimes you will smell or taste something that reminds you of a person, place, or event from your past, even your distant past? What scents and tastes make you want to praise God?
- What scents or tastes bring back bad memories? What does God want you to do with those memories?

Lord God, may I not just see and hear that you are good, may I experience you in all five senses. Amen.

YOU ARE OPPOSED

Many are the afflictions of the righteous,
but the LORD delivers him out of them all.

—Psalm 34:9

In many of his psalms, David says that God blesses the righteous. Here are some examples: "For you bless the righteous, O LORD; you cover him with favor as with a shield" (5:11). "The righteous shall inherit the land and dwell upon it forever" (37:29). "Light is sown for the righteous, and joy for the upright in heart" (97:11).

So why are the righteous afflicted? As we endure event after event that breaks our hearts, our confidence that we matter to God and that he means us well is eroded. After all, why didn't God heal your mom? Save your marriage? Get you married? Help you out more? Or, as John Eldredge writes, why is life so difficult?

> Either (a) we're blowing it, or (b) God is holding out on us. Or some combination of both, which is where most people land. Think about it. Isn't this where you land, with all the things that haven't gone the way you'd hoped and wanted?[22]

The truth is that we are afflicted because we are opposed. As C. S. Lewis writes:

> One of the things that surprised me when I first read the New Testament seriously was that it talked so much about a Dark Power in the universe—a mighty evil spirit who was held to be the Power behind death and disease, and sin. The difference is that Christianity thinks this Dark Power was created by God, and was good when he was created, and went wrong. Christianity agrees with Dualism that this universe is at war. But it does not think this is a war between independent powers. It thinks it is a civil war, a rebellion, and that we are living in a part of the universe occupied by the rebel.[23]

You may have many afflictions in life, but God is on your side. Trust in him, and he will deliver you out of them all.

Passage: Verse in Context — Psalm 34:15–22

The eyes of the LORD are toward the righteous and his ears toward their cry. The face of the LORD is against those who do evil, to cut off the memory of them from the earth. When the righteous cry for help, the LORD hears and delivers them out of all their troubles. The LORD is near to the brokenhearted and saves the crushed in spirit. Many are the afflictions of the righteous, but the LORD delivers him out of them all. He keeps all his bones; not one of them is broken. Affliction will slay the wicked, and those who hate the righteous will be condemned. The LORD redeems the life of his servants; none of those who take refuge in him will be condemned.

Related Passage — 1 Peter 5:6–11

Humble yourselves, therefore, under the mighty hand of God so that at the proper time he may exalt you, casting all your anxieties on him, because he cares for you. Be sober-minded; be watchful. Your adversary the devil prowls around like a roaring lion, seeking someone to devour. Resist him, firm in your faith, knowing that the same kinds of suffering are being experienced by your brotherhood throughout the world. And after you have suffered a little while, the God of all grace, who has called you to his eternal glory in Christ, will himself restore, confirm, strengthen, and establish you. To him be the dominion forever and ever. Amen.

Questions for Reflection and Application

- When you are afflicted, what is your first response?
- When do you find yourself feeling that either you're blowing it or God is holding out on you? How do you overcome that feeling?
- Part of comedian Flip Wilson's routine was the phrase "the devil made me do it." How seriously do you treat the forces of evil and what role they play in your life?
- How has God delivered you from afflictions?

Father, help me to recognize when I am afflicted why it happens (I am opposed) and who will deliver me (you). Amen.

THE DESIRES OF YOUR HEART

Delight yourself in the LORD,
and he will give you the desires of your heart.
—Psalm 37:4

For the Jews of David's time, delighting in God's Law was synonymous with delighting in God. Delighting in God's Law is not like coming close to the speed limit if you think that there might be a policeman or trooper with radar nearby. It is not following the rules because you fear the repercussions. God gave us the Law not to keep us in line but so that we would appreciate him and his love for us. After all, Jesus said that "all the Law and the Prophets" (Matthew 22:40) hang on two commandments: (1) Love the Lord your God with all your heart and with all your soul and with all your mind and (2) Love your neighbor as yourself. (See Matthew 22:36–40.)

The apostle Paul recognized that he could not keep the Law on his own. In Romans 7, he laments that, while he wants to do what is right, he lacks the ability to carry it out. The "law of sin" within him keeps causing him to do the evil that he doesn't want to do, until he cries out, "Wretched man that I am! Who will deliver me from this body of death?" (Romans 7:23–24). The answer, of course, is Jesus.

"For the law of the Spirit of life has set you free in Christ Jesus from the law of sin and death. For God has done what the law, weakened by the flesh, could not do. By sending his own Son in the likeness of sinful flesh and for sin, he condemned sin in the flesh, in order that the righteous requirement of the law might be fulfilled in us, who walk not according to the flesh but according to the Spirit" (Romans 8:2–5).

Thanks be to God! We can delight in his law and in him by delighting in his Son. When we do, God will give us the desires of our heart, and those desires will bear an uncanny resemblance to the desires of God's heart.

Passage: Verse in Context — Psalm 37:3–7, 16–19

Trust in the LORD, and do good; dwell in the land and befriend faithfulness. Delight yourself in the LORD, and he will give you the desires of your heart.

Commit your way to the LORD; trust in him, and he will act. He will bring forth your righteousness as the light, and your justice as the noonday.

Be still before the LORD and wait patiently for him; fret not yourself over the one who prospers in his way, over the man who carries out evil devices! ...

Better is the little that the righteous has than the abundance of many wicked. For the arms of the wicked shall be broken, but the LORD upholds the righteous.

The LORD knows the days of the blameless, and their heritage will remain forever; they are not put to shame in evil times; in the days of famine they have abundance.

Questions for Reflection and Application

- Which parts of the Law make you appreciate God more? Which parts of the Law seem to put an obstacle between you and God?
- Which parts of the Law do you have the most trouble keeping? Why?
- What does it mean for you to walk "according to the Spirit"? What disciplines are you practicing to do that more consistently? What disciplines are you not practicing—or not practicing consistently enough?

Father, I love your law because I love your Son. When my heart aligns with yours, you give me the desires of my heart. Amen.

STAND UP EIGHT

The steps of a man are established by the LORD,
when he delights in his way; though he fall,
he shall not be cast headlong, for the LORD upholds his hand.
—*Psalm 37:23–24*

Nobody likes to fall, but everyone does.

In 2008, a popular television commercial for Converse basketball shoes featured NBA star Dwayne Wade. The first half of the commercial was a montage of Wade getting knocked to the basketball floor, usually via a hard foul from the opposing team. After one of those times, the camera lingered on Wade, face down on the floor.

After the montage, there were scenes of Wade getting up after his spills. The tagline was a Japanese proverb: Fall seven times. Stand up eight.

Some people believe that if you follow God and have enough faith then you won't fall—you won't suffer calamities or even disappointments. To these people, falling is evidence of a lack of faith. If you fall, then it's your own fault.

David, a man after God's own heart (Acts 13:22), had his share of "falls." Some of these certainly were David's fault, but many were not. In Psalm 37, David, now an old man, states from experience that, even when you are a consistent follower of God, you still will fall. And falling, or suffering, is no fun. It leaves you bruised and battered—maybe not physically, but certainly emotionally. Emotional scars can last a long time. Even when you are able to get back in the game, you may not want to, because you could get knocked down again.

But God is at your side, holding your hand. You may not realize it, but he has softened your fall. He has kept you from going off the cliff. He has shielded you from jagged rocks. He has kept you on the path. You can get back up again. He will help you do that. And once you are back on your feet, he'll stay at your side.

Fall seven times. Stand up eight. Just keep holding onto his hand. Don't let go.

Passage: Verse in Context — Psalm 37:23–31, 39–40

The steps of a man are established by the LORD, when he delights in his way; though he fall, he shall not be cast headlong, for the LORD upholds his hand.

I have been young, and now am old, yet I have not seen the righteous forsaken or his children begging for bread. He is ever lending generously, and his children become a blessing.

Turn away from evil and do good; so shall you dwell forever. For the LORD loves justice; he will not forsake his saints. They are preserved forever, but the children of the wicked shall be cut off. The righteous shall inherit the land and dwell upon it forever. The mouth of the righteous utters wisdom, and his tongue speaks justice. The law of his God is in his heart; his steps do not slip. …

The salvation of the righteous is from the LORD; he is their stronghold in the time of trouble. The LORD helps them and delivers them; he delivers them from the wicked and saves them, because they take refuge in him.

Questions for Reflection and Application

- How do you know if you are following the path that God wants you to follow or your own path?
- Think about some recent times when you have "fallen." Why did you fall? Where was God? How did the experience affect your relationship with God?
- After you fall, do you always get back in the game? If so, how? If not, why not?
- What emotional scars do you bear because of past failures? How are you dealing with them?

Father, every time I fall, you help me stand up again. Every time. You never tire of helping me up. Amen.

THE PATIENCE OF JOSEPH

I waited patiently for the Lord; he inclined to me and heard my cry.
He drew me up from the pit of destruction, out of the miry bog,
and set my feet upon a rock, making my steps secure.
—Psalm 40:1–2

People often mention "the patience of Job," but Joseph was the poster child of patience.

His patience began when he was seventeen and his brothers sold him as a slave. He was taken to Egypt, where he ended up serving Potiphar, Pharaoh's captain of the guard. Recognizing that God was with Joseph, Potiphar made Joseph the overseer of his house. But Joseph still was a slave.

Potiphar's wife decided that she wanted Joseph. When he resisted all her advances, she framed him for attempted rape, and Potiphar threw Joseph in prison. God helped Joseph gain favor with the keeper of the prison, who put Joseph in charge of all the other prisoners. But Joseph still was in prison.

Pharaoh's chief cupbearer and chief baker end up in prison. Both had dreams, which God enabled Joseph to interpret. Knowing that the cupbearer would be reinstated, Joseph asked the cupbearer to tell Pharaoh about Joseph. But the cupbearer forgot about Joseph, and Joseph remained in prison.

Two years later, when Pharaoh had dreams that no one could interpret, the cupbearer finally remembered Joseph and told Pharaoh about him. After Joseph interpreted Pharaoh's dreams, Pharaoh made Joseph second in command in Egypt.

Joseph spent thirteen years as a slave and prisoner before God set his feet upon a rock. But those years were necessary for God's plan. The betrayal of Joseph's brothers brought Joseph to Egypt. The false accusation by Potiphar's wife put Joseph in Pharaoh's prison. Interpreting the cupbearer's dream gave Joseph an ally in Pharaoh's court. Interpreting Pharaoh's dreams about a coming famine put Joseph in a position where God could use him to save thousands of people, including Joseph's family—God's chosen people—from starvation.

When you wait patiently, God will come through, not just for you but also for others.

Passage: Verse in Context — Psalm 40:1–4

I waited patiently for the LORD; he inclined to me and heard my cry. He drew me up from the pit of destruction, out of the miry bog, and set my feet upon a rock, making my steps secure. He put a new song in my mouth, a song of praise to our God. Many will see and fear, and put their trust in the LORD. Blessed is the man who makes the LORD his trust, who does not turn to the proud, to those who go astray after a lie!

Related Passage — Genesis 50:15–21

When Joseph's brothers saw that their father was dead, they said, "It may be that Joseph will hate us and pay us back for all the evil that we did to him." So they sent a message to Joseph, saying, "Your father gave this command before he died: 'Say to Joseph, "Please forgive the transgression of your brothers and their sin, because they did evil to you."' And now, please forgive the transgression of the servants of the God of your father." Joseph wept when they spoke to him. His brothers also came and fell down before him and said, "Behold, we are your servants." But Joseph said to them, "Do not fear, for am I in the place of God? As for you, you meant evil against me, but God meant it for good, to bring it about that many people should be kept alive, as they are today. So do not fear; I will provide for you and your little ones." Thus he comforted them and spoke kindly to them.

Questions for Reflection and Application

- Joseph spent thirteen years as a slave and a prisoner. Thirteen years! What is the longest time that you have suffered? How did you make it through that period?
- Consider some tough times that you have endured. How did God use those times as a part of his plan? How patient were you with God? If you could go back and live through those periods again, what would you do differently?
- What disciplines can you undertake to increase your patience?

Father, my life seems to be one trial after another. Grant me the patience of Joseph, and help me to trust in your plan for me, as he trusted in you. Amen.

A MIGHTY FORTRESS

God is our refuge and strength, a very present help in trouble.

—*Psalm 46:1*

In 1517, Martin Luther started the Protestant Reformation by posting his "Ninety-Five Theses," or "Disputation on the Power of Indulgences," on the door of All Saints' Church in Wittenberg, Germany. But Luther was much more than a theologian. Among his many other gifts and talents, he was a musician with a desire to restore worship to the German church.

Luther worked with other musicians to write thirty-six hymns that were designed to revive congregational singing. The most widely known of his hymns is "Ein Feste Burg Ist Unser Gott" or, in English, "A Mighty Fortress Is Our God." Written in 1527, the hymn was instantly popular throughout Germany and, nearly five hundred years later, remains a favorite of many. Its vivid German proved difficult to translate, although at least eighty English versions are available. Even though it was penned by a leader of the Protestant Reformation, the hymn is popular even in the Roman Catholic Church.

Based on Psalm 46, the hymn celebrates the power of God over all enemies, earthly and spiritual. David starts the psalm by calling God our refuge and strength. Luther starts the hymn with even more vivid imagery—God is a mighty fortress with (in German) plenty of weapons for us to use against our enemies.

Here is the first verse of the most popular English translation, by Frederick H. Hedge, dated 1853:

A mighty fortress is our God, A bulwark never failing;
Our helper He amid the flood Of mortal ills prevailing:
For still our ancient foe Doth seek to work us woe;
His craft and power are great, And, armed with cruel hate,
On earth is not his equal.[24]

The hymn and the psalm on which it is based remind us that we will have trouble in this life because our "ancient foe" wants it that way. Regardless of what Satan throws at us, God will remain our refuge and strength, and he will help us through the storm.

Passage: Verse in Context — Psalm 46:1–11

God is our refuge and strength, a very present help in trouble. Therefore we will not fear though the earth gives way, though the mountains be moved into the heart of the sea, though its waters roar and foam, though the mountains tremble at its swelling.

There is a river whose streams make glad the city of God, the holy habitation of the Most High. God is in the midst of her; she shall not be moved; God will help her when morning dawns. The nations rage, the kingdoms totter; he utters his voice, the earth melts. The LORD of hosts is with us; the God of Jacob is our fortress.

Come, behold the works of the LORD, how he has brought desolations on the earth. He makes wars cease to the end of the earth; he breaks the bow and shatters the spear; he burns the chariots with fire. "Be still, and know that I am God. I will be exalted among the nations, I will be exalted in the earth!"

The LORD of hosts is with us; the God of Jacob is our fortress.

Questions for Reflection and Application

- What is your favorite hymn or worship song? Why is it your favorite?
- A fortress combines a refuge (safety) with strength (weapons). How does God protect you from the forces of evil? With what weapons does God supply you? How can you become more effective at using those weapons?
- In addition to describing God as a fortress, Psalm 46 states that the Lord of hosts—the God of angel armies—is with us. Which is more compelling for you? Why?

God, you are my mighty fortress, always protecting me when the foe seeks to work me woe. Amen.

IT IS WELL

Cast your cares on the LORD and he will sustain you;
he will never let the righteous be shaken.
—*Psalm 55:22 (NIV)*

Things were going well for the Spafford family. Horatio, a prosperous Chicago lawyer, was making shrewd investments in properties along Lake Michigan. He and his wife, Anna, were blessed with four daughters and a son and living comfortably in the Lakeview neighborhood on the city's north side.

Then a series of tragedies struck. First, the Spaffords' four-year-old son died of scarlet fever. A short time later, the great Chicago fire of 1871 caused extensive damage to the properties that the Spaffords owned. The economic downturn of 1873 dealt a further blow to Horatio's business interests.

In late 1873, needing a break, the family decided to travel to Europe. Needing to stay in Chicago to resolve some fire-related zoning problems, Horatio sent Anna and the girls ahead on the S.S. *Ville du Havre*. On November 22, the ship was struck by an English vessel in the Atlantic and sank quickly. Anna, who stayed afloat by clinging to debris, was one of only forty-seven people who survived. Her four daughters drowned. When she reached Cardiff, Wales, Anna sent her husband a telegram: "Saved alone."

The grieving father hastily traveled to meet his grieving wife. As his ship passed the area where his daughters had died, Horatio, a devout Christian, wrote the hymn "It Is Well." Here are the first and last verses:

When peace like a river attendeth my way,
When sorrows like sea billows roll;
Whatever my lot, Thou hast taught me to say,
"It is well, it is well with my soul."
And, Lord, haste the day when the faith shall be sight,
The clouds be rolled back as a scroll,
The trump shall resound, and the Lord shall descend,
"Even so"—it is well with my soul.[25, 26]

How was Horatio Spafford able to deal with tragedies of this magnitude? He cast his cares on the Lord, and the Lord sustained him.

Passage: Verse in Context — Psalm 55:1–5, 16–22

Give ear to my prayer, O God, and hide not yourself from my plea for mercy! Attend to me, and answer me; I am restless in my complaint and I moan, because of the noise of the enemy, because of the oppression of the wicked. For they drop trouble upon me, and in anger they bear a grudge against me. My heart is in anguish within me; the terrors of death have fallen upon me. Fear and trembling come upon me, and horror overwhelms me. …

But I call to God, and the LORD will save me. Evening and morning and at noon I utter my complaint and moan, and he hears my voice. He redeems my soul in safety from the battle that I wage, for many are arrayed against me. God will give ear and humble them, he who is enthroned from of old, because they do not change and do not fear God.

My companion stretched out his hand against his friends; he violated his covenant. His speech was smooth as butter, yet war was in his heart; his words were softer than oil, yet they were drawn swords.

Cast your burden on the LORD, and he will sustain you; he will never permit the righteous to be moved.

Questions for Reflection and Application

- At the start of Psalm 55, David's heart is in anguish. Later, however, he declares that God will save, sustain, and restore him. How was David able to overcome his anguish? How do you deal with tragedies in your life?
- In his song, Spafford declares that his soul is "well," but he also looks forward to the day when he will be rewarded for his faith and see his Savior face-to-face. What questions might Spafford ask Jesus? What do you want to ask Jesus? How do you think Jesus will respond?
- How has God sustained you during the worst times in your life?

Lord God, whether I am floating down a peaceful river or flailing under sea billows, it is well with my soul—because my soul is secure with you. Amen.

IN GOD WE TRUST

When I am afraid, I put my trust in you. In God,
whose word I praise, in God I trust; I shall not be afraid.
—Psalm 56:3–4a

David knew that when he was afraid he needed to put his trust in God and then his fear would disappear. But how did David know that he could put his trust in God? In other words, why did David trust God?

"IN GOD WE TRUST" is the United States national motto, and every bill and coin of US currency includes the phrase. According to the US Department of the Treasury, the motto first appeared on coins as a result of "increased religious sentiment" during the Civil War. The Secretary of the Treasury heard from many devout US citizens that the government should "recognize the Deity on United States coins." So Congress passed a law, and the motto began appearing on all US coins.

Nearly a century later, Congress took action again, and the motto began to appear on paper money:

In a law passed by the 84th Congress (P.L. 84–140) and approved by the president on July 30, 1956, the president approved a Joint Resolution of the 84th Congress, declaring IN GOD WE TRUST the national motto of the United States. [27]

Apparently, every American trusts God. After all, it's the national motto.

Of course, trusting someone is not as easy as simply saying, "I trust you." When David was afraid, he remembered God's Word. That Word included not just God's Law but also the history of how God had helped his people—those who, like David, feared God. Remembering that God had helped in the past reassured David that God would help now and gave David the confidence that he could trust God. David's trust conquered his fears. Ours can do the same.

IN GOD WE TRUST. As a result, we are not afraid.

Passage: Verse in Context — Psalm 56:1–4, 8–11

Be gracious to me, O God, for man tramples on me; all day long an attacker oppresses me; my enemies trample on me all day long, for many attack me proudly. When I am afraid, I put my trust in you. In God, whose word I praise, in God I trust; I shall not be afraid. What can flesh do to me? ... You have kept count of my tossings; put my tears in your bottle. Are they not in your book? Then my enemies will turn back in the day when I call. This I know, that God is for me. In God, whose word I praise, in the LORD, whose word I praise, in God I trust; I shall not be afraid. What can man do to me?

Related Passage — Mark 9:17–18a, 21–24

And someone from the crowd answered him, "Teacher, I brought my son to you, for he has a spirit that makes him mute. And whenever it seizes him, it throws him down, and he foams and grinds his teeth and becomes rigid." ... And Jesus asked [the child's] father, "How long has this been happening to him?" And he said, "From childhood. And it has often cast him into fire and into water, to destroy him. But if you can do anything, have compassion on us and help us." And Jesus said to him, " 'If you can'! All things are possible for one who believes." Immediately the father of the child cried out and said, "I believe; help my unbelief!"

Questions for Reflection and Application

- Who has broken your trust? Were you able to trust that person again? If so, how?
- Whose trust have you broken? Were you able to rebuild that person's trust in you? If so, how?
- Do you ever have trouble believing in or trusting God? If so, why?
- In Mark 9, the father expresses doubt that Jesus can help his son. How does Jesus respond? (Read Mark 9:25–29.) How do you think God feels when we have doubts about him?

Father, when I doubt, remind me of how many times you have helped me and saved me in the past. I put my trust in you for today and tomorrow. Amen.

THE BEST THINGS IN LIFE

Because your steadfast love is better than life, my lips will praise you.

—*Psalm 63:3*

In 1927, the songwriting team of Buddy DeSylva, Lew Brown (lyrics), and Ray Henderson (music) wrote songs for the musical *Good News*. One of those songs, "The Best Things in Life Are Free," enjoyed a revival after World War II and has been covered by many artists. The song mentions six of the best things in life—the moon, the stars, springtime flowers, songbirds, sunbeams, and love—that are freely available to everyone.

When you consider the best things in your life, flowers and birds may not leap to your mind. Love may, depending on your situation. You may picture a wonderful vacation spot, your child's first steps, a delicious meal, watching your favorite sports team win a championship, hearing a beautiful concert, the picturesque view at the top of a mountain, or one of a thousand other things.

Life has many good things to offer that don't cost us a dime.

David experienced wonderful things in his life. Certainly, he had his share of problems and hardships, but he was a king, and God blessed him richly. David recognized, however, that even the best things in life can't hold a candle to the steadfast love of God. At the beginning of Psalm 63, David expresses the fact that, without God, his life is hollow and empty: "O God, you are my God; earnestly I seek you; my soul thirsts for you; my flesh faints for you, as in a dry and weary land where there is no water" (v. 1).

God wants us to enjoy our lives on earth. After all, he designed our first home here—the garden of Eden—to be a paradise. But without God, even a paradise is unsatisfying.

The best things in life are free. The very best thing in life is God.

Passage: Verse in Context — Psalm 63:1–11

O God, you are my God; earnestly I seek you; my soul thirsts for you; my flesh faints for you, as in a dry and weary land where there is no water. So I have looked upon you in the sanctuary, beholding your power and glory.

Because your steadfast love is better than life, my lips will praise you. So I will bless you as long as I live; in your name I will lift up my hands.

My soul will be satisfied as with fat and rich food, and my mouth will praise you with joyful lips, when I remember you upon my bed, and meditate on you in the watches of the night; for you have been my help, and in the shadow of your wings I will sing for joy. My soul clings to you; your right hand upholds me.

But those who seek to destroy my life shall go down into the depths of the earth; they shall be given over to the power of the sword; they shall be a portion for jackals. But the king shall rejoice in God; all who swear by him shall exult, for the mouths of liars will be stopped.

Questions for Reflection and Application

- Take three to five minutes to make a list of the best things in your life. How many items are on the list? How many more could you add if you took another five minutes?
- Of the best things in your life, what percentage are things that you purchased or worked hard to attain, and what percentage were free?
- Is the steadfast love of God better than the best things in your life? How can you develop a deeper appreciation for the fact that God loves you, sent Jesus that you may have life to the full, and has prepared a place for you in heaven?

Father, the best things in life are free because you gave your Son freely. Amen.

(GOOD) NEWS FLASH!

The LORD gives the word;
the women who announce the news are a great host.
—*Psalm 68:11*

At the time of David, and for centuries before, women celebrated the victories of the Israelites with music, songs, and dances. They also announced any good news or joyful event to the people at large. In Psalm 68, the news is coming directly from God, and God is entrusting the women to announce the news to everyone.

One thousand years later, God again entrusted women to announce great news. This time the news was the resurrection of Jesus. On Easter Sunday morning, all of Jesus' disciples were in hiding. The only followers who came near the tomb of Jesus were women: Mary Magdalene, Joanna, and Mary the mother of James. When they returned from the tomb, they had an amazing announcement for the disciples: the stone was rolled away, the tomb was empty, and angels had told them that Jesus was alive.

Most of the disciples did not believe the women, but Peter and John ran to the tomb and saw the strips of linen and cloth that had been wrapped around his body and head. The two returned to the other disciples and told them that the tomb was empty, thereby verifying the report of the women.

Mary Magdalene returned to the tomb and stood outside it, weeping. After speaking briefly with two angels, she turned and saw Jesus, whom she recognized as soon as he said her name. She returned to the disciples and exclaimed, "I have seen the Lord" (John 20:18).

The first people to see and report on the empty tomb were women. The first person to see the risen Jesus was a woman. God entrusted women to announce the most important news in history.

Passage: Verse in Context — Psalm 68:7–13

O God, when you went out before your people, when you marched through the wilderness, the earth quaked, the heavens poured down rain, before God, the One of Sinai, before God, the God of Israel. Rain in abundance, O God, you shed abroad; you restored your inheritance as it languished; your flock found a dwelling in it; in your goodness, O God, you provided for the needy. The LORD gives the word; the women who announce the news are a great host: "The kings of the armies—they flee, they flee!" The women at home divide the spoil—though you men lie among the sheepfolds—the wings of a dove covered with silver, its pinions with shimmering gold.

Related Passage — Luke 24:1–10

But on the first day of the week, at early dawn, they went to the tomb, taking the spices they had prepared. And they found the stone rolled away from the tomb, but when they went in they did not find the body of the Lord Jesus. While they were perplexed about this, behold, two men stood by them in dazzling apparel. And as they were frightened and bowed their faces to the ground, the men said to them, "Why do you seek the living among the dead? He is not here, but has risen. Remember how he told you, while he was still in Galilee, that the Son of Man must be delivered into the hands of sinful men and be crucified and on the third day rise." And they remembered his words, and returning from the tomb they told all these things to the eleven and to all the rest. Now it was Mary Magdalene and Joanna and Mary the mother of James and the other women with them who told these things to the apostles.

Questions for Reflection and Application

- What are at least three reasons God chose women to announce the resurrection of Jesus?
- What are the strengths of the women in your life? What do they do better than you?
- How can you affirm and encourage the women in your life?

Father, you give a voice to the voiceless to proclaim your good work. May I know that, no matter how powerless I feel, you make me powerful. Amen.

DOUBTING DISCIPLES

You ascended on high, leading a host of captives in your train.
—*Psalm 68:18a*

Here is how the Gospel of Luke records the ascension of Jesus: "And he led them out as far as Bethany, and lifting up his hands he blessed them. While he blessed them, he parted from them and was carried up into heaven. And they worshiped him and returned to Jerusalem with great joy, and were continually in the temple blessing God" (24:50–53).

Sounds fairly cut and dry. Jesus blessed the disciples and ascended. Excited, the disciples headed to Jerusalem and started the church.

Near the end of the Gospel of Matthew, however, there is an odd statement about the disciples: "[They] went to Galilee, to the mountain to which Jesus had directed them. And when they saw him they worshiped him, but some doubted" (28:16–17). Some doubted? Doubted what? Luke provides a clue in the opening to the book of Acts: "So when they had come together, they asked him, 'Lord, will you at this time restore the kingdom to Israel?' He said to them, 'It is not for you to know times or seasons that the Father has fixed by his own authority. But you will receive power when the Holy Spirit has come upon you, and you will be my witnesses in Jerusalem and in all Judea and Samaria, and to the end of the earth' " (1:6–8).

After Jesus died and rose, all eleven disciples saw him. They knew he was alive. But some of them doubted … that he was the Messiah. After all, the Messiah was going to overthrow the Romans and restore the kingdom of Israel. After Jesus ascended, they stared at the sky, hoping he'd come back and fulfill his real mission.

But his mission was not to overthrow the Romans. His mission was to liberate people who are captives of sin—including you and me. And he had accomplished that mission. The disciples who didn't understand got the message from the Holy Spirit a few weeks later at Pentecost.

And then they started the church.

Passage: Verse in Context — Psalm 68:15–20

O mountain of God, mountain of Bashan; O many-peaked mountain, mountain of Bashan! Why do you look with hatred, O many-peaked mountain, at the mount that God desired for his abode, yes, where the LORD will dwell forever? The chariots of God are twice ten thousand, thousands upon thousands; the LORD is among them; Sinai is now in the sanctuary. You ascended on high, leading a host of captives in your train and receiving gifts among men, even among the rebellious, that the LORD God may dwell there. Blessed be the LORD, who daily bears us up; God is our salvation. Our God is a God of salvation, and to God, the LORD, belong deliverances from death.

Related Passage — Acts 2:1–4, 14, 36

When the day of Pentecost arrived, they were all together in one place. And suddenly there came from heaven a sound like a mighty rushing wind, and it filled the entire house where they were sitting. And divided tongues as of fire appeared to them and rested on each one of them. And they were all filled with the Holy Spirit and began to speak in other tongues as the Spirit gave them utterance. ... But Peter, standing with the eleven, lifted up his voice and addressed them: "Men of Judea and all who dwell in Jerusalem, let this be known to you, and give ear to my words. ... Let all the house of Israel therefore know for certain that God has made him both Lord and Christ, this Jesus whom you crucified."

Questions for Reflection and Application

- Why did the disciples deny and abandon Jesus when he was put on trial and executed? Why did so many followers of Jesus misunderstand his true identity and mission? When and why have you denied and abandoned Jesus or misunderstood his identity and mission?
- Write down the names of people you know who have questions about Jesus. How can you help them know him more?

Father, sometimes I don't get it. I place you in a box and think you'll work in a way that molds to my plan. Send your Spirit to give me clarity, just as you did with the doubting disciples. Amen.

YOU CAN DEPEND ON ME

Be to me a rock of refuge, to which I may continually come;
you have given the command to save me, for you are my rock and my fortress.
—*Psalm 71:3*

One of the most popular film genres of all time is the western. Westerns became popular because Americans romanticized the frontier spirit of the Old West, where people succeeded because of hard work, determination, rugged independence, and self-reliance.

The icon of the western was Marion Morrison, better known as John Wayne. He appeared in 142 films, most of them westerns, and was a top box office draw for three decades. Wayne's hit films included *Red River*, *The Longest Day*, *How the West Was Won*, and *True Grit*. Here are some famous lines uttered by Wayne in films:

- "Well, there are some things a man just can't run away from."
- "Sorry don't get it done, Dude."
- "Well, son, since you haven't learned to respect your elders, it's time you learned to respect your betters." [28]

In the films of John Wayne, dependence is a sign of weakness. In the world of David, dependence was a necessity.

David was the king of Israel. During his forty-year reign, he ruled over a united kingdom, led them to victory in many battles, expanded the area of the kingdom, and paved the way for his son, Solomon, to build the Temple. David recognized, however, that his successes in life were blessings from God. He owed his accomplishments, his position, his possessions, and his very life to God.

In Psalm 71, David admits that he needs God, every day. He prays that he can depend on God continually, as he has done throughout his life. David is not ashamed of his dependence on God; instead, he celebrates it. After all, the "God of angel armies" (see April 27–28) has commanded his troops to protect David.

God is the rock of refuge to which you can come any time you need to, Pilgrim.

Passage: Verse in Context — Psalm 71:1–12

In you, O LORD, do I take refuge; let me never be put to shame! In your righteousness deliver me and rescue me; incline your ear to me, and save me! Be to me a rock of refuge, to which I may continually come; you have given the command to save me, for you are my rock and my fortress.

Rescue me, O my God, from the hand of the wicked, from the grasp of the unjust and cruel man. For you, O LORD, are my hope, my trust, O LORD, from my youth. Upon you I have leaned from before my birth; you are he who took me from my mother's womb. My praise is continually of you.

I have been as a portent to many, but you are my strong refuge. My mouth is filled with your praise, and with your glory all the day. Do not cast me off in the time of old age; forsake me not when my strength is spent. For my enemies speak concerning me; those who watch for my life consult together and say, "God has forsaken him; pursue and seize him, for there is none to deliver him."

O God, be not far from me; O my God, make haste to help me!

Questions for Reflection and Application

- How much value do you place on hard work, determination, rugged independence, and self-reliance? How much of your self-worth comes from what you have achieved and accomplished?
- How do you feel when you are unable to do something on your own and must depend on others?
- For what things are you completely dependent on God? For what additional things should you be?

Father, our world in the Western Hemisphere has the western movie mentality that dependence means weakness. Remind me that reliance on you equals strength. Amen.

A ROCK BECOMES A FAILURE

My flesh and my heart may fail, but God is the strength
of my heart and my portion forever.
—*Psalm 73:26*

His name was Simon, son of Jonah. Jesus had given him a new name: Peter, which means "Rock." And Jesus said that he would build his church on that rock! But Peter didn't feel like a rock now. He felt like a failure. No, he *was* a failure.

It all happened so fast. Just after the Passover meal that evening, Jesus stated that before the rooster crowed, Peter would deny three times that he knew Jesus. Peter was aghast. "Lord, I am ready to go with you both to prison and to death," he protested (Luke 22:33).

A few hours later, a huge band of soldiers arrested Jesus. Peter tried to fight for Jesus, even grabbing a sword and cutting off the ear of the high priest's servant, but Jesus did not fight. He went away quietly.

Peter followed at a distance. When they reached the high priest's house, he joined others at a fire in the courtyard. A servant girl challenged him first, saying that he was with Jesus. Peter denied it. Someone else said that Peter was "one of them." "Man, I am not," Peter snapped back (v. 58).

An hour later, another person, catching Peter's Galilean accent, insisted that Peter was a follower of Jesus. Peter invoked a curse on himself and swore that he didn't know Jesus. He didn't know the man whom he had declared as the Messiah. He didn't know the man for whom he said he was willing to die.

A rooster crowed and Jesus looked at Peter, who ran out of the courtyard and wept bitterly.

King David had his own share of failures, as everyone does. He took comfort in the knowledge that, even when he failed, God would remain the strength—or literally, the rock—of his heart. God would sustain him, get him back on his feet, and supply him with whatever he needed to make it through.

God will do the same for you.

Passage: Verse in Context — Psalm 73:1–5, 21–28

Truly God is good to Israel, to those who are pure in heart. But as for me, my feet had almost stumbled, my steps had nearly slipped. For I was envious of the arrogant when I saw the prosperity of the wicked. For they have no pangs until death; their bodies are fat and sleek. They are not in trouble as others are; they are not stricken like the rest of mankind. ...

When my soul was embittered, when I was pricked in heart, I was brutish and ignorant; I was like a beast toward you. Nevertheless, I am continually with you; you hold my right hand. You guide me with your counsel, and afterward you will receive me to glory.

Whom have I in heaven but you? And there is nothing on earth that I desire besides you. My flesh and my heart may fail, but God is the strength of my heart and my portion forever.

For behold, those who are far from you shall perish; you put an end to everyone who is unfaithful to you. But for me it is good to be near God; I have made the LORD God my refuge, that I may tell of all your works.

Questions for Reflection and Application

- Why did Jesus rename Simon to Peter?
- Why did God choose David to be king?
- For what has God chosen you? Why did God choose you?
- When you fail, how do you act toward others? How do you act privately? How does God want you to act? What does God want you to learn from your failures?
- What can you do to put God at the center of your life and enable him to be the strength, or rock, of your heart?

Father, even when I fail, you remain a steadfast Rock—solid, unwavering, immovable, unfailing. Amen.

A GERMAN REQUIEM

How lovely is your dwelling place, O LORD of hosts!
—*Psalm 84:1*

A requiem mass is a liturgical worship service in honor of someone who has died. It often includes these elements:

- Introit: "Grant them eternal rest, O Lord, and let perpetual light shine upon them …"
- Kyrie eleison: "Lord have mercy; Christ have mercy; Lord have mercy."
- Sequence (Dies Irae): "The day of wrath, that day will dissolve the world in ashes …"
- Sanctus: "Holy, Holy, Holy, Lord God of Hosts …"
- Agnus Dei: "Lamb of God, who takes away the sins of the world, grant them rest …"
- Pie Jesu: "Merciful Lord Jesus, grant them rest; grant them eternal rest."
- Libera me: "Deliver me, O Lord, from death eternal on that fearful day …"
- In paradisum: "May the angels lead you into paradise …"[29]

Many famous composers have set the texts of the requiem mass to music to produce "Requiems." In 1868, Johannes Brahms completed the score for *Ein Deutches Requiem*, or *A German Requiem*, but his work followed few of the conventions of other Requiems to date. Its text is in German, the language of his people, not Latin, the language of the church at that time. The texts of its movements do not match the texts of a requiem mass. Instead, Brahms used various Bible passages that provide comfort and consolation to those who are mourning the death of a loved one, as Brahms was doing for his mother, who had died a few years earlier.

Movement IV of Brahms *Requiem* uses Psalm 84, verses 1, 2, and 4. Here it is, in English: "How lovely is your dwelling place, O Lord of hosts! My soul longs, yes, faints for the courts of the Lord; my heart and flesh sing for joy to the living God. … Blessed are those who dwell in your house, ever singing your praise!"

Ein Deutches Requiem continues to touch people today. Of all choral-orchestral works, only Handel's *Messiah* is performed more.[30] Both are lovely, but neither compares to the beauty of our dwelling place in heaven.

Passage: Verse in Context — Psalm 84:1–7

How lovely is your dwelling place, O LORD of hosts! My soul longs, yes, faints for the courts of the LORD; my heart and flesh sing for joy to the living God.

Even the sparrow finds a home, and the swallow a nest for herself, where she may lay her young, at your altars, O LORD of hosts, my King and my God. Blessed are those who dwell in your house, ever singing your praise!

Blessed are those whose strength is in you, in whose heart are the highways to Zion. As they go through the Valley of Baca they make it a place of springs; the early rain also covers it with pools. They go from strength to strength; each one appears before God in Zion.

Related Passage — John 14:1–6

"Let not your hearts be troubled. Believe in God; believe also in me. In my Father's house are many rooms. If it were not so, would I have told you that I go to prepare a place for you? And if I go and prepare a place for you, I will come again and will take you to myself, that where I am you may be also. And you know the way to where I am going." Thomas said to him, "Lord, we do not know where you are going. How can we know the way?" Jesus said to him, "I am the way, and the truth, and the life. No one comes to the Father except through me."

Questions for Reflection and Application

- When a loved one dies, what Bible verses bring you the most comfort?
- What do you think heaven is like? What are you hoping is there? Why?
- What elements in David's and Jesus' descriptions of heaven resonate the most with you? Why?

Father, I cannot imagine the beauty of heaven—even the best classical music cannot capture its splendor. Amen.

GROUNDHOG DAY

For a day in your courts is better than a thousand elsewhere.
—*Psalm 84:10a*

Imagine a few days in the vacation spot of your dreams. Now imagine a month there. Six months. A year. Over two-and-a-half years. One day in the presence of God is better than one thousand days there.

In the film *Groundhog Day*, TV weatherman Phil Connors spends at least a thousand days not in God's courts, or even in his ideal vacation spot, but in Punxsutawney, Pennsylvania, a town that he hates. Every day he wakes up in Punxsutawney on February 2, or Groundhog Day. He is doomed to repeat the same day, in the same place, over and over again.

After learning that his actions have no consequences (no matter what he does, including killing himself, he always wakes up the next morning and it's February 2 again), Phil decides to seduce his producer, Rita, by talking with her and learning what she likes. When that fails, Phil begins to consider what he can do to help others in the town. Along the way, he learns a variety of skills, such as playing the piano, speaking French, and sculpting ice.

Eventually, Phil becomes a beloved man in Punxsutawney, even though to all of the townspeople he is there only one day. He also wins over Rita and, near the end of the film, he confesses to her, "No matter what happens tomorrow, or for the rest of my life, I'm happy now, because I love you."

The more we appreciate God and all that he has done, and does every day for us, the more that we want to worship him, talk with him, study his Word, and just be with him. We want to be in his courts. The good news for us is that we can be in his courts at any time and all the time, regardless of where we happen to be on this earth.

Even in Punxsutawney.

Passage: Verse in Context — Psalm 84:1–13

How lovely is your dwelling place, O LORD of hosts! My soul longs, yes, faints for the courts of the LORD; my heart and flesh sing for joy to the living God.

Even the sparrow finds a home, and the swallow a nest for herself, where she may lay her young, at your altars, O LORD of hosts, my King and my God. Blessed are those who dwell in your house, ever singing your praise!

Blessed are those whose strength is in you, in whose heart are the highways to Zion. As they go through the Valley of Baca they make it a place of springs; the early rain also covers it with pools. They go from strength to strength; each one appears before God in Zion.

O LORD God of hosts, hear my prayer; give ear, O God of Jacob! Behold our shield, O God; look on the face of your anointed!

For a day in your courts is better than a thousand elsewhere. I would rather be a doorkeeper in the house of my God than dwell in the tents of wickedness. For the LORD God is a sun and shield; the LORD bestows favor and honor. No good thing does he withhold from those who walk uprightly. O LORD of hosts, blessed is the one who trusts in you!

Questions for Reflection and Application

- What is the vacation spot of your dreams? What would you do there?
- What is your favorite way to spend time with God? How often do you do that?
- How can you be more disciplined in spending time with God? What are some ways that you can remind yourself of what God has done for you, especially when you are busy or stressed?

Father, your unbelievable goodness is all around me, and yet I choose to complain. Forgive me! Thank you for allowing me to be in your courts, right now. Amen.

FORGIVING EVERY PENNY

For you, O LORD, are good and forgiving,
abounding in steadfast love to all who call upon you.
—Psalm 86:5

Do you ever get tired of forgiving someone? Peter certainly did.

After Jesus explained to his disciples how to respond when "your brother sins against you" (Matthew 18:15), with the goal of getting your brother to repent so that you can forgive him, Peter asked, "Lord, how often will my brother sin against me, and I forgive him? As many as seven times?" (v. 21). He was stunned by Jesus' response: not seven times but seventy-seven times—or, in some translations, seventy times seven times (v. 22).

Jesus then told a parable about a king who wants to settle accounts with servants who owe him money. One servant owes the equivalent of two hundred thousand years' wages for a laborer. (If a laborer earns $25,000 a year, then the servant owes $5 billion.) Incredibly, the king forgives the entire debt.

As soon as he leaves the presence of his unbelievably gracious king, the forgiven servant finds a fellow servant who owes him one hundred days' wages (or using our previous math, about $8,000). The forgiven servant demands that his $8,000 debt be paid. When it can't, he has his fellow servant thrown in prison. When the king finds out, he throws the first servant in prison for the rest of his life. Jesus ended the parable with this sobering statement: "So also my heavenly Father will do to every one of you, if you do not forgive your brother from your heart" (v. 35).

Why does God command us to forgive those who sin against us? Every time? Because God forgives us. Every time. He never gets tired of forgiving us, because he is good and forgiving, abounding in steadfast love to all who call on him. The debt that each of us has accumulated with God is more than $5 billion. A lot more. We can't count it all.

And he forgives every penny.

Passage: Verse in Context — Psalm 86:1–10

Incline your ear, O Lord, and answer me, for I am poor and needy. Preserve my life, for I am godly; save your servant, who trusts in you—you are my God. Be gracious to me, O Lord, for to you do I cry all the day. Gladden the soul of your servant, for to you, O Lord, do I lift up my soul. For you, O Lord, are good and forgiving, abounding in steadfast love to all who call upon you. Give ear, O Lord, to my prayer; listen to my plea for grace. In the day of my trouble I call upon you, for you answer me.

There is none like you among the gods, O Lord, nor are there any works like yours. All the nations you have made shall come and worship before you, O Lord, and shall glorify your name. For you are great and do wondrous things; you alone are God.

Related Passage — Matthew 18:15–17

"If your brother sins against you, go and tell him his fault, between you and him alone. If he listens to you, you have gained your brother. But if he does not listen, take one or two others along with you, that every charge may be established by the evidence of two or three witnesses. If he refuses to listen to them, tell it to the church. And if he refuses to listen even to the church, let him be to you as a Gentile and a tax collector."

Questions for Reflection and Application

- Why doesn't God get tired of forgiving you?
- What sins do you tend to commit over and over? Why do you do that? How can you break yourself of your patterns of sin?
- Think of some people who have sinned against you repeatedly. Why have they done that? How do their sins against you compare to your sins against others?

Father, when I refuse to forgive someone's sins against me, remind me of how much you paid to forgive mine. Amen.

MARVELOUS THINGS

Oh sing to the LORD a new song, for he has done marvelous things!
His right hand and his holy arm have worked salvation for him.

—Psalm 98:1

The word "marvelous" isn't used much these days. When most people hear "marvel," they probably think of Marvel Comics, creators of superheroes whose stories have been cleaning up at the box office for over a decade. When you marvel at something, you are filled with wonder and astonishment. Your jaw drops. You simply can't believe what you are seeing or experiencing.

Throughout the Bible, God does things that inspire awe and wonder. Here are some examples:

- When the Israelites are trapped by the Red Sea, with Pharaoh's troops racing toward them, God opens the Red Sea, allows the Israelites to walk across, and then drowns Pharaoh's army. (Exodus 14)
- After Joshua's army marches around the walled city of Jericho for six straight days and then marches around it seven times on the seventh day, the walls come tumbling down. (Joshua 6)
- When Daniel's friends are thrown into a furnace so hot that the flames consume the guards who throw them in, the friends walk around and emerge unharmed. (Daniel 3)
- After Jesus dies a horrible death on a cross and is placed in a tomb where the entrance is blocked by a heavy stone, on the third day he rises from the dead and appears to many. (Matthew 27–28; Mark 15–16; Luke 23–24; John 19–21)

But what marvelous things has God done lately? Why should we sing him a new song? It depends on what you consider marvelous.

David certainly had seen some amazing things, starting as a teenager when he killed the giant Goliath with a slingshot. But in Psalm 139, David marvels at himself. He sees his body—every part of it, how all the parts work together in harmony, and the simple fact that he moves, breathes, and is alive—as a miracle. He is fearfully and wonderfully made by a God, who has loved him and cared about him since before he was born.

David was a marvelous thing, created by God. And so are you.

Passage: Verse in Context — Psalm 98:1–9

Oh sing to the LORD a new song, for he has done marvelous things! His right hand and his holy arm have worked salvation for him. The LORD has made known his salvation; he has revealed his righteousness in the sight of the nations. He has remembered his steadfast love and faithfulness to the house of Israel. All the ends of the earth have seen the salvation of our God.

Make a joyful noise to the LORD, all the earth; break forth into joyous song and sing praises! Sing praises to the LORD with the lyre, with the lyre and the sound of melody! With trumpets and the sound of the horn make a joyful noise before the King, the LORD!

Let the sea roar, and all that fills it; the world and those who dwell in it! Let the rivers clap their hands; let the hills sing for joy together before the LORD, for he comes to judge the earth. He will judge the world with righteousness, and the peoples with equity.

Related Passage — Job 5:8–11

"As for me, I would seek God, and to God would I commit my cause, who does great things and unsearchable, marvelous things without number: he gives rain on the earth and sends waters on the fields; he sets on high those who are lowly, and those who mourn are lifted to safety."

Questions for Reflection and Application

- What are some marvelous things that God has done in your life? List as many as you can.
- What are some "ordinary" things in your life that, when you really think about them, actually are quite marvelous? Try to list at least a dozen.
- Why don't you marvel more at the things that God has done or created? How can you get into the habit of praising God for his mighty deeds and works?

God, from knitting us together in the womb to helping us defeat giants, everything you do is marvelous. Amen.

A JOYFUL NOISE

Make a joyful noise to the LORD, all the earth!
—*Psalm 100:1*

There are many ways to worship God, both publicly and privately. Reading and studying the Bible can be an act of worship. So can praying. So can an act of love or service. But God takes great pleasure in our singing. The Bible contains hundreds of references to singing. The book of Psalms is a book of songs that were sung to God. After the Last Supper, when he was less than a few hours from the arrest that would lead to his crucifixion, Jesus sang a hymn with his disciples.

The Bible commands Christians to sing when they meet together. Two examples are Ephesians 5: 19 and Colossians 3:16. One of the reasons for this command is that remembering words, phrases, and concepts is easier when they are set to music. Singing praise songs and hymns can help us learn and remember biblical passages and the truths of our faith. It is believed that Philippians 2:5–11, which describes Christ's humble obedience and subsequent exaltation, is the text of an early Christian hymn.

But what should you do if you don't sing well? God knows that some of us can't carry a tune, but he tells us to sing anyway, and to sing from the heart.

Psalm 150 lists musical instruments that were used to accompany singing—trumpets, lutes, harps, strings, and pipes. All of those made sweet, melodic music. But also included in the list is cymbals, which are described as "sounding cymbals" and "loud clashing cymbals" (v. 5). Cymbals are not subtle. They are not melodic. They are simply noisy, especially when you are playing them with all of your might.

Any praise to God is sweet music to his ears. So if you don't like to sing or your singing isn't the best, don't let that stop you. If the person next to you gives you a look, then smile and point up, to remind him that you are singing to God.

Make some noise!

Passage: Verse in Context — Psalm 100

Make a joyful noise to the LORD, all the earth! Serve the LORD with gladness! Come into his presence with singing! Know that the LORD, he is God! It is he who made us, and we are his; we are his people, and the sheep of his pasture.

Enter his gates with thanksgiving, and his courts with praise! Give thanks to him; bless his name! For the LORD is good; his steadfast love endures forever, and his faithfulness to all generations.

Related Passage — Psalm 150

Praise the LORD! Praise God in his sanctuary; praise him in his mighty heavens! Praise him for his mighty deeds; praise him according to his excellent greatness!

Praise him with trumpet sound; praise him with lute and harp! Praise him with tambourine and dance; praise him with strings and pipe! Praise him with sounding cymbals; praise him with loud clashing cymbals! Let everything that has breath praise the LORD! Praise the LORD!

Questions for Reflection and Application

- What is your favorite way to worship God? Why is that your favorite?
- Why does Psalm 100 use the word "noise"? Why does Psalm 150 encourage us to praise God with "loud clashing cymbals"?
- How comfortable are you in praising God at the top of your lungs? What would make you more comfortable doing that? What would be the impact on others if you praised God more vociferously?

God, I can't praise you with the voice of an angel, but I can praise you with the voice that you gave me. With my actions. With my all. Because all is a gift from you. Give me the courage not to hold back when I worship you. Amen.

FOREVER

For the LORD is good; his steadfast love endures forever,
and his faithfulness to all generations.
—Psalm 100:5

Written over four hundred years ago, the hymn "All People that on Earth Do Dwell" is set to the tune known as "Old Hundredth" because the lyrics come from Psalm 100. It opens this way:

All people that on earth do dwell,
Sing to the Lord with cheerful voice;
Him serve with mirth, His praise forth tell,
Come ye before Him and rejoice.[31]

The first three verses of the hymn—like the first four verses of the psalm—command us to sing to, serve, trust in, submit to, praise, and thank God. The final verse of the psalm, and the hymn, explains why: God is good. He loves you. He always will. He always will be faithful. Forever.

In our fast-paced world—where a film earns half of its box office revenue in the first weekend, where the vast majority of the downloads of a popular app occur in the first month after its release, and where a band goes from hot to forgotten in less than a year—the concept of forever is increasingly difficult to grasp. The word "forever" appears over four hundred times in the Bible, including 145 times in Psalms. Thirty-six of those are in Psalm 136, where David goes on a "forever kick" and uses the phrase "for his steadfast love endures forever" in every verse. And people complain about how contemporary Christian praise songs are repetitious!

Certainly David's world was not nearly as fast-paced as ours, but David saw the need to remind himself and others that no matter how much things change, God remains the same. New and flashy may be captivating, but faithful and true are reassuring. And encouraging.

God: Always steadfast. Always faithful. Always just. Always righteous. Always loving. Always forgiving. Always there for you. Forever.

Passage: Verse in Context — Psalm 100

Make a joyful noise to the LORD, all the earth! Serve the LORD with gladness! Come into his presence with singing! Know that the LORD, he is God! It is he who made us, and we are his; we are his people, and the sheep of his pasture.

Enter his gates with thanksgiving, and his courts with praise! Give thanks to him; bless his name! For the LORD is good; his steadfast love endures forever, and his faithfulness to all generations.

Related Passage — Psalm 136:1–7

Give thanks to the LORD, for he is good, for his steadfast love endures forever. Give thanks to the God of gods, for his steadfast love endures forever. Give thanks to the LORD of lords, for his steadfast love endures forever; to him who alone does great wonders, for his steadfast love endures forever; to him who by understanding made the heavens, for his steadfast love endures forever; to him who spread out the earth above the waters, for his steadfast love endures forever; to him who made the great lights, for his steadfast love endures forever.

Questions for Reflection and Application

- Why does David repeat the statement that God's steadfast love endures forever so many times? What are some phrases that you like to repeat? Why?
- What are some things that you wish could last forever or, at least, for a very long time?
- When do you most need the reassurance that God's love and faithfulness are reliable and steadfast?

Father, thank you for being our permanence in an ever-changing world. Amen.

FIELD OF PEACE

Bless the LORD, O my soul, and forget not all his benefits,
who forgives all your iniquity, who heals all your diseases.
—*Psalm 103:2–3*

"If you build it, he will come." So says "the voice" to Iowa farmer Ray Kinsella in the film *Field of Dreams*. Ray figures out that if he builds a baseball field in his cornfield, then his dad's favorite baseball player, Shoeless Joe Jackson—who, along with seven other Chicago White Sox players, was banned from baseball for throwing the 1919 World Series—will get to come back and play ball again.

Ray builds the field and Jackson appears, along with other players from that era, to play baseball. But "the voice" is not done. First it directs Ray to Boston to ease the pain of Terrence Mann, a Pulitzer Prize-winning author who secretly loved baseball. Then it sends Ray and Terrence to Minnesota to find a ball-player who, after never getting the chance to swing a bat in the Majors, became a much-loved small-town doctor.

As they drive back to Iowa, Ray shares how his dad tried and failed to make it as a ballplayer and how, as a teenager, Ray had called his dad's favorite player a criminal. Ray left home in anger at seventeen and never saw his father alive again. He lived with regret ever since. And even after Shoeless Joe comes to play baseball again, Ray has no peace.

All of us have done things that we regret. We have hurt those we love with our words and our actions. We can't take back the words, and we can't undo the actions. Regrets are the stains that we can't get out, no matter how hard we try.

God knows our regrets and their impacts on our lives. He forgives all our iniquity. He washes away the stains that have permeated our souls, robbing us of peace. He heals us and frees us.

We don't have to plow under a cornfield to make it happen. We just have to ask.

Passage: Verse in Context — Psalm 103:1–5

Bless the LORD, O my soul, and all that is within me, bless his holy name! Bless the LORD, O my soul, and forget not all his benefits, who forgives all your iniquity, who heals all your diseases, who redeems your life from the pit, who crowns you with steadfast love and mercy, who satisfies you with good so that your youth is renewed like the eagle's.

Related Passage — Psalm 51:1–2, 7–12

Have mercy on me, O God, according to your steadfast love; according to your abundant mercy blot out my transgressions. Wash me thoroughly from my iniquity, and cleanse me from my sin! ...

Purge me with hyssop, and I shall be clean; wash me, and I shall be whiter than snow. Let me hear joy and gladness; let the bones that you have broken rejoice. Hide your face from my sins, and blot out all my iniquities. Create in me a clean heart, O God, and renew a right spirit within me. Cast me not away from your presence, and take not your Holy Spirit from me. Restore to me the joy of your salvation, and uphold me with a willing spirit.

Questions for Reflection and Application

- What have you done or said that you regret? Who was hurt by your words or actions?
- If those you hurt are still alive, then have you asked for their forgiveness? If so, what happened? If not, why not? What will help you to walk down that path?
- If those you hurt are dead, then what can you do about it?
- How is regret robbing you of peace and life?

Father, you heal our hurts and restore the peace robbed by regret. Amen.

SCHINDLER'S PIT

[The LORD] redeems your life from the pit [and]
crowns you with steadfast love and mercy.
—*Psalm 103:4*

Oskar Schindler was irreligious and immoral, a sinful man through and through. An alcoholic and member of the Nazi Party, he smoked, cursed, and cheated on his wife numerous times. When Germany invaded Poland near the beginning of World War II, Schindler moved to Poland to make a fortune as a war profiteer. The German Intelligence Agency recruited Schindler to collect information about Poles, and Schindler willingly obliged.

Moving to Krakow, Schindler took over a Jewish family's apartment. Using bribes, Schindler gained control of a Jewish-owned enameled-goods factory close to the Jewish ghetto. Employing primarily Jewish workers, whom he could pay slave wages, Schindler converted the factory to a manufacturer of munitions. On his way to making a fortune, Schindler had no sympathy for the Polish Jews who were being systematically eradicated by the Nazis.

But when he saw the liquidation of the Krakow Ghetto, Schindler changed. The man who previously had cared only about himself and his own fortune suddenly began spending that fortune to do whatever he could—including bribing Nazi officials—to protect and save Jews from death in Auschwitz. His efforts saved the lives of more than 1,200 Jews.

After spending much of his life in a self-absorbed pit of his own making, Oskar Schindler allowed God to pull him out of that pit, and he became a hero to Jews everywhere. In the early 1960s, Schindler was honored in Israel and invited to plant a tree in The Avenue of the Righteous. A memorial honors him in the Park of Heroes. [32]

You may feel that your life is in a pit and that there is no way out. But no pit is too deep for God. His arms are long enough to reach to the bottom of any pit. He can pull you out, redeem your life, and crown you with steadfast love and mercy.

Passage: Verse in Context — Psalm 103:1–5

Bless the LORD, O my soul, and all that is within me, bless his holy name! Bless the LORD, O my soul, and forget not all his benefits, who forgives all your iniquity, who heals all your diseases, who redeems your life from the pit, who crowns you with steadfast love and mercy, who satisfies you with good so that your youth is renewed like the eagle's.

Related Passage — Psalm 40:1–5

I waited patiently for the LORD; he inclined to me and heard my cry. He drew me up from the pit of destruction, out of the miry bog, and set my feet upon a rock, making my steps secure. He put a new song in my mouth, a song of praise to our God. Many will see and fear, and put their trust in the LORD.

Blessed is the man who makes the LORD his trust, who does not turn to the proud, to those who go astray after a lie! You have multiplied, O LORD my God, your wondrous deeds and your thoughts toward us; none can compare with you! I will proclaim and tell of them, yet they are more than can be told.

Questions for Reflection and Application

- Was Oskar Schindler a righteous man? Why or why not? What encouragement does his story offer you?
- Has God pulled you out of a pit? If so, then compare your life in the pit to your life now. How did God pull you out? Why did he do that? Do people know your story?
- If you feel that you are in a pit now, then what do you plan to do? What help do you need? Who can supply that help?

Father, no pit is too deep, no sin too great, for your redeeming work. Amen.

A SPIRITUAL DIET

[The LORD] satisfies you with good so that
your youth is renewed like the eagle's.
—*Psalm 103:5*

You Gotta Eat[SM]. For years, that was the slogan of the Checkers° drive-through restaurant chain and its sister chain, Rally's° restaurants. Of course, people don't just *have* to eat. We *love* to eat. Unfortunately, many of us love to eat too much, especially too much of foods that are not the best for us.

Unhealthy eating habits have contributed to a broad range of health issues in the western world. Of all adults who live in the United States, age twenty and over, 37.9 percent were obese and 70.7 percent were overweight in 2014, compared to 22.3 percent and 54.9 percent twenty years earlier.[33] Losing weight can improve your overall health, reduce your risk for heart disease, diabetes, and cancer, increase your energy, and even improve your memory.[34]

Most of us can lose weight and get healthier if we simply eat less and exercise more, but that doesn't stop millions of us from buying books on eating every year. Diet books have been lucrative since 1972, when *Dr. Atkins' Diet Revolution* was published. Over 20 million copies of that book and its spin-offs have been purchased. Similar sales have been seen by *The South Beach Diet* (2003), which sold 14.5 million copies in its first two years alone.[35] In the first half of 2016, five of the top ten print books in the United Kingdom were on cooking and eating.

God wants us to be healthy physically, but it is more important to him that we are healthy spiritually. Our bodies are temporary, but our lives are eternal. Just as God provides plenty of food that is good for our bodies, he provides plenty of spiritual nourishment that is good for our souls. In all things, God satisfies us with good so that we feel as young and vibrant as an eagle in flight.

The latest bestseller may have the recipe you need for healthy eating. The all-time bestseller, the Bible, has the recipe that you need for healthy living.

You gotta read it. Every day.

Passage: Verse in Context — Psalm 103:1–5

Bless the LORD, O my soul, and all that is within me, bless his holy name! Bless the LORD, O my soul, and forget not all his benefits, who forgives all your iniquity, who heals all your diseases, who redeems your life from the pit, who crowns you with steadfast love and mercy, who satisfies you with good so that your youth is renewed like the eagle's.

Related Passage — Isaiah 40:28–31

Have you not known? Have you not heard? The LORD is the everlasting God, the Creator of the ends of the earth. He does not faint or grow weary; his understanding is unsearchable. He gives power to the faint, and to him who has no might he increases strength. Even youths shall faint and be weary, and young men shall fall exhausted; but they who wait for the LORD shall renew their strength; they shall mount up with wings like eagles; they shall run and not be weary; they shall walk and not faint.

Questions for Reflection and Application

- How much time do you spend each week playing sports, exercising, and otherwise trying to stay in shape physically? How disciplined are you with eating healthy foods?
- How much time do you spend each week keeping yourself in shape spiritually? How disciplined are you spiritually?
- How challenging is it for you to read your Bible every day? Have you tried alternatives, such as listening to an audio Bible in your car or on your phone? What works best for you? Why?
- What is the ideal Bible study for you? Do you like listening to a teacher and taking notes, or do you prefer a lively discussion? When is the last time you were in your ideal type of Bible study?

Father, may I immerse myself in your Word every day, fulfilling the requirements of a healthy spiritual diet. Amen.

FIGHTING FOR JUSTICE

The LORD works righteousness and justice for all who are oppressed.
—*Psalm 103:6*

William Wilberforce was born into a rich merchant family in 1759. When his father died, young William spent two years with his aunt and uncle in London. His aunt embraced the emerging Methodist movement, which emphasized social reform, including the abolition of slavery and the slave trade. A frequent visitor to the London home was John Newton, a former slave-ship captain who became a Christian and the writer of the hymn "Amazing Grace."

When William went back home to Hull, his interest in Christianity faded. While at Cambridge University, he was elected to Parliament and began a lifelong friendship with William Pitt (the Younger), who became Prime Minister.

A year after winning his first reelection to Parliament, Wilberforce became a Christian. He reconnected with Newton, who encouraged him to serve God in public life. Wilberforce began to use his position in Parliament to attack vices, such as drinking and gambling, that afflicted the poor. When antislavery activist Thomas Clarkson showed him the appalling conditions under which slaves were transported from Africa to the West Indies, Wilberforce became an abolitionist.

In 1791, Wilberforce introduced a bill to abolish the slave trade, but it was defeated because port cities depended on income generated by the slave trade. Year after year, Wilberforce reintroduced his bill, only to watch it be defeated. After tabling his bill for a decade during Britain's war with France, Wilberforce won approval for a clever anti-French law that gutted the revenues of many in the slave trade.

By 1807, with the pro-slavery lobby low on funds and with public sentiment against slavery, both houses of Parliament passed Wilberforce's bill, the Slave Trade Act, by large margins, ending nearly four hundred years of the slave trade in the British Empire. A year later, the United States passed its own law banning the slave trade.[36] [37]

The Lord worked righteousness and justice for the oppressed by inspiring an ordinary person, William Wilberforce, to act on his behalf.

Passage: Verse in Context — Psalm 103:6–14

The LORD works righteousness and justice for all who are oppressed. He made known his ways to Moses, his acts to the people of Israel. The LORD is merciful and gracious, slow to anger and abounding in steadfast love. He will not always chide, nor will he keep his anger forever. He does not deal with us according to our sins, nor repay us according to our iniquities. For as high as the heavens are above the earth, so great is his steadfast love toward those who fear him; as far as the east is from the west, so far does he remove our transgressions from us. As a father shows compassion to his children, so the LORD shows compassion to those who fear him. For he knows our frame; he remembers that we are dust.

Related Passage — Micah 6:6–8

"With what shall I come before the LORD, and bow myself before God on high? Shall I come before him with burnt offerings, with calves a year old? Will the LORD be pleased with thousands of rams, with ten thousands of rivers of oil? Shall I give my firstborn for my transgression, the fruit of my body for the sin of my soul?" He has told you, O man, what is good; and what does the LORD require of you but to do justice, and to love kindness, and to walk humbly with your God?

Questions for Reflection and Application

- It took Wilberforce sixteen years to get Parliament to pass his bill to abolish the slave trade. What causes inspire enough passion in you that you would persist for sixteen years to achieve your goal?
- Wilberforce lived out his Christian faith in his workplace. How do you do that? Where can you improve?
- Wilberforce was a crafty legislator who used anti-French sentiments to persuade Parliament to pass a law that weakened his opponents. Given that Jesus advised us to be "wise as serpents" (Matthew 10:16) when dealing with the world, how can you use your cleverness to gain ground for the kingdom?

God, lead me to bring justice to today's thoroughly unjust world. Amen.

TO INFINITY, AND BEYOND

As far as the east is from the west,
so far does he remove our transgressions from us.
—*Psalm 103:12*

How far is the east from the west?

Let's say you are on the western border of your city and the eastern border is five miles away. Traveling in a car, you can be on the eastern border in less than half an hour. Even traveling by foot, you can get there in a few hours. When you reach the eastern border however, you're really not in "the east," because you still can travel further east.

Let's say you are on the western border of a state. How far is it to the eastern border of that state? How long would it take you to get there? When you get there, you're really not in "the east," because you still can travel further east.

Heading from the western border of a country to its eastern border? Same deal. When you get there, you still can go further east.

Of course, you can extend this analogy only so far on the earth, because the earth is not flat but a sphere. If you keep traveling east on the earth, then eventually you go around the globe and end up where you started. Does that mean that the distance from the east to the west is half the circumference of the earth?

Nope. Sorry, but David was speaking in theoretical terms. The distance between the east and the west is infinite. You can't get there from here.

While the concept of infinity may give you a headache, the application of infinity to your sins should warm your heart. How far has God removed your sins from you? Infinitely far. Even though you still remember your sins, God does not. Jesus bore the penalty for your sins. Once you repent of them, God not only forgives your sins but also forgets them. They are infinitely far from his mind.

He can't get there from here.

Passage: Verse in Context — Psalm 103:6–14

The LORD works righteousness and justice for all who are oppressed. He made known his ways to Moses, his acts to the people of Israel. The LORD is merciful and gracious, slow to anger and abounding in steadfast love. He will not always chide, nor will he keep his anger forever. He does not deal with us according to our sins, nor repay us according to our iniquities. For as high as the heavens are above the earth, so great is his steadfast love toward those who fear him; as far as the east is from the west, so far does he remove our transgressions from us. As a father shows compassion to his children, so the LORD shows compassion to those who fear him. For he knows our frame; he remembers that we are dust.

Related Passage — Ephesians 3:14–19

For this reason I bow my knees before the Father, from whom every family in heaven and on earth is named, that according to the riches of his glory he may grant you to be strengthened with power through his Spirit in your inner being, so that Christ may dwell in your hearts through faith—that you, being rooted and grounded in love, may have strength to comprehend with all the saints what is the breadth and length and height and depth, and to know the love of Christ that surpasses knowledge, that you may be filled with all the fullness of God.

Questions for Reflection and Application

- Think about some of the worst things you have done in life, the worst sins you have committed. How does it feel to realize that once you repent of them, God not only forgives you but also forgets that you ever committed them?
- How does God see you? What does God see when he looks at you?
- God gave us his Law. He has very high standards for our conduct. Why is God "merciful and gracious, slow to anger and abounding in steadfast love"? Why does God forgive you when you repent?

Father, thank you for moving my sins so far away that even you can't get to them. Amen.

RUNNING AWAY NAKED

Who can proclaim the mighty acts of the Lord
or fully declare his praise?
—*Psalm 106:2*

When you think about great characters of the Bible, you probably don't think of Mark, author of the second Gospel.

Mark probably was the young man mentioned in chapter 14 of that Gospel. That man witnessed the arrest of Jesus from a distance, wearing only a linen cloth, then left the cloth behind and ran away naked. Sixteen or seventeen years later, after Paul and Barnabas (who was Mark's cousin) visited Jerusalem, they took Mark with them back to Antioch. Mark then accompanied Paul, Barnabas, and others on their first missionary journey. But when the group set sail from Paphos (on Cyprus) to Perga in Pamphylia, Mark left them and returned to Jerusalem. Paul considered it a desertion. A few years later, when Barnabas suggested that they take Mark on their second missionary journey, Paul became so angry with Barnabas that they parted company—Paul departed with Silas, and Barnabas took Mark and headed for Cyprus. Paul never saw Barnabas again.

Eventually, Paul patched things up with Mark. In Colossians 4 and Philemon, Paul lists Mark among his "fellow workers for the kingdom of God" who "have been a comfort" to him (v. 11). In Paul's last letter, 2 Timothy, he asks Timothy to bring Mark because "he is very useful to me for ministry" (4:11). The early church stated consistently that in addition to helping Paul, Mark helped Peter in Rome and wrote the second Gospel, primarily based on Peter's account of what Jesus had said and done.

Has God done amazing and miraculous things in your life? Do people hang on every word of your testimony? No? Then maybe God wants you to be a present-day Mark by serving others for God and telling others about the mighty acts of God; not focused on your own life, but focused on the lives of those around you.

After all, the second Gospel was written by a guy whose claims to fame were that he ran away naked and made the apostle Paul really mad.

Passage: Verse in Context — Psalm 106:1–8

Praise the LORD! Oh give thanks to the LORD, for he is good, for his steadfast love endures forever! Who can utter the mighty deeds of the LORD, or declare all his praise? Blessed are they who observe justice, who do righteousness at all times!

Remember me, O LORD, when you show favor to your people; help me when you save them, that I may look upon the prosperity of your chosen ones, that I may rejoice in the gladness of your nation, that I may glory with your inheritance.

Both we and our fathers have sinned; we have committed iniquity; we have done wickedness. Our fathers, when they were in Egypt, did not consider your wondrous works; they did not remember the abundance of your steadfast love, but rebelled by the sea, at the Red Sea. Yet he saved them for his name's sake, that he might make known his mighty power.

Related Passage — 2 Timothy 4:9–11

Do your best to come to me soon. For Demas, in love with this present world, has deserted me and gone to Thessalonica. Crescens has gone to Galatia, Titus to Dalmatia. Luke alone is with me. Get Mark and bring him with you, for he is very useful to me for ministry.

Questions for Reflection and Application

- We're not sure why Mark left Paul and Barnabas and headed home. Maybe he was homesick or overwhelmed by what he has witnessed with Paul. What are some things you did when you were younger that you now regret? How have you worked to overcome those actions? How can you repair relationships that were broken by your words or actions?
- What types of people are most likely to be affected by how God has worked in your life? How can you communicate most effectively with them?

Lord God, you can use me, despite past embarrassments and failures, to bring glory to your name, just as you did with Mark. Amen.

INTROVERTS UNITE!

With my mouth I will give great thanks to the LORD; I will praise him
in the midst of the throng. For he stands at the right hand of the needy one,
to save him from those who condemn his soul to death.

—Psalm 109:30–31

If you're an introvert, then these T-shirt slogans probably make you chuckle and
nod knowingly:

- Introverts Unite! Separately. In your own homes.
- Introverts Unite! We're here. We're uncomfortable. And we want to
  go home.

When you read Psalm 109, you may stop at "I will praise him in the midst
of the throng" and consider what it would be like to praise God with the eyes of
dozens or even hundreds of people on you. And start to sweat.

According to Professor Susan Krauss Whitbourne, there is unwarranted
stigma with being an introvert. Many people wrongly assume that introverts
don't like other people, and introverts often give a first impression of being aloof
or arrogant. The reality is that introverts and extroverts are equally warm and
caring—they just interact with others differently, especially in groups. Signs that
you may be an introvert include: you enjoy having time to yourself and think
best that way; you rarely voice your opinion unless asked; you receive more
calls, texts, and emails than you make; and you don't initiate small talk with
others with whom you have casual contact.[38]

So how does an introvert praise God in the midst of the throng? One way is
to get the throng to praise God with you. When everyone else is praising God,
you feel less like a soloist and more like a member of the choir. Another is to
get everyone else to focus on the object of your praise, not you. Praising God
often involves telling a story about God. Consider the story you will tell and how
other people will be able to identify with that story. After all, God is working in
their lives too.

The introverts in the throng will thank you. And so will the extroverts.

Passage: Verse in Context — Psalm 109:1–5, 26–31

Be not silent, O God of my praise! For wicked and deceitful mouths are opened against me, speaking against me with lying tongues. They encircle me with words of hate, and attack me without cause. In return for my love they accuse me, but I give myself to prayer. So they reward me evil for good, and hatred for my love. …

Help me, O LORD my God! Save me according to your steadfast love! Let them know that this is your hand; you, O LORD, have done it! Let them curse, but you will bless! They arise and are put to shame, but your servant will be glad! May my accusers be clothed with dishonor; may they be wrapped in their own shame as in a cloak!

With my mouth I will give great thanks to the LORD; I will praise him in the midst of the throng. For he stands at the right hand of the needy one, to save him from those who condemn his soul to death.

Questions for Reflection and Application

- You don't have to be an introvert to be uncomfortable with praising God in front of a bunch of people. What aspects of praising God or sharing your faith make you the most uncomfortable? Why? How can you overcome your fears or misgivings in these areas?
- With what people are you most comfortable discussing your faith, including any doubts or struggles you have? Why?
- What can you do to make others more willing to discuss matters of faith with you?
- In Psalm 109, David speaks about people who accuse him falsely. How do you respond when someone lies about you?

Father, you made me the way that you want me. My personality enables me to reach out to, and to reach, people who are like me, and thereby bring glory to you. Amen.

DRINKING LIKE DOGS

The LORD is on my side; I will not fear.
What can man do to me?
—*Psalm 118:6*

Everyone loves an underdog, but this was ridiculous.

For seven years, the Midianites forced the people of Israel to live in caves, stole their crops, and slaughtered their sheep, oxen, and donkeys. For seven years, the Israelites cried out to God for help. God responded by calling Gideon to lead the Israelites against the people of Midian and their allies. A large army of Israel's enemies were encamped in the Valley of Jezreel. To the south was Gideon's force of thirty-two thousand men: Israelites, Abiezrites, and men from Manasseh, Asher, Zebulun, and Naphtali.

Thirty-two thousand men were too many for God's liking. If Israel were to win with that number, then Israel would boast that it didn't need God to win. So God told Gideon, "Whoever is fearful and trembling, let him return home and hurry away from Mount Gilead" (Judges 7:3). Twenty-two thousand men left but, let's face it, fearful and trembling men aren't terrific on the battlefield.

Ten thousand men were too many for God. He instructed Gideon to take all ten thousand to the water, watch how they drink, and keep only those who lap water with their tongues, like a dog.

Wait! What? God told Gideon to take on the massive Midianite army with three hundred men who drink like dogs. They weren't just hopelessly outnumbered, but they *lapped water with their tongues.*

Recognizing that Gideon's confidence had plummeted, God told him to sneak into the enemy camp and listen to a conversation. When Gideon did, he heard a man tell his dream and his comrade interpreted that dream as meaning that God had given the Midianite force to Gideon. That helped with their confidence and God's battle plan did the rest.

Gideon's paltry band of three hundred men prevailed over the mighty Midianite army. The underdog won.

When God is on your side, there is no reason to fear. Even when you're leading a badly outnumbered band of men who were chosen for the sole reason that they drink like dogs.

Passage: Verse in Context — Psalm 118:1–9

Oh give thanks to the LORD, for he is good; for his steadfast love endures forever! Let Israel say, "His steadfast love endures forever." Let the house of Aaron say, "His steadfast love endures forever." Let those who fear the LORD say, "His steadfast love endures forever." Out of my distress I called on the LORD; the LORD answered me and set me free. The LORD is on my side; I will not fear. What can man do to me? The LORD is on my side as my helper; I shall look in triumph on those who hate me. It is better to take refuge in the LORD than to trust in man. It is better to take refuge in the LORD than to trust in princes.

Related Passage — Psalm 124:1–8

If it had not been the LORD who was on our side—let Israel now say—if it had not been the LORD who was on our side when people rose up against us, then they would have swallowed us up alive, when their anger was kindled against us; then the flood would have swept us away, the torrent would have gone over us; then over us would have gone the raging waters. Blessed be the LORD, who has not given us as prey to their teeth! We have escaped like a bird from the snare of the fowlers; the snare is broken, and we have escaped! Our help is in the name of the LORD, who made heaven and earth.

Questions for Reflection and Application

- Why did God reduce Gideon's force from thirty-two thousand men to three hundred men who drank water like dogs?
- From what challenging or seemingly impossible situations have you emerged victorious? How did God pull you through?
- "It is better to take refuge in the LORD than to trust in man." In what men, or women, do you sometimes put your trust? How can you break yourself of that tendency?

Father, you choose underdogs and the least worthy men to do your greatest works. I am honored and humbled that you are on my side every moment. Amen.

SALVATION ON A MOUNTAIN

The LORD is my strength and my song; he has become my salvation.
—*Psalm 118:14*

God wanted Abraham to sacrifice his only son, who had been promised when Abraham was seventy-five years old but didn't arrive until Abraham was one hundred. Abraham had been really old then. He was ancient now. He had to obey, so the ancient man headed to the mountains with Isaac and two servants.

When they reached the place for the sacrifice, Abraham and Isaac left the servants behind. Isaac carried the wood for the burnt offering; Abraham carried the fire and the knife. "Where is the lamb for a burnt offering?" asked Isaac (Genesis 22:7). Abraham kept his answer simple: God would provide the lamb.

In his mind, Abraham asked God some other obvious questions. If Isaac were sacrificed, then how would God keep his promise that Abraham would be the father of many nations? Would Sarah, now well over one hundred, get pregnant again? Would God raise Isaac from the dead? Hearing no answers, Abraham came to a simple conclusion: God would provide an heir.

Abraham built the altar and laid the wood on it. He bound his son, Isaac, and laid him on the altar. Taking the knife, he raised it to kill Isaac.

But an angel stopped him. Abraham looked up and saw a ram, his horns caught in a thicket. Instead, he sacrificed the ram, and he named the place "The LORD will provide."

God kept his promise to Abraham, a promise that had been made nearly a half-century earlier. Isaac would be Abraham's heir. Isaac's son, Jacob, whom God would rename Israel, would be the father of the nation of Israel. Because of Abraham's faithfulness, people from many nations would come to faith in God and receive salvation. God spared Abraham's son that day because God's ultimate plan was to sacrifice his own Son, Jesus, to pay the penalty that no other sacrifice would cover.

God had been Abraham's strength and his song. On the mountain, God became his salvation. And ours too.

Passage: Verse in Context — Psalm 118:14–24

The LORD is my strength and my song; he has become my salvation. Glad songs of salvation are in the tents of the righteous: "The right hand of the LORD does valiantly, the right hand of the LORD exalts, the right hand of the LORD does valiantly!" I shall not die, but I shall live, and recount the deeds of the LORD. The LORD has disciplined me severely, but he has not given me over to death.

Open to me the gates of righteousness, that I may enter through them and give thanks to the LORD. This is the gate of the LORD; the righteous shall enter through it. I thank you that you have answered me and have become my salvation. The stone that the builders rejected has become the cornerstone. This is the LORD's doing; it is marvelous in our eyes. This is the day that the LORD has made; let us rejoice and be glad in it.

Related Passage — Genesis 22:6–8

And Abraham took the wood of the burnt offering and laid it on Isaac his son. And he took in his hand the fire and the knife. So they went both of them together. And Isaac said to his father Abraham, "My father!" And he said, "Here I am, my son." He said, "Behold, the fire and the wood, but where is the lamb for a burnt offering?" Abraham said, "God will provide for himself the lamb for a burnt offering, my son." So they went both of them together.

Questions for Reflection and Application

- As men, we usually don't want to be saved or rescued. Why is that?
- From what has God saved you? How did God do that? Who knows your story? Who should know it but does not?
- Why do you think God tested Abraham? How has God tested you? How did you do?

Almighty God, Abraham trusted that you would provide and you did. Help me to trust you in all things, big and small. Amen.

REDEMPTION IN HICKORY

It is good for me that I was afflicted,
that I might learn your statutes.
—*Psalm 119:71*

Norman Dale was a successful college basketball coach until he struck a player and received a lifetime coaching ban in the college ranks. As the film *Hoosiers* opens, Dale is hired as a teacher by his friend, the principal at Hickory High School in rural southeast Indiana. Dale's only hope for a successful season is to persuade Jimmy Chitwood—the best player in the area and one of the best in the state—to play ball. But teacher Myra Fleener, who is looking after Chitwood, warns Dale to leave him alone, and Dale heeds her warning.

Without Chitwood, the team has only six players. Dale drills the six endlessly in fundamentals, conditioning, and discipline. At the first game, when a player disobeys the coach, Dale benches him. When another player fouls out, Dale refuses to put the disobedient player back in the game, forcing the Huskers to finish the game with only four players on the floor. The basketball-crazed townspeople are infuriated.

After the team loses several more games, the townspeople call an emergency town meeting to vote Dale out. As the vote is being counted, Chitwood enters the hall and says that he will play, but only if Dale remains as coach. Dale stays. The team starts winning and, when the state playoffs begin, Hickory advances all the way to the state finals, where one of the smallest schools in the state will meet a big-school powerhouse, the defending state champions.

Rather than giving them an inspirational speech before the final game, Dale sits with his players and tells them that he loves them. The college coach who once struck a player has become a high school coach with a greater appreciation for the game and a love for each of his players. His affliction, a lifetime ban from coaching in college, was good for him.

When you are afflicted, consider what God may be trying to teach you.

Passage: Verse in Context — Psalm 119:65–74

You have dealt well with your servant, O LORD, according to your word. Teach me good judgment and knowledge, for I believe in your commandments. Before I was afflicted I went astray, but now I keep your word. You are good and do good; teach me your statutes. The insolent smear me with lies, but with my whole heart I keep your precepts; their heart is unfeeling like fat, but I delight in your law. It is good for me that I was afflicted, that I might learn your statutes. The law of your mouth is better to me than thousands of gold and silver pieces.

Your hands have made and fashioned me; give me understanding that I may learn your commandments. Those who fear you shall see me and rejoice, because I have hoped in your word.

Related Passage — 2 Corinthians 4:16–18

So we do not lose heart. Though our outer self is wasting away, our inner self is being renewed day by day. For this light momentary affliction is preparing for us an eternal weight of glory beyond all comparison, as we look not to the things that are seen but to the things that are unseen. For the things that are seen are transient, but the things that are unseen are eternal.

Questions for Reflection and Application

- How have you been afflicted in your life? What did you learn from your afflictions?
- Does an affliction draw you closer to God—causing you to look to the things that are unseen—or pull you away? Why do you respond that way?
- In the 2 Corinthians passage, Paul implies that enduring an affliction increases the "weight" of your glory. What does that mean? How do you feel about that?

God, I hate going through a tough time. I just want it to be over. Help me not to grit my teeth and endure it but to consider what you want to teach me through it. Then help me get through it! Amen.

SWORD OF THE SPIRIT

Your word is a lamp to my feet and a light to my path.
—*Psalm 119:105*

Trying to grow spiritually can feel like hiking in unfamiliar woods on a moonless night. You have a general feeling for where you should be going but it's pitch black. There are plenty of things around you that can cause you an injury if you bang into them or even brush against them, and there are plenty of things underfoot that can trip you up and send you sprawling. Without a light, it's going to be slow going, and you could get hurt.

When you are just trying to stay steady spiritually, an unexpected challenge or sudden source of stress can be like a nighttime power outage at home. You're in a familiar place, but you can't see anything, and flipping a light switch has no effect. A few wrong steps could send you down some stairs or into the corner of a table.

Even when you think that you're in a familiar setting in broad daylight, you may be mistaken. Our enemy is called the prince of darkness because, in the spiritual realm, he wants us to operate in darkness, as Paul describes in Ephesians: "Finally, be strong in the Lord and in the strength of his might. Put on the whole armor of God, that you may be able to stand against the schemes of the devil. For we do not wrestle against flesh and blood, but against the rulers, against the authorities, against the cosmic powers over this present darkness, against the spiritual forces of evil in the heavenly places" (6:10–12).

The armor consists of a belt, a breastplate, shoes, a shield, and a helmet. The only weapon mentioned is "the sword of the Spirit, which is the word of God" (v. 17). God's Word, the Bible, pierces the darkness of uncertainty, doubt, and afflictions, giving us a light to our path and the confidence that we can make it to our destination. The more we use it, the more effective a weapon it is in our hands.

Passage: Verse in Context — Psalm 119:103–112

How sweet are your words to my taste, sweeter than honey to my mouth! Through your precepts I get understanding; therefore I hate every false way.

Your word is a lamp to my feet and a light to my path. I have sworn an oath and confirmed it, to keep your righteous rules. I am severely afflicted; give me life, O LORD, according to your word! Accept my freewill offerings of praise, O LORD, and teach me your rules. I hold my life in my hand continually, but I do not forget your law. The wicked have laid a snare for me, but I do not stray from your precepts. Your testimonies are my heritage forever, for they are the joy of my heart. I incline my heart to perform your statutes forever, to the end.

Related Passage — Hebrews 4:9–12

So then, there remains a Sabbath rest for the people of God, for whoever has entered God's rest has also rested from his works as God did from his. Let us therefore strive to enter that rest, so that no one may fall by the same sort of disobedience. For the word of God is living and active, sharper than any two-edged sword, piercing to the division of soul and of spirit, of joints and of marrow, and discerning the thoughts and intentions of the heart.

Questions for Reflection and Application

- How has the devil masqueraded as light in your life and led you astray?
- How stressed are you right now? What is causing stress in your life? How are you dealing with it?
- How do troubles in your life affect your walk with God?
- What role does the Bible play in your key decisions in life? What role does prayer play? What about the counsel of trusted Christian friends?

Lord, the stress in my life makes everything dark. I need the light of your Word to find my way. Instill in me a desire to pursue your Word with passion. Amen.

THE BIBLE'S KNUCKLEHEADS

You are my hiding place and my shield; I hope in your word.
—*Psalm 119:114*

There are many reasons to hope in God's Word, the Bible. One of them is that the Bible is filled with stories of knuckleheads, such as these:

- **Abraham:** Twice when he was afraid, he said that his wife, Sarah, was his sister.
- **Judah:** He slept with his daughter-in-law because he thought she was a prostitute.
- **David:** He slept with the wife of a loyal military officer, got her pregnant, and then had the officer killed.
- **Solomon:** He married hundreds of foreign women, clung to them, and allowed them to turn his heart away from God.

Even the disciples of Jesus were knuckleheads. That includes John, who wrote the fourth Gospel. Consider two accounts of an event on Easter morning. In Luke's account, after Mary Magdalene and some other women return from Jesus' tomb and claim that it is empty and he is risen, Peter runs to the tomb, sees the discarded linen cloths and marvels. In John's account, after Mary Magdalene returns and says that the tomb is empty, both Peter and John run to the tomb. John gets there first and sees the linen cloths. Then Peter arrives, barges into the tomb, and sees the cloths. John then goes in, sees, and believes.

Apparently, John had to set the record straight by telling us that he was there too. Oh, and he was faster than Peter. And he believed first. Maybe John still was trying to live down his mother's impertinent request that he and his brother James sit at Jesus' right and left hand in the kingdom. Or the time when a Samaritan village rejected Jesus and James and John asked Jesus, "Lord, do you want us to tell fire to come down from heaven and consume them?" (Luke 9:54).

John was a knucklehead. Peter was too. So were Thomas, Philip, and the rest of the disciples. So was the apostle Paul. And so are we. Knuckleheads, every one of us. There's hope for all of us.

Passage: Verse in Context — Psalm 119:108–117

Accept my freewill offerings of praise, O LORD, and teach me your rules. I hold my life in my hand continually, but I do not forget your law. The wicked have laid a snare for me, but I do not stray from your precepts. Your testimonies are my heritage forever, for they are the joy of my heart. I incline my heart to perform your statutes forever, to the end.

I hate the double-minded, but I love your law. You are my hiding place and my shield; I hope in your word. Depart from me, you evildoers, that I may keep the commandments of my God. Uphold me according to your promise, that I may live, and let me not be put to shame in my hope! Hold me up, that I may be safe and have regard for your statutes continually!

Related Passage — Romans 5:1–5

Therefore, since we have been justified by faith, we have peace with God through our Lord Jesus Christ. Through him we have also obtained access by faith into this grace in which we stand, and we rejoice in hope of the glory of God. Not only that, but we rejoice in our sufferings, knowing that suffering produces endurance, and endurance produces character, and character produces hope, and hope does not put us to shame, because God's love has been poured into our hearts through the Holy Spirit who has been given to us.

Questions for Reflection and Application

- How do you feel about the great saints of the Bible being referred to as knuckleheads?
- Do you consider yourself a knucklehead? How does God feel about you?
- What does it mean to hope in the Word of God? What does it mean to rejoice in hope of the glory of God? What does it mean that hope "does not put us to shame"?

God, I admit it: I'm a knucklehead. I keep making the same mistakes, committing the same sins, and relying on myself instead of turning to you. I don't know why you are so patient with me, but I praise you that you are. Amen.

GOOD NEWS FOR THE SIMPLE

The unfolding of your words gives light;
it imparts understanding to the simple.
—Psalm 119:130

No one likes to be called stupid. Not even the title character of the film *Forrest Gump*, who had an IQ of 75 and admitted that he was "not a smart man." Whenever someone said or implied that Forrest was stupid, he always gave the same firm retort, "Stupid is as stupid does."

No one likes to be called simple either. The adjective "simple" can have very positive connotations. For example, when you are wrestling with a problem, you prefer a simple solution to a complex one. But in the modern vernacular, calling a person simple is akin to calling that person a simpleton, which means that he lacks intelligence, common sense, and good judgment.

In Psalm 116, David says, "The LORD preserves the simple; when I was brought low, he saved me" (v. 6). Why does David refer to himself as "simple"? He certainly wasn't a simpleton. The Hebrew word that he used, both there and in Psalm 119:130, can be translated as "one who is open to persuasion" or "one who can be enticed or seduced." Ouch. That's applicable not just to David but also to all of us. After all, the Bible often refers to us as sheep who can be led astray quite easily.

To avoid heading down the wrong path, we need the "unfolding"—the opening, the insight, the guidance—of God's Word. We need to allow God's Word to penetrate our hearts and change us. For many of us, that can be difficult, especially when a passage of the Bible is not terribly straightforward or applicable.

Fortunately, we have help. The Hebrew word for "unfolding" means an entrance, such as a gate. In John chapter 10, Jesus describes himself not only as the good shepherd, but also as the door, or the gate, for the sheep. Jesus, the embodiment of God's Word, enables that Word to penetrate our hearts.

That's good news for all of us simple folks.

Passage: Verse in Context — Psalm 119:125–135

I am your servant; give me understanding, that I may know your testimonies! It is time for the LORD to act, for your law has been broken. Therefore I love your commandments above gold, above fine gold. Therefore I consider all your precepts to be right; I hate every false way. Your testimonies are wonderful; therefore my soul keeps them. The unfolding of your words gives light; it imparts understanding to the simple. I open my mouth and pant, because I long for your commandments. Turn to me and be gracious to me, as is your way with those who love your name. Keep steady my steps according to your promise, and let no iniquity get dominion over me. Redeem me from man's oppression, that I may keep your precepts. Make your face shine upon your servant, and teach me your statutes.

Related Passage — 1 Corinthians 1:20–25

Where is the one who is wise? Where is the scribe? Where is the debater of this age? Has not God made foolish the wisdom of the world? For since, in the wisdom of God, the world did not know God through wisdom, it pleased God through the folly of what we preach to save those who believe. For Jews demand signs and Greeks seek wisdom, but we preach Christ crucified, a stumbling block to Jews and folly to Gentiles, but to those who are called, both Jews and Greeks, Christ the power of God and the wisdom of God. For the foolishness of God is wiser than men, and the weakness of God is stronger than men.

Questions for Reflection and Application

- Are you simple like David, open to persuasion and able to be enticed or seduced? When have you been persuaded or enticed to go down the wrong path?
- How does God's Word penetrate your heart and change you? What can you do to make that a more frequent occurrence?
- What is "the foolishness of God"? What is "the weakness of God"?

Father, you sent your Son so that your Word can penetrate the hearts of simple folks such as me. Thank you for being my light when I lived in darkness. Amen.

SMELLING THE COLOR NINE

*In my distress I called to the L*ORD*, and he answered me.*
—Psalm 120:1

If you are like most people, then you've called out to the Lord and waited for an answer. And waited. And waited. Is God silent? Is he answering? Why can't you hear his answer? Why does the Bible make it sound so easy to hear from God when many of us rarely do?

In his song "Smell the Color 9," Chris Rice says that trying to connect with God can seem like, well, trying to smell the color nine. At the song's outset, Rice is miffed that God seems to speak and give signs to everyone else but him. He longs to hear God's voice, and the fact that he doesn't may mean that he doesn't know God as well as other people do. But Rice is committed to believing and trusting in God anyway. He knows God always is near and leading him, imparting wisdom in ways other than burning bushes and "divine graffiti."

Maybe our difficulties in finding God are not God's fault. After all, the disciples were with Jesus for three full years and still didn't understand that he was "Word made flesh" (John 1:14), even when Jesus told them directly. Consider this exchange from John chapter 14 when Jesus said to Thomas, " 'I am the way, and the truth, and the life. No one comes to the Father except through me. If you had known me, you would have known my Father also. From now on you do know him and have seen him.' Philip said to him, 'Lord, show us the Father, and it is enough for us.' Jesus said to him, 'Have I been with you so long, and you still do not know me, Philip? Whoever has seen me has seen the Father' " (vv. 6–9).

God hears our cries, and he answers. When we're expecting a booming voice, we get a whisper. When we're hoping for a burning bush, we get a much subtler sign. Or a gut feeling. Or something else. But we get an answer.

Passage: Verse in Context — Psalm 120:1–4

In my distress I called to the LORD, and he answered me. Deliver me, O LORD, from lying lips, from a deceitful tongue.

What shall be given to you, and what more shall be done to you, you deceitful tongue? A warrior's sharp arrows, with glowing coals of the broom tree!

Related Passage — 1 Kings 19:11–13

And he said, "Go out and stand on the mount before the LORD." And behold, the LORD passed by, and a great and strong wind tore the mountains and broke in pieces the rocks before the LORD, but the LORD was not in the wind. And after the wind an earthquake, but the LORD was not in the earthquake. And after the earthquake a fire, but the LORD was not in the fire. And after the fire the sound of a low whisper. And when Elijah heard it, he wrapped his face in his cloak and went out and stood at the entrance of the cave. And behold, there came a voice to him and said, "What are you doing here, Elijah?"

Questions for Reflection and Application

- How does God answer your prayers? How does God give you wisdom and insight into his will for your life?
- Has God spoken, directly and audibly, to you? If not, then how do you feel when people say that God has spoken directly to them? Do you wish that God spoke directly to you, or spoke to you more often? Why or why not?
- Why does God sometimes make you hunt for his response and hunt for him? How do you deal with times where trying to find God seems like trying to smell the color nine?

Father, I know that you hear my prayers and I know that you respond, but sometimes it is difficult to hear you. Help me to tune out distractions and tune into you. Amen.

SPECIAL AGENT

My help comes from the LORD, who made heaven and earth.
—*Psalm 121:2*

Founded in 1865 to combat the counterfeiting of United States currency, the U.S. Secret Service has been protecting top federal government officials—including current and former presidents—since 1901. To earn the position of Secret Service Special Agent, an individual must meet stringent physical requirements, qualify for a Top Secret clearance, undergo rigorous training, and pass a series of tests. Once in the position, an agent must be willing to sacrifice his or her life to protect the president or another protected person.[39] In short, a Secret Service Special Agent must be qualified, capable, and willing.

The last member of the US Secret Service to take a bullet for the president was Tim McCarthy, who was shot in the abdomen when John Hinckley Jr. tried to assassinate President Ronald Reagan on March 30, 1981. McCarthy survived and, after recovering from the gunshot, he served on the Reagan security detail for six years total.

The Reagans, of course, were forever grateful for McCarthy's sacrifice. The agent got to know the president and his wife well after the shooting, but on March 30, 1981 he put his life on the line for a complete stranger. In a 2016 interview, McCarthy gave a simple summary of his heroics: "I did what I was trained to do, and I did it correctly."[40]

Presidents rely on the Secret Service for their protection. David relied on God, not just for his protection but also for his health, his well-being, and his eternal destiny. He trusted that God was qualified, capable, and willing.

In other Psalms, David extols the willingness of God to do anything and everything for God's people. In Psalm 121, David gives God's qualifications for the position. And, like Tim McCarthy, David keeps it simple: God is qualified because God made everything. God doesn't need any special training, because everything that God does is perfect—and done right the first time.

And he already took a bullet for you. On the cross.

Passage: Verse in Context — Psalm 121

I lift up my eyes to the hills. From where does my help come? My help comes from the LORD, who made heaven and earth. He will not let your foot be moved; he who keeps you will not slumber. Behold, he who keeps Israel will neither slumber nor sleep.

The LORD is your keeper; the LORD is your shade on your right hand. The sun shall not strike you by day, nor the moon by night. The LORD will keep you from all evil; he will keep your life. The LORD will keep your going out and your coming in from this time forth and forevermore.

Related Passage — Hebrews 1:1–4

Long ago, at many times and in many ways, God spoke to our fathers by the prophets, but in these last days he has spoken to us by his Son, whom he appointed the heir of all things, through whom also he created the world. He is the radiance of the glory of God and the exact imprint of his nature, and he upholds the universe by the word of his power. After making purification for sins, he sat down at the right hand of the Majesty on high, having become as much superior to angels as the name he has inherited is more excellent than theirs.

Questions for Reflection and Application

- Tim McCarthy was a hero, taking a bullet for President Reagan. What people do you consider heroes? Who has been a hero in your life?
- Would anyone consider you a hero? Why?
- How does God provide you with help? What steps have you taken to rely on God instead of yourself?
- What does it mean that Jesus sat down at the right hand of God the Father?

God, you sent your Son, Jesus, who was qualified, capable, and willing to bear the punishment for my sins on the cross and conquer death by rising to new life. Amen.

A WONDERFUL LIFE

The LORD has done great things for us, and we are filled with joy.
—*Psalm 126:3 (NIV)*

"I'm worth more dead than alive." So says George Bailey in the classic film *It's a Wonderful Life.*

After his father's sudden death leaves George in charge of the family business, a small-town building and loan, George fights a lifelong battle to keep his family's head above water financially. Things get ugly when George's Uncle Billy misplaces $8,000—a huge amount of money in 1946—instead of depositing it in the bank. The most powerful man in town, Henry F. Potter, ends up with the cash. George takes responsibility for the debt to the bank, and Potter has a warrant issued for George's arrest.

Seeing no escape from his predicament, George decides to kill himself so that his family can gain the benefit of his $15,000 life insurance policy. A guardian angel, Clarence, intervenes to prevent George's suicide. Clarence explains that George has had a tremendously positive impact on the lives of many people, but George rejects that notion. "I wish I'd never been born," he says.

Clarence grants him his wish, and George sees how his actions, many of which seemed insignificant, have blessed many lives. In a world without George Bailey:

- His brother Harry is dead, because George didn't save Harry from drowning as a child.
- Dozens of servicemen were killed because Harry didn't shoot down two enemy planes.
- The town pharmacist spent years in prison because George didn't prevent him from accidentally poisoning a child.
- The Bailey family business shut down after his father's death, and many who would have lived in homes financed by the building and loan instead live in slums controlled by Potter.
- George's wife, Mary, is an "old maid" who works at the library.

Before the visit by Clarence, George Bailey feels that his life is worthless. After the visit, he realizes that God has done great things for him and through him, and he is filled with joy. And Clarence gets his wings.

Passage: Verse in Context — Psalm 126

When the LORD restored the fortunes of Zion, we were like those who dream. Then our mouth was filled with laughter, and our tongue with shouts of joy; then they said among the nations, "The LORD has done great things for them." The LORD has done great things for us; we are glad.

Restore our fortunes, O LORD, like streams in the Negeb! Those who sow in tears shall reap with shouts of joy! He who goes out weeping, bearing the seed for sowing, shall come home with shouts of joy, bringing his sheaves with him.

Related Passage — Psalm 71:17–21

O God, from my youth you have taught me, and I still proclaim your wondrous deeds. So even to old age and gray hairs, O God, do not forsake me, until I proclaim your might to another generation, your power to all those to come. Your righteousness, O God, reaches the high heavens. You who have done great things, O God, who is like you? You who have made me see many troubles and calamities will revive me again; from the depths of the earth you will bring me up again. You will increase my greatness and comfort me again.

Questions for Reflection and Application

- What great things has God done for you? Make a list, focusing on the things that God has done in the past few years. How often do you think about these things?
- What things have made your life wonderful? Why don't you consider these blessings more often?
- What changed George's perspective on his life? Has there been a time in your life where your perspective changed radically? What caused the change? How can you keep an eternal perspective instead of complaining about your life or being jealous of other men's lives?

Father, you have created me in your image, which gives me worth. Help me to recognize that even on days when I believe I have nothing to offer. Amen.

STEADFAST AND PLENTIFUL

O Israel, hope in the LORD! For with the LORD there is steadfast love,
and with him is plentiful redemption.
—Psalm 130:7

God offers us love and redemption. Our enemy wants us to believe that we can be cut off from God's love and that our actions can cause God to refuse to forgive us. But as Paul explains in Romans 8, we never can be separated from God's steadfast love: "Who shall separate us from the love of Christ? Shall tribulation, or distress, or persecution, or famine, or nakedness, or danger, or sword? ... No, in all these things we are more than conquerors through him who loved us. For I am sure that neither death nor life, nor angels nor rulers, nor things present nor things to come, nor powers, nor height nor depth, nor anything else in all creation, will be able to separate us from the love of God in Christ Jesus our Lord" (v. 35, 37–39).

In the previous chapter, Paul reassures us that, even when we sin repeatedly, God offers us redemption: "For I have the desire to do what is right, but not the ability to carry it out. For I do not do the good I want, but the evil I do not want is what I keep on doing. Now if I do what I do not want, it is no longer I who do it, but sin that dwells within me. So I find it to be a law that when I want to do right, evil lies close at hand. For I delight in the law of God, in my inner being, but I see in my members another law waging war against the law of my mind and making me captive to the law of sin that dwells in my members. Wretched man that I am! Who will deliver me from this body of death? Thanks be to God through Jesus Christ our Lord!" (7:18b–25a).

Our hope is in a God who offers us what we need: steadfast love and plentiful redemption.

Passage: Verse in Context — Psalm 130

Out of the depths I cry to you, O Lord! O Lord, hear my voice! Let your ears be attentive to the voice of my pleas for mercy! If you, O Lord, should mark iniquities, O Lord, who could stand? But with you there is forgiveness, that you may be feared.

I wait for the Lord, my soul waits, and in his word I hope; my soul waits for the Lord more than watchmen for the morning, more than watchmen for the morning. O Israel, hope in the Lord! For with the Lord there is steadfast love, and with him is plentiful redemption. And he will redeem Israel from all his iniquities.

Related Passage — Psalm 36:5–9

Your steadfast love, O Lord, extends to the heavens, your faithfulness to the clouds. Your righteousness is like the mountains of God; your judgments are like the great deep; man and beast you save, O Lord. How precious is your steadfast love, O God! The children of mankind take refuge in the shadow of your wings. They feast on the abundance of your house, and you give them drink from the river of your delights. For with you is the fountain of life; in your light do we see light.

Questions for Reflection and Application

- When have you felt closest to God? When have you felt cut off from God's love and redemption? What are the primary differences between those two experiences?
- Paul struggled with the fact that he wanted to do the right things but lacked the ability to do them and kept doing evil. What are some things that, even though you know they are wrong, you keep doing them anyway? Why do you do that?
- How will Jesus deliver you from your predicament? What evidence do you have that he has done so already?

God, thank you that nothing can separate me from your love because you won't allow it. Amen.

KNITTED TOGETHER

For you formed my inward parts; you knitted me together in my mother's
womb. I praise you, for I am fearfully and wonderfully made.
—*Psalm 139:13–14a*

Within twenty-four hours after being fertilized, a human egg begins dividing
rapidly into many cells. After three days, the rapidly dividing blastocyst moves
from the fallopian tube to the uterus where it implants. Here are some highlights of the first three months of a baby's development:

Area	Month 1	Month 2	Month 3
head and face	A primitive face takes form.	Eyes and ears begin to form.	Ears form fully. Teeth begin to form. The baby can open and close its mouth.
arms and legs		Arms, legs, fingers, and toes begin to form. Bone starts to replace cartilage.	Arms, legs, hands, feet, fingers, and toes are fully formed.
nervous system	The first nerve cells form in the first three weeks.	The brain, spinal cord, and tissue of the central nervous system form.	
circulatory system	Blood cells take shape. A tiny "heart" tube beats.	At about six weeks, the baby's heartbeat can be detected.	The circulatory system is fully functioning.
other		The digestive tract begins to form.	All organs form. The urinary system works.

After three months in the womb, a baby measures just four inches and weighs
just one ounce, but it is a fully-formed human being. Fearfully and wonderfully
made by a loving Creator.

Passage: Verse in Context — Psalm 139:7–18

Where shall I go from your Spirit? Or where shall I flee from your presence? If I ascend to heaven, you are there! If I make my bed in Sheol, you are there! If I take the wings of the morning and dwell in the uttermost parts of the sea, even there your hand shall lead me, and your right hand shall hold me. If I say, "Surely the darkness shall cover me, and the light about me be night," even the darkness is not dark to you; the night is bright as the day, for darkness is as light with you.

For you formed my inward parts; you knitted me together in my mother's womb. I praise you, for I am fearfully and wonderfully made. Wonderful are your works; my soul knows it very well. My frame was not hidden from you, when I was being made in secret, intricately woven in the depths of the earth. Your eyes saw my unformed substance; in your book were written, every one of them, the days that were formed for me, when as yet there was none of them.

How precious to me are your thoughts, O God! How vast is the sum of them! If I would count them, they are more than the sand. I awake, and I am still with you.

Questions for Reflection and Application

- What traits did you inherit from your mother? What traits did you inherit from your father? For which of your traits is the origin a mystery?
- What are your primary physical or mental gifts, such as athletic ability or a high IQ? Which of these gifts have you tried to develop? How much effort have you put into developing them? Why? Which gifts have you not invested enough in? Why?
- What are your primary physical or mental liabilities? How have you tried to overcome these? Take some time to thank God for the miracle that you are, warts and all.

Father, I praise you, for I am fearfully and wonderfully made! Amen.

LIFT UP YOUR VOICE IN PRAISE

Praise the LORD! For it is good to sing praises to our God;
for it is pleasant, and a song of praise is fitting.
—*Psalm 147:1*

One of the oldest hymns still sung in Christian churches is "All Creatures of Our God and King," which in English begins with these words:

All creatures of our God and King,
Lift up your voice and with us sing Alleluia, Alleluia!
Thou burning sun with golden beam,
Thou silver moon with softer gleam,
O praise Him, O praise Him, Alleluia, Alleluia, Alleluia!

The original text of the hymn was written in 1225 by Giovanni Bernardone, better known as St. Francis of Assisi. Born into a wealthy family in 1182, St. Francis led an indulgent life until he was twenty-five, when he decided to serve God by imitating the selfless life of Christ. St. Francis began to deny himself all but the most meager necessities and dedicated himself to evangelism, preaching, and helping the poor. At the age of twenty-eight, he founded the Franciscan Order of Friars, which became a large movement of young men (and some women) who adopted his religious beliefs and ascetic lifestyle.

Perhaps the best-known of St. Francis' writings begins with this:

Make me an instrument of Thy peace. Where there is hatred, let me
sow love. Where there is injury, pardon. Where there is discord, unity.
Where there is doubt, faith. Where there is error, truth. Where there
is despair, hope. Where there is sadness, joy. Where there is darkness,
light.

St. Francis loved to sing and believed strongly in the importance of church music. He wrote over sixty hymns, completing "All Creatures of Our God and King" a year before he died, when he was very ill and had lost his eyesight.[41]

Even when he was suffering, St. Francis knew that a song of praise to God was fitting.

Passage: Verse in Context — Psalm 147:1–6

Praise the LORD! For it is good to sing praises to our God; for it is pleasant, and a song of praise is fitting. The LORD builds up Jerusalem; he gathers the outcasts of Israel. He heals the brokenhearted and binds up their wounds. He determines the number of the stars; he gives to all of them their names. Great is our LORD, and abundant in power; his understanding is beyond measure. The LORD lifts up the humble; he casts the wicked to the ground.

Related Passage — Psalm 148:1–6

Praise the LORD! Praise the LORD from the heavens; praise him in the heights! Praise him, all his angels; praise him, all his hosts!

Praise him, sun and moon, praise him, all you shining stars! Praise him, you highest heavens, and you waters above the heavens!

Let them praise the name of the LORD! For he commanded and they were created. And he established them forever and ever; he gave a decree, and it shall not pass away.

Questions for Reflection and Application

- Have you—or do you know someone who has—made a radical change such as that made by St. Francis? What caused the change? How did God bless it?
- Which of the elements in St. Francis' best-known writing do you try to emulate? Why?
- How often do you praise God when you are suffering or struggling mightily in your life? How can you be more consistent in praising God?

Lord God, even when he was nearing death and blind, St. Francis still praised you. Forgive me for not doing the same. Amen.

A CITY UNDER SIEGE

He heals the brokenhearted and binds up their wounds.
—Psalm 147:3

Born in 1586 in Eilenberg, Germany, Martin Rinkart was the son of a poor coppersmith. As a young adult, Rinkart completed his studies at the University of Leipzig and was ordained as a Lutheran minister. At thirty-one, he was called to be the pastor in his hometown, just when the Thirty Years' War was starting.

Because Eilenberg was a walled city, it became an overcrowded refuge for political and military fugitives. As armies marched through the city, waves of pestilence, famine, and death often followed. Even though Rinkart had trouble providing sufficient food and clothing for his own family, he allowed his home to serve as a refuge for victims of war and its associated ills. The plague of 1637 was dreadfully severe. Rinkart was the only remaining minister in the city, and he conducted as many as fifty funeral services daily.

In spite of the suffering and death all around him, Rinkart wrote uplifting dramatic productions and hymns. His sixty-six hymns include "Now Thank We All Our God," which is based on Psalm 147.

Near the end of the war, Eilenberg was invaded and occupied by the Swedish army, which demanded that a large tribute payment be made by the impoverished citizens of Eilenberg. Rinkart and his parishioners met with the Swedish commander and asked that the tribute amount be reduced. When the commander refused, Rinkart dropped to his knees and led his congregation in prayer and the singing of a familiar hymn. Moved by this demonstration of faith, the commander decided to accept the request for a lower tribute amount.[42]

Rinkart was a minister to people who were surrounded by pain and death. While he could do only so much to alleviate their physical suffering, he pointed them to God, who heals the most important wounds of all—those to the heart. Rinkart demonstrated to the people of a besieged city how to do something very difficult: rejoice and thank God in the midst of our sufferings.

Passage: Verse in Context — Psalm 147:1–6

Praise the LORD! For it is good to sing praises to our God; for it is pleasant, and a song of praise is fitting.

The LORD builds up Jerusalem; he gathers the outcasts of Israel. He heals the brokenhearted and binds up their wounds. He determines the number of the stars; he gives to all of them their names.

Great is our LORD, and abundant in power; his understanding is beyond measure. The LORD lifts up the humble; he casts the wicked to the ground.

Related Passage — Psalm 34:15–18

The eyes of the LORD are toward the righteous and his ears toward their cry. The face of the LORD is against those who do evil, to cut off the memory of them from the earth. When the righteous cry for help, the LORD hears and delivers them out of all their troubles. The LORD is near to the brokenhearted and saves the crushed in spirit.

Questions for Reflection and Application

- When has your heart been broken? How did God help you? How have you used that experience to help others?
- What people in your life are brokenhearted? How can you pray for them right now? What else can you do this week to help them?
- Rinkart encouraged people to praise God, even while they were suffering. Paul did the same in Romans 5, telling us to rejoice in our sufferings. Why are we to do that?

Father, you heal in the midst of every situation in which the enemy brings hurt. You heal always. Amen.

BIGGER THAN THE BOOGIE MAN

Great is our LORD, and abundant in power;
his understanding is beyond measure.
—Psalm 147:5

"God is bigger than the boogie man, and he's watching out for you and me!" So sang Junior Asparagus in 1993's debut video in the VeggieTales animated series—the brainchild of Phil Vischer. In 1994, Vischer's company, Big Idea Productions, sold seven million videos and a reported revenue of $44 million. Its 210 employees worked furiously to release its first feature film, *Jonah*.

But Big Idea was in trouble. Costs began spiraling out of control and revenues flattened. When an $11 million lawsuit judgment went against Big Idea, Vischer's company declared bankruptcy, ten years after the first video was released.

Yet Vischer was strangely happy. Profoundly affected by his dad's leaving home when he was nine, Vischer had driven himself to create a company whose positive messages strengthened families. The self-imposed stress led to pericarditis, an infection of the tissues around the heart, then strep, and then shingles. And that was before the Big Idea business took a downturn and Vischer had to start laying-off employees, whom he considered family.

Just after the lawsuit trial ended, Vischer heard a Bible conference session that asked: What does it mean when God gives you a dream and the dream comes to life, and then the dream dies? The answer: God wants to see if you can live without the dream, depending only on him for meaning. Vischer realized that he had pursued cultural influence instead of pursuing God.

Today, Vischer does voices for the VeggieTales characters in exchange for a small percentage of royalties from the VeggieTales videos created by Big Idea. Those royalties have given Vischer the freedom to pursue a range of creative ventures, all in service to God.[43] [44]

God is not just great and powerful but also all-knowing. He is bigger than the boogie man … the failed business … the failed marriage … the devastating loss … the dream that flourishes and then dies. And he's watching out for you and me.

Passage: Verse in Context — Psalm 147:1–6

Praise the LORD! For it is good to sing praises to our God; for it is pleasant, and a song of praise is fitting.

The LORD builds up Jerusalem; he gathers the outcasts of Israel. He heals the brokenhearted and binds up their wounds. He determines the number of the stars; he gives to all of them their names.

Great is our LORD, and abundant in power; his understanding is beyond measure. The LORD lifts up the humble; he casts the wicked to the ground.

Related Passage — Romans 11:33–36

Oh, the depth of the riches and wisdom and knowledge of God! How unsearchable are his judgments and how inscrutable his ways!

"For who has known the mind of the Lord, or who has been his counselor?"

"Or who has given a gift to him that he might be repaid?"

For from him and through him and to him are all things. To him be glory forever. Amen.

Questions for Reflection and Application

- Why did God allow Vischer to fall? What did Vischer learn?
- When has God allowed you to fall or fail? What did you learn? How did you respond?
- What experiences have left you frustrated with God because you still don't know why you had to go through them? Write down a prayer to God for those experiences, a prayer that you can pray consistently until God brings you insight and peace.
- Who are the "boogie men" in your life right now? How should you enlist God's help with them?

God, you're bigger, stronger, more powerful, and infinitely better than any child—or adult—can comprehend. Amen.

LORD, HAVE MERCY

The LORD lifts up the humble;
he casts the wicked to the ground.
—*Psalm 147:6*

It's time once again for '80s music trivia! No search engines allowed! Ready?

> This song hit #1 on the Billboard Hot 100 in March 1986, three months after the band's song "Broken Wings" did the same in late 1985. Each line of the chorus of the group's second smash hit repeats the Greek phrase for "Lord, have mercy on us." Name the band and the song.

The answer: Mr. Mister, "Kyrie." The song's lyricist, John Lang, said that he was inspired by "singing it as a kid in an Episcopal church in Phoenix."[45] While band front man Richard Page initially was reluctant "to make a religious statement with pop music," he grew to appreciate the song and considers it a prayer in musical form.[46]

Jesus told a parable of a man who wanted God to have mercy on him: "Two men went up into the temple to pray, one a Pharisee and the other a tax collector. The Pharisee, standing by himself, prayed thus: 'God, I thank you that I am not like other men, extortioners, unjust, adulterers, or even like this tax collector. I fast twice a week; I give tithes of all that I get.' But the tax collector, standing far off, would not even lift up his eyes to heaven, but beat his breast, saying, 'God, be merciful to me, a sinner!'" (Luke 18:10–13).

Which of the two men went home justified? The tax collector, Jesus said. "For everyone who exalts himself will be humbled, but the one who humbles himself will be exalted" (v. 14).

Humbling yourself is no fun, but God knows your sin anyway. And he is waiting to wash you clean. As James 4:10 says: "Humble yourselves before the Lord, and he will exalt you."

Down the road that you must travel. Through the darkness of the night. Where you're going, he will follow ... or lead, if you let him.

Kyrie eleison.

Passage: Verse in Context — Psalm 147:1–6

Praise the LORD! For it is good to sing praises to our God; for it is pleasant, and a song of praise is fitting.

The LORD builds up Jerusalem; he gathers the outcasts of Israel. He heals the brokenhearted and binds up their wounds. He determines the number of the stars; he gives to all of them their names.

Great is our LORD, and abundant in power; his understanding is beyond measure. The LORD lifts up the humble; he casts the wicked to the ground.

Related Passage — Ephesians 2:1–9

And you were dead in the trespasses and sins in which you once walked, following the course of this world, following the prince of the power of the air, the spirit that is now at work in the sons of disobedience—among whom we all once lived in the passions of our flesh, carrying out the desires of the body and the mind, and were by nature children of wrath, like the rest of mankind. But God, being rich in mercy, because of the great love with which he loved us, even when we were dead in our trespasses, made us alive together with Christ—by grace you have been saved—and raised us up with him and seated us with him in the heavenly places in Christ Jesus, so that in the coming ages he might show the immeasurable riches of his grace in kindness toward us in Christ Jesus. For by grace you have been saved through faith. And this is not your own doing; it is the gift of God, not a result of works, so that no one may boast.

Questions for Reflection and Application

- In what situations do you struggle with humbling yourself before God and asking for his mercy? When do you prefer to justify your actions or compare yourself favorably to others? Why?
- How do you feel about God's grace being offered to someone who has committed horrible crimes but repents on his deathbed?
- What kind of road has God put you on now? Well-lit and smooth, or challenging and covered in darkness? How dependent are you on God? What is God trying to teach you?

Lord, have mercy on me wherever I go. Amen.

UNBROKEN IN CHRIST

His delight is not in the strength of the horse,
nor his pleasure in the legs of a man, but the LORD takes pleasure in
those who fear him, in those who hope in his steadfast love.
—*Psalm 147:10–11*

The film *Unbroken* tells the story of Louis Zamperini, the Olympic distance runner who survived on a life raft for forty-seven days and endured a harsh imprisonment. But Zamperini's struggles continued even after World War II ended.

In May 1943, after their plane crashed in the Pacific, Zamperini and two other United States soldiers survived in a life raft. One died after thirty-three days. Fourteen days later, Zamperini and the other soldier, clinging to life, were captured by the Japanese. Zamperini was shuttled from one prison to another and, for a time, was in the brutal hands of Mutsuhiro Watanabe, later classified as a war criminal, who subjected Zamperini and others to relentless physical and emotional torment.

Zamperini was liberated at war's end, but his battles were not over. Recurring nightmares of war and memories of torture tormented him. Angry and bitter, he turned to alcohol. Considering divorce, his wife, Cynthia, attended a multi-week Billy Graham rally in Los Angeles, where she accepted Jesus as her Lord and Savior. Returning home, she begged Louis to attend the rally. He finally agreed, but he got angry at Graham's words and stormed out.

A few days later, he returned. When Graham gave the invitation, Louis recalled that, in the life raft, he had promised God, "If you will save me, I will serve you forever." He finally made good on his promise. He became a Christian. His nightmares ended. He gave up alcohol and opened Victory Boys Camp to help troubled boys, many of whom were renewed and reformed, enabling them to live productive lives.[47][48]

It takes a strong man to survive forty-seven days in a life raft and two years of torture in POW camps. But God's delight is not in the strength of a man but in those who hope in his steadfast love.

Passage: Verse in Context — Psalm 147:7–18

Sing to the LORD with thanksgiving; make melody to our God on the lyre! He covers the heavens with clouds; he prepares rain for the earth; he makes grass grow on the hills. He gives to the beasts their food, and to the young ravens that cry. His delight is not in the strength of the horse, nor his pleasure in the legs of a man, but the LORD takes pleasure in those who fear him, in those who hope in his steadfast love.

Praise the LORD, O Jerusalem! Praise your God, O Zion! For he strengthens the bars of your gates; he blesses your children within you. He makes peace in your borders; he fills you with the finest of the wheat. He sends out his command to the earth; his word runs swiftly. He gives snow like wool; he scatters frost like ashes. He hurls down his crystals of ice like crumbs; who can stand before his cold? He sends out his word, and melts them; he makes his wind blow and the waters flow.

Questions for Reflection and Application

- Why does God take pleasure in those who fear and hope in him rather than in those who are strong?
- Have you ever made a promise to God like the one that Zamperini made in the raft? Did you follow through? Why or why not?
- What are your biggest struggles in life? About what things are you most angry and even bitter? How can you turn these things over completely to God?

Father, may I be encouraged by Louis' story, knowing that, when he trusted in you, you gave him the strength he needed to overcome his anger and bitterness. Amen.

A DAZZLING ADORNMENT

For the LORD takes pleasure in his people;
he adorns the humble with salvation.
—*Psalm 149:4*

In his first Letter, Peter writes that we always should be "prepared to make a defense to anyone who asks you for a reason for the hope that is in you" (3:15). Author John Eldredge comments that this passage is strange because "no one ever asks":

> When was the last time someone stopped you to inquire about the reason for the hope that lies within you? You're at the market, say, in the frozen food section. A friend you haven't seen for some time comes up to you, grasps you by both shoulders and pleads, "Please, you've got to tell me. Be honest now. How can you live with such hope? Where does it come from? I must know the reason." In talking with hundreds of Christians, I've met only one or two who have experienced something like this.[49]

Many of us treat our salvation as an insurance policy—a "fire insurance policy," as the old joke goes. We tuck it into our back pockets, ready to pull it out on Judgment Day.

Psalm 149:4 should stop us in our tracks. God loves his people so much that he adorns us with salvation. Adorns us! An adornment is something you wear proudly, especially when it is a gift from someone special. Of course, salvation is an adornment that you can't wear. It happens inside of you; it's an adornment of your soul. It won't be seen by others unless it shines through you—your words, actions, and even attitude.

Historians report that those who persecuted the early Christians marveled at the hope of those Christians. Nothing the persecutors did could diminish that hope. The hope of the early Christians was an adornment that dazzled.

We've been given the greatest gift ever. Let's live in such a way that people can't help but see it.

Passage: Verse in Context — Psalm 149

Praise the LORD! Sing to the LORD a new song, his praise in the assembly of the godly!

Let Israel be glad in his Maker; let the children of Zion rejoice in their King! Let them praise his name with dancing, making melody to him with tambourine and lyre!

For the LORD takes pleasure in his people; he adorns the humble with salvation.

Let the godly exult in glory; let them sing for joy on their beds. Let the high praises of God be in their throats and two-edged swords in their hands, to execute vengeance on the nations and punishments on the peoples, to bind their kings with chains and their nobles with fetters of iron, to execute on them the judgment written! This is honor for all his godly ones.

Praise the LORD!

Related Passage — 1 Peter 3:14–16

But even if you should suffer for righteousness' sake, you will be blessed. Have no fear of them, nor be troubled, but in your hearts honor Christ the Lord as holy, always being prepared to make a defense to anyone who asks you for a reason for the hope that is in you; yet do it with gentleness and respect, having a good conscience, so that, when you are slandered, those who revile your good behavior in Christ may be put to shame.

Questions for Reflection and Application

- "Preach the Gospel at all times, and if necessary use words." This quote is often attributed, some say falsely, to St. Francis of Assisi, a man who demonstrated that he followed Christ in both his words and his actions. How effectively do your actions preach the gospel?
- When is the last time you recognized that you are a Christian because of how you live? How can your salvation, the adornment of your soul, shine through you so that it cannot be missed?
- Peter wrote to people who were being persecuted and suffering greatly. What is your attitude when you go through a rough period? How can your attitude reflect your salvation instead of your circumstances?

God, the salvation that you have given me should shine through me like the sun. Spur me to offer hope to people who have none. Amen.

RISKING THE DEN

But whoever listens to me will dwell secure
and will be at ease, without dread of disaster.
—*Proverbs 1:33*

Daniel was an old man who had lived nearly his entire life in captivity in Babylon. The current king, Darius the Mede, made Daniel one of three high officials who oversaw one hundred and twenty satraps, or provincial rulers. When Darius made Daniel second-in-command over the whole kingdom, the other two high officials and many of the satraps were furious. Unable to find grounds for a complaint against Daniel, they decided to trick Darius into creating one. They persuaded him to sign a thirty-day ordinance that anyone who prayed to a god or a man other than the king would be thrown into a den of lions.

Daniel was not about to suspend his prayers to God for thirty days. He could have prayed in secret, but that's not how he operated. He continued his practice of praying to God three times a day, in front of open windows in his home.

He was caught and brought before Darius, who was bound by the ordinance to have Daniel thrown into the den of lions. Darius spent a sleepless night fasting. As soon as the sun appeared, he raced to the den and cried out to Daniel, desperately hoping to hear a response.

He did. Daniel was alive and unharmed. As soon as Daniel was out of the den, the lions had some new guests: all of the men who had accused Daniel, along with their wives and children. And Darius signed a decree that everyone in the kingdom would worship Daniel's God.

If Daniel had played it safe, then he may have survived thirty days without getting caught praying to God. Because Daniel didn't play it safe, the heart of a king, and the hearts of many in the kingdom, were changed.

How was Daniel able to risk the den? How could he dwell secure and be at ease, without dread of disaster? He did what he always did: he listened to God and was obedient.

Passage: Verse in Context — Proverbs 1:29–33

"Because they hated knowledge and did not choose the fear of the Lord, would have none of my counsel and despised all my reproof, therefore they shall eat the fruit of their way, and have their fill of their own devices. For the simple are killed by their turning away, and the complacency of fools destroys them; but whoever listens to me will dwell secure and will be at ease, without dread of disaster."

Related Passage — Daniel 6:16–22

Then the king commanded, and Daniel was brought and cast into the den of lions. The king declared to Daniel, "May your God, whom you serve continually, deliver you!" And a stone was brought and laid on the mouth of the den, and the king sealed it with his own signet and with the signet of his lords, that nothing might be changed concerning Daniel. Then the king went to his palace and spent the night fasting; no diversions were brought to him, and sleep fled from him.

Then, at break of day, the king arose and went in haste to the den of lions. As he came near to the den where Daniel was, he cried out in a tone of anguish. The king declared to Daniel, "O Daniel, servant of the living God, has your God, whom you serve continually, been able to deliver you from the lions?" Then Daniel said to the king, "O king, live forever! My God sent his angel and shut the lions' mouths, and they have not harmed me, because I was found blameless before him; and also before you, O king, I have done no harm."

Questions for Reflection and Application

- There's not much flash or glory in obedience. It requires discipline and faith. How are you doing on the obedience front? What helps you stay obedient? What is most disruptive?
- How do you listen to and follow God when you are under tremendous pressure? What practices help you to "keep your head" when, as Kipling wrote, "all about you are losing theirs and blaming it on you"?

Father, may I not "play it safe" when it comes to sharing my faith or anything else that you want me to do. If I keep my eyes on you, then I will have no fear, because no earthly lion can stand up to the Lion of Judah. Amen.

THE VALUE OF WISDOM

*For the L*ORD *gives wisdom; from his mouth
come knowledge and understanding.*
—*Proverbs 2:6*

God wants to hear your prayers. In Philippians, Paul encourages us "in everything by prayer and supplication with thanksgiving let your requests be made known to God" (4:6). In 1 Thessalonians, he tells us to "pray without ceasing" (5:17). In Matthew, Jesus says, "Ask, and it will be given to you; seek, and you will find; knock, and it will be opened to you" (7:7).

For what should you pray? If you could make one request to God, and you know that God would grant that request, then what would your request be?

Solomon became the king of Israel when David died. Wanting to follow in his father's footsteps of loving and following God, Solomon went to Gibeon to offer a sacrifice. God appeared to Solomon in a dream and said that he would grant Solomon one request. Here is Solomon's response to God: "You have shown great and steadfast love to your servant David my father, because he walked before you in faithfulness, in righteousness, and in uprightness of heart toward you. And you have kept for him this great and steadfast love and have given him a son to sit on his throne this day. And now, O LORD my God, you have made your servant king in place of David my father. ... And your servant is in the midst of your people whom you have chosen, a great people, too many to be numbered or counted for multitude. Give your servant therefore an understanding mind to govern your people, that I may discern between good and evil, for who is able to govern this your great people?" (1 Kings 3:6–7a, 8–9).

Solomon prayed for wisdom and God gave it to him. And because God was so pleased with Solomon's request, God also gave Solomon riches and honor and made a promise that if Solomon kept God's commandments, then he would live a long life.

True wisdom comes from God. The closer we are to God, the wiser we become.

Passage: Verse in Context — Proverbs 2:1–15

My son, if you receive my words and treasure up my commandments with you, making your ear attentive to wisdom and inclining your heart to understanding; yes, if you call out for insight and raise your voice for understanding, if you seek it like silver and search for it as for hidden treasures, then you will understand the fear of the LORD and find the knowledge of God. For the LORD gives wisdom; from his mouth come knowledge and understanding; he stores up sound wisdom for the upright; he is a shield to those who walk in integrity, guarding the paths of justice and watching over the way of his saints.

Then you will understand righteousness and justice and equity, every good path; for wisdom will come into your heart, and knowledge will be pleasant to your soul; discretion will watch over you, understanding will guard you, delivering you from the way of evil, from men of perverted speech, who forsake the paths of uprightness to walk in the ways of darkness, who rejoice in doing evil and delight in the perverseness of evil, men whose paths are crooked, and who are devious in their ways.

Questions for Reflection and Application

- How much do you prize wisdom? Where is it on your list of the things that you most desire from God?
- Do people consider you wise? Why or why not?
- How would you compare your level of wisdom from where it was five years ago?
- We live in an information age, where facts and figures are just a tap away. Has increased information increased your wisdom? What things do increase your wisdom?
- How can you get closer to God in the next year? In the next month? Today?

God, you are the source of all good things. Grant me wisdom and discernment that I may know your will and strive to do it. Amen.

PEACE ON THE BATTLEFIELD

My son, do not forget my teaching, but let your heart keep my commandments,
for length of days and years of life and peace they will add to you.
—Proverbs 3:1–2

Special military operators must be trained to perform well in challenging situations, including when operating in hostile enemy territory, where stress can be severe and effective performance can mean the difference between life and death. The army and navy use training to ensure that these operators can perform well while under stress on the battlefield. Stress inoculation training uses a three-stage approach, where the trainer:

- Explains how stress affects emotions, thoughts, decision-making, and performance.
- Increases operators' repertoire of behavioral and cognitive skills that can aid performance under stress.
- Enables operators to practice these new skills under stressful conditions.[50]

You may not think of yourself as a soldier, but you were born into a world at war and you are operating in enemy territory. Jesus called Satan "the ruler of this world" (John 12:31) and said that he "comes only to steal and kill and destroy" (John 10:10). Paul wrote that Satan is "the god of this world" and "has blinded the minds of the unbelievers" (2 Corinthians 4:4). Peter wrote "the devil prowls around like a roaring lion, seeking someone to devour" (1 Peter 5:8).

How do we battle the devil on a daily basis? We need training and we need to follow that training. Our training manual is all of God's commandments in the Bible. Our trainer is Jesus, who modeled the disciplines and behaviors that we should adopt. Right after he was baptized, Jesus went into the wilderness by himself and fasted for forty days and nights, which made him incredibly weak, tired, and hungry. He then was tempted by the devil.

How did Jesus resist temptation under such tremendous stress? Each time the devil tempted him, Jesus responded with a passage of Scripture. When we keep God's commandments, we have peace, even when things get rough on the daily battlefield.

Passage: Verse in Context — Proverbs 3:1–4

My son, do not forget my teaching, but let your heart keep my commandments, for length of days and years of life and peace they will add to you. Let not steadfast love and faithfulness forsake you; bind them around your neck; write them on the tablet of your heart. So you will find favor and good success in the sight of God and man.

Related Passage — Mark 12:28–34

And one of the scribes came up and heard them disputing with one another, and seeing that he answered them well, asked him, "Which commandment is the most important of all?" Jesus answered, "The most important is, 'Hear, O Israel: The Lord our God, the Lord is one. And you shall love the Lord your God with all your heart and with all your soul and with all your mind and with all your strength.' The second is this: 'You shall love your neighbor as yourself.' There is no other commandment greater than these." And the scribe said to him, "You are right, Teacher. You have truly said that he is one, and there is no other besides him. And to love him with all the heart and with all the understanding and with all the strength, and to love one's neighbor as oneself, is much more than all whole burnt offerings and sacrifices." And when Jesus saw that he answered wisely, he said to him, "You are not far from the kingdom of God." And after that no one dared to ask him any more questions.

Questions for Reflection and Application

- How did Jesus train for his temptation in the wilderness? How did Jesus train for the challenges of his ministry? How did Jesus prepare himself for the cross?
- How are you training yourself to keep God's commandments and withstand the attacks of the devil?
- When is the last time you truly felt at peace? What robs you of peace?

Father, every day I fight battles and every night I am weary from the struggle and the realization that I must do it all over again tomorrow. Give me the focus I need to follow your commandments and be obedient to your will. Amen.

THE TRUST OF ANANIAS

Trust in the LORD with all your heart, and do not lean on your
own understanding. In all your ways acknowledge him,
and he will make straight your paths.
—*Proverbs 3:5–6*

Trusting God can be difficult, especially when God asks you to do something that doesn't make sense to you.

After observing and approving of the stoning of Stephen, Saul of Tarsus decided to rid the world of as many followers of Jesus as he could. The high priest gave him the authority to go to Damascus, root out those who belonged to "the Way" (Acts 9:2), arrest them, and bring them back to Jerusalem for trial and execution.

Then Jesus intervened. As Saul and his band approached Damascus, Jesus blinded Saul and told him that he was persecuting followers of the Messiah. By the time Saul got to Damascus, he was a convert to Christianity. The problem was that no one on earth knew that except Saul. To Christians everywhere, Saul still was Enemy #1.

Imagine the surprise of Ananias, a disciple of Jesus in Damascus, when God told him in a vision to go to Saul of Tarsus in Damascus and lay his hands on Saul so that Saul could regain his sight. What sense did it make for Ananias to help the world's greatest persecutor of Christians? God told Ananias that he had made Saul "a chosen instrument of mine to carry my name before the Gentiles and kings and the children of Israel" (Acts 9:15).

Ananias didn't understand completely, but he trusted in God and was obedient. He went to Saul, laid his hands on Saul, and told Saul that Jesus wanted Saul to regain his sight and be filled with the Holy Spirit. And all of this happened. Because Ananias trusted God, other disciples in Damascus trusted Saul and helped him. Saul became the apostle Paul, spreading Christianity in Damascus and throughout the Roman Empire.

When you trust in God with all your heart and lean on God instead of your own understanding, God makes great things happen. Just ask Ananias.

Passage: Verse in Context — Proverbs 3:5–8

Trust in the LORD with all your heart, and do not lean on your own understanding. In all your ways acknowledge him, and he will make straight your paths. Be not wise in your own eyes; fear the LORD, and turn away from evil. It will be healing to your flesh and refreshment to your bones.

Related Passage — Philemon 17–22

So if you consider me your partner, receive him as you would receive me. If he has wronged you at all, or owes you anything, charge that to my account. I, Paul, write this with my own hand: I will repay it—to say nothing of your owing me even your own self. Yes, brother, I want some benefit from you in the Lord. Refresh my heart in Christ.

Confident of your obedience, I write to you, knowing that you will do even more than I say. At the same time, prepare a guest room for me, for I am hoping that through your prayers I will be graciously given to you.

Questions for Reflection and Application

- How do you usually make decisions? How much do you rely on your intellect and experiences? How much do you rely on the prompting of God?
- When you make a good decision—one that pans out well—do you acknowledge God, or do you pat yourself on the back? How can you become more consistent in consulting with God, trusting him, and giving him all the glory?
- When you feel that God is telling you to do something, especially something that you normally wouldn't do (or that doesn't make sense), how do you know that it is God speaking to you? What are appropriate ways for you to "test the spirits"? (See 1 John 4:1–3.)

Father, when you ask me to do something that seems counterintuitive, help me to trust and obey. Amen.

STILL STANDING AFTER FIFTEEN

My son, do not despise the LORD's discipline or be weary of his reproof,
for the LORD reproves him whom he loves,
as a father the son in whom he delights.

—Proverbs 3:11–12

On Thanksgiving Day as a publicity stunt, world heavyweight boxing champion Apollo Creed selects unknown Philadelphia fighter Rocky Balboa as his opponent for a New Year's Day bout in the film *Rocky*. With only five weeks to prepare, Rocky needs an experienced trainer. Mickey Goldmill, who runs the gym where Rocky trains, is the best choice. But Mickey has never helped Rocky before because he was disappointed in Rocky's lack of devotion to the sport.

A few days after Thanksgiving, the seventy-six-year-old Mickey comes to Rocky's apartment and offers to be his manager. But Rocky rejects Mickey's offer: "I needed your help about ten years ago. Ten years ago, you never helped me. You didn't care." After Mickey leaves, Rocky has a change of heart, chases Mickey down, and agrees to let Mickey manage him.

Getting Rocky ready to fight Apollo appears to be an impossible task. But Mickey trains Rocky as if he were a legitimate contender. He is hard on Rocky but also encouraging. When he uses a technique to improve Rocky's balance, Mickey says that famous champion Rocky Marciano had the same balance problem and cured it with this technique. As an exhausted Rocky continues to throw punches at the end of a marathon day of training, Mickey buoys Rocky with his words: "You'll be able to spit nails, kid. … You're gonna become a very dangerous person."

Mickey's training enables Rocky to become the first fighter to go the distance with Apollo Creed and remain standing after fifteen rounds.

God disciplines us because he loves us. Our prize is better than the satisfaction of going the distance in a title bout. It's a crown of righteousness, placed on our heads by God himself.

So cue the theme song, and let's get training!

Passage: Verse in Context — Proverbs 3:9–12

Honor the LORD with your wealth and with the firstfruits of all your produce; then your barns will be filled with plenty, and your vats will be bursting with wine. My son, do not despise the LORD's discipline or be weary of his reproof, for the LORD reproves him whom he loves, as a father the son in whom he delights.

Related Passage — Hebrews 12:7–11

It is for discipline that you have to endure. God is treating you as sons. For what son is there whom his father does not discipline? If you are left without discipline, in which all have participated, then you are illegitimate children and not sons. Besides this, we have had earthly fathers who disciplined us and we respected them. Shall we not much more be subject to the Father of spirits and live? For they disciplined us for a short time as it seemed best to them, but he disciplines us for our good, that we may share his holiness. For the moment all discipline seems painful rather than pleasant, but later it yields the peaceful fruit of righteousness to those who have been trained by it.

Questions for Reflection and Application

- What story of discipline is most inspiring to you?
- How has God disciplined you in the past? How is he disciplining you today?
- How do you respond to God's discipline? How can you develop a greater appreciation for it?
- What spiritual disciplines are you subjecting yourself to? How is that going? In what areas do you need to be more disciplined? What are some steps that you can take in those areas beginning today?

Thank you God, that as my trainer you will go tough on me and will prepare me to accomplish things I could never do in my own power. Amen.

THE WISDOM OF HAZEL

Blessed is the one who finds wisdom, and the one who gets understanding,
for the gain from her is better than gain from silver and her profit better than gold.
—*Proverbs 3:13–14*

Hazel does not stand out from the other rabbits in his warren. He does not see visions, is not the strongest fighter, and now that he is injured from a gunshot wound obtained on a raid to free some rabbits from a farm, he is not as fast as the others.

But he is wise. His wisdom has earned him the position of leader, or Chief Rabbit, of the warren on Watership Down, formed by a ragtag group of rabbits that Hazel led from a doomed warren a few months earlier. Wise decisions by Hazel, including befriending a wounded bird and nursing it back to health, have helped his warren survive and thrive.

Under Hazel's leadership, the warren has been able to obtain some rabbits, including some sorely needed ones, from Efrafa, a warren led by a militaristic warlord, General Woundwort. Now a company under Woundwort is tracking Hazel's band and planning to attack Hazel's warren. Hazel approaches Woundwort. Thinking Hazel is a messenger, Woundwort demands the return of all the rabbits that left Efrafa. Hazel responds with a radical idea: the two warrens should form a partnership:

> At that moment, in the sunset on Watership Down, there was offered to General Woundwort the opportunity to show whether he was really the leader of vision and genius which he believed himself to be, or whether he was no more than a tyrant with the courage and cunning of a pirate. For one beat of his pulse the lame rabbit's idea shone clearly before him.

Woundwort rejects Hazel's proposal and proceeds to attack Hazel's warren. But his attack fails because Hazel, in his wisdom, bites through the rope of a dog on Nuthanger Farm, and another rabbit leads the dog to Woundwort.[51]

Blessed is the rabbit, or the person, who finds wisdom and receives understanding.

Passage: Verse in Context — Proverbs 3:13–27

Blessed is the one who finds wisdom, and the one who gets understanding, for the gain from her is better than gain from silver and her profit better than gold. She is more precious than jewels, and nothing you desire can compare with her. Long life is in her right hand; in her left hand are riches and honor. Her ways are ways of pleasantness, and all her paths are peace. She is a tree of life to those who lay hold of her; those who hold her fast are called blessed.

The Lord by wisdom founded the earth; by understanding he established the heavens; by his knowledge the deeps broke open, and the clouds drop down the dew.

My son, do not lose sight of these—keep sound wisdom and discretion, and they will be life for your soul and adornment for your neck. Then you will walk on your way securely, and your foot will not stumble. If you lie down, you will not be afraid; when you lie down, your sleep will be sweet. Do not be afraid of sudden terror or of the ruin of the wicked, when it comes, for the Lord will be your confidence and will keep your foot from being caught. Do not withhold good from those to whom it is due, when it is in your power to do it.

Questions for Reflection and Application

- What is your vision for your life? From where did that vision come? What is your strategy to achieve that vision? What role does wisdom play in that strategy?
- Hazel's wisdom enabled him to see strengths and opportunities, even in unlikely places. Consider the challenges you now face. What opportunities may be there? How can God help you to realize those opportunities for his glory?
- A wise person looks past the weaknesses in others to see their strengths and how to harness those strengths for the good of others. Consider four or five key people in your life. What are their strengths? How do those strengths complement yours? How is God calling you to lead, or serve, among these people?

Father, I often forget the merit of wisdom—how it far surpasses strength, speed, and talent. Grant me wisdom today. Amen.

SHADING OUR EYES

But the path of the righteous is like the light of dawn,
which shines brighter and brighter until full day.
—*Proverbs 4:18*

Have you had a "mountaintop experience" with God? Was it when you became a Christian? Rediscovered your faith? Went on a missions trip and felt incredibly close to God as you served others for him? Regardless of when and how it happened, that experience changed you and how you live your life.

What happened next when you came down off the mountaintop? Did the radiance of God grow brighter in your life over the coming months and years? Or did the light slowly fade as you went back to "business as usual" in your life?

Charlie Peacock asks questions like those in his song "Is the Brightness Still in Me?". A long-time Christian, Peacock looks back on his life and asks whether or not the light of God shines in him as brightly as it did when he was young and first believed. Peacock reflects in his song that God's light, like God's grace, is given to every sinner who relies on God completely.

The light of God—the Holy Spirit—is given to us once but lasts forever. How brightly it shines depends not on God but on us. On the mountaintop, where we feel close to God and rely on him completely, we are dazzled with that light. But when we rely on ourselves, the light can seem to fade. Peacock asks the Holy Spirit to speak for him when his light grows weak, so that he can shine brightly every day.

It takes discipline to follow the path of righteousness every day. When you do, the light of God on the mountaintop will begin to seem like the sun at dawn. Sure, it was brighter than the darkness that preceded it, but the midmorning light is much brighter, and you'll have to shade your eyes for the midday sun.

And the brightness of the midday sun can illuminate your life—and the lives of those around you—for the rest of your days.

Passage: Verse in Context — Proverbs 4:10–23

Hear, my son, and accept my words, that the years of your life may be many. I have taught you the way of wisdom; I have led you in the paths of uprightness. When you walk, your step will not be hampered, and if you run, you will not stumble. Keep hold of instruction; do not let go; guard her, for she is your life.

Do not enter the path of the wicked, and do not walk in the way of the evil. Avoid it; do not go on it; turn away from it and pass on. For they cannot sleep unless they have done wrong; they are robbed of sleep unless they have made someone stumble. For they eat the bread of wickedness and drink the wine of violence. But the path of the righteous is like the light of dawn, which shines brighter and brighter until full day. The way of the wicked is like deep darkness; they do not know over what they stumble.

My son, be attentive to my words; incline your ear to my sayings. Let them not escape from your sight; keep them within your heart. For they are life to those who find them, and healing to all their flesh. Keep your heart with all vigilance, for from it flow the springs of life.

Questions for Reflection and Application

- All too often, the brilliance of a "mountaintop experience" with God fades in the ensuing weeks. Why is that?
- According to Solomon, the light on the path of the righteous gets brighter and brighter the longer you walk on it. When have you experienced this? In what areas of your life is God's radiance shining most brightly? In what areas has it faded? What is the difference?
- How can you stay on the path of righteousness, especially when you face adversity? How can you avoid complacency in your faith?

Lord, help me to be disciplined in following you so that, even after the glow from the mountaintop experience fades, I can stay "bright" in serving you. Amen.

SURPRISE!

For a man's ways are before the eyes of the LORD,
and he ponders all his paths.
—*Proverbs 5:21*

People love surprises—in murder mysteries, but not in real life.

Every year, mystery novels have higher sales than any other book genre except romance novels. The best-selling fiction author of all time, Agatha Christie (1890–1976), wrote over ninety books that achieved sales of around four billion dollars. The books were popular primarily because of their surprising plot twists that kept the reader guessing until the very end.

After some of her books were dramatized into plays and films, Christie decided to write her own plays. By the end of World War II, she was as well-known for her plays as for her books. *The Mousetrap*, in which the snowbound guests at a country house include a murderer, is the world's longest-running play, having been continually on stage since its debut in 1952.

Christie's writing became a way of escaping from two unfortunate surprises in her life in 1926. First, her beloved mother died. While Christie was still grieving, her husband of twelve years asked for a divorce. After that double whammy, Christie went from an occasional amateur writer to a prolific professional, averaging three full novels a year. Her friend, the historian A. L. Rowse, said that 1926 "left its traces all through her work. It also made her the great woman she became."[52] [53]

Surprises in our life can be devastating or elating, debilitating or motivating. They can show us that we are on the right track or convince us that we need to pursue a new path. As much as an event may catch us off guard however, it is never a surprise to God.

An author of a mystery novel knows the ending and how the characters arrive there. God knows the same for each of our lives. He studies all the possible outcomes of our decisions. At every juncture, he knows the right path for us to take. The closer we are to God, the fewer surprises we'll encounter … except in murder mysteries.

Passage: Verse in Context — Proverbs 5:1–4, 20–23

My son, be attentive to my wisdom; incline your ear to my understanding, that you may keep discretion, and your lips may guard knowledge. For the lips of a forbidden woman drip honey, and her speech is smoother than oil, but in the end she is bitter as wormwood, sharp as a two-edged sword. …

Why should you be intoxicated, my son, with a forbidden woman and embrace the bosom of an adulteress? For a man's ways are before the eyes of the LORD, and he ponders all his paths. The iniquities of the wicked ensnare him, and he is held fast in the cords of his sin. He dies for lack of discipline, and because of his great folly he is led astray.

Related Passage — Psalm 16:7–11

I bless the LORD who gives me counsel; in the night also my heart instructs me. I have set the LORD always before me; because he is at my right hand, I shall not be shaken. Therefore my heart is glad, and my whole being rejoices; my flesh also dwells secure. For you will not abandon my soul to Sheol, or let your holy one see corruption. You make known to me the path of life; in your presence there is fullness of joy; at your right hand are pleasures forevermore.

Questions for Reflection and Application

- In Proverbs 5, Solomon laments that, too often, a man is led astray by a "forbidden woman" or "iniquities of the wicked" (vv. 20, 22). What things have led you astray? Why?
- In the past few years, what unexpected things have happened to you? How did you respond? Did they draw you closer to God or push you away?
- When something unexpected happens to you, how quickly do you turn to God? How often do you try to deal with the surprise on your own first?

Father, it should come as no surprise to me that you have carved out a perfect plan for my life. I pray that I stay close to you at every turn. Amen.

A STRAIGHT-A STUDENT

The fear of the LORD is the beginning of wisdom,
and the knowledge of the Holy One is insight.
—*Proverbs 9:10*

Contrary to the sentiments of the trendy respondent in Billy Joel's song "It's Still Rock and Roll to Me," there is nothing wrong with being a straight-A student. Good grades in high school can get you a college scholarship, which may result in a job where you earn enough to get some "pink sidewinders and a bright orange pair of pants" (if you really want to).

Gaining knowledge is good. Gaining wisdom is better. But wisdom is beneficial only if you use it … wisely. Solomon, who wrote the majority of the book of Proverbs, asked God for wisdom so that he could put it into practice and be an effective leader of God's people, one who governed well by making good decisions.

Christians often are instructed that they should spend a lot of time reading God's Word, the Bible. By studying the Bible regularly, you can gain a lot of knowledge about God, which results in insight. But the real purpose of reading Scripture is to be changed by it. Paul says that Scripture is useful for teaching, reproof, correction, and training in righteousness. James expresses similar sentiments more succinctly: "Do not merely listen to the word, and so deceive yourselves. Do what it says" (1:22, NIV)

Jesus starts one of his parables with this question: "Why do you call me 'Lord, Lord,' and not do what I tell you?" (Luke 6:46). He then proceeds to say that someone who hears his words and does them is like a wise man who built a house on a rock; whereas someone who hears his words and does not do them is like a man who built a house on the sand. When a storm brought a flood, the wise man's house survived; the foolish man's house was ruined.

The fear of God is the beginning of wisdom, and reading Scripture can make you wise. But following Jesus will get you through the storms of life with your house intact.

Passage: Verse in Context — Proverbs 9:7–12

Whoever corrects a scoffer gets himself abuse, and he who reproves a wicked man incurs injury. Do not reprove a scoffer, or he will hate you; reprove a wise man, and he will love you. Give instruction to a wise man, and he will be still wiser; teach a righteous man, and he will increase in learning. The fear of the LORD is the beginning of wisdom, and the knowledge of the Holy One is insight. For by me your days will be multiplied, and years will be added to your life. If you are wise, you are wise for yourself; if you scoff, you alone will bear it.

Related Passage — James 1:22–25

But be doers of the word, and not hearers only, deceiving yourselves. For if anyone is a hearer of the word and not a doer, he is like a man who looks intently at his natural face in a mirror. For he looks at himself and goes away and at once forgets what he was like. But the one who looks into the perfect law, the law of liberty, and perseveres, being no hearer who forgets but a doer who acts, he will be blessed in his doing.

Questions for Reflection and Application

- How were your grades in school? What kind of effort did you give in your classes? Why?
- What is your primary motivation for reading the Bible? When you read it consistently, what changes do you see in your life? What changes would you like to see?
- What helps you feel closest to God? Prayer? Bible reading? Music? Being outdoors? How can reading your Bible draw you closer to God?
- What instructions in Scripture are the most difficult for you to follow (or do)? Why?

Lord God, help me to do more than listen to and read your Word. Help me to do what it says and to follow you faithfully through the storms of life. Amen.

KEEPING YOUR HANDS CLEAN

The wicked earns deceptive wages,
but one who sows righteousness gets a sure reward.
—*Proverbs 11:18*

At the beginning of the 1993 film *The Firm*, Mitch McDeere begins work at Bendini, Lambert & Locke (BL&L), a small Memphis firm that specializes in accounting and tax law. The firm demands complete loyalty, strict confidentiality, and a willingness to charge exceptional fees for its services, which are designed to help wealthy clients avoid taxes by hiding large amounts of money in off-shore shell corporations.

After passing the bar exam, Mitch begins working long hours, which puts a strain on his marriage. While on a trip to the Cayman Islands, Mitch is seduced by a local woman and cheats on his wife. The encounter is a setup that is photographed so that the firm's security chief can blackmail Mitch to keep him quiet. Mitch soon learns why: the firm's biggest client is the Morolto Mafia family from Chicago, and the firm's partners, as well as most of the associates, are complicit in a massive tax fraud and money laundering scheme.

The FBI approaches Mitch and pressures him to provide evidence that the FBI can use to go after the Moroltos and bring down BL&L. If he keeps silent, then he likely will end up in jail. If he discloses information about the firm's clients to the FBI however, he will break attorney-client privilege and be disbarred. How can Mitch stay alive, remain a lawyer, and bring down the firm?

While you likely have never worked for a truly wicked employer such as BL&L, you probably have encountered some shady business practices along the way. No one's wages are labeled as "deceptive" or "legitimate"— all money is the same color, regardless of how it is earned or obtained.

In every work environment, God challenges us to keep our hands clean, even when the hands around us are dirty. Staying righteous in the workplace may not net us a higher income, but God promises a better reward: His favor. It's a sure thing. In Memphis and everywhere else.

Passage: Verse in Context — Proverbs 11:10–22

When it goes well with the righteous, the city rejoices, and when the wicked perish there are shouts of gladness. By the blessing of the upright a city is exalted, but by the mouth of the wicked it is overthrown. Whoever belittles his neighbor lacks sense, but a man of understanding remains silent. Whoever goes about slandering reveals secrets, but he who is trustworthy in spirit keeps a thing covered.

Where there is no guidance, a people falls, but in an abundance of counselors there is safety. Whoever puts up security for a stranger will surely suffer harm, but he who hates striking hands in pledge is secure. A gracious woman gets honor, and violent men get riches. A man who is kind benefits himself, but a cruel man hurts himself. The wicked earns deceptive wages, but one who sows righteousness gets a sure reward.

Whoever is steadfast in righteousness will live, but he who pursues evil will die. Those of crooked heart are an abomination to the LORD, but those of blameless ways are his delight. Be assured, an evil person will not go unpunished, but the offspring of the righteous will be delivered. Like a gold ring in a pig's snout is a beautiful woman without discretion.

Questions for Reflection and Application

- "Cheaters never prosper." Except when they do. When have you seen people who bend the rules get ahead? When have you seen them get caught and punished? Why does God allow some cheaters to prosper? What is God calling you to do when you witness people bending or breaking the rules to get ahead?
- Think about times that you have been tempted to cheat at work or elsewhere. When did you succumb to the temptation? What happened as a result? What has God called you to do with respect to cheating? If you have not heeded his call, how can you get started on that this week?

Father, give me clean hands and a pure heart. Amen.

A GOOD NEIGHBOR

A generous person will prosper;
whoever refreshes others will be refreshed.
—*Proverbs 11:25 (NIV)*

Complete this phrase: "Like a good neighbor, _____ is there."

If you said "the Good Samaritan", then you've been looking ahead.

In Luke's Gospel, Jesus tells a lawyer that he is correct when stating that loving God and loving his neighbor will lead to eternal life. When the lawyer asks who his neighbor is, Jesus tells the parable of the Good Samaritan: "A man was going down from Jerusalem to Jericho, and he fell among robbers, who stripped him and beat him and departed, leaving him half dead. Now by chance a priest was going down that road, and when he saw him he passed by on the other side. So likewise a Levite, when he came to the place and saw him, passed by on the other side. But a Samaritan, as he journeyed, came to where he was, and when he saw him, he had compassion. He went to him and bound up his wounds, pouring on oil and wine. Then he set him on his own animal and brought him to an inn and took care of him. And the next day he took out two denarii [a day's wage] and gave them to the innkeeper, saying, 'Take care of him, and whatever more you spend, I will repay you when I come back'" (10:29–35).

The parable shocked Jesus' audience for two reasons. First, Jews and Samaritans had hated each other for centuries. Second, the part of the Law that mentions loving your neighbor implies that your neighbor is your fellow Jew, but Jesus made it clear that the Samaritan "proved to be a neighbor to the man who fell among the robbers" and instructed the lawyer to "go, and do likewise" (vv. 36–37).

To whom should you be a good neighbor? To whom should you be generous? Whom should you refresh? It depends on how much you want to be blessed. God is insanely generous with each of us. He smiles at us and says, "Give it a try!"

Passage: Verse in Context — Proverbs 11:23–30

The desire of the righteous ends only in good, the expectation of the wicked in wrath. One gives freely, yet grows all the richer; another withholds what he should give, and only suffers want. Whoever brings blessing will be enriched, and one who waters will himself be watered. The people curse him who holds back grain, but a blessing is on the head of him who sells it.

Whoever diligently seeks good seeks favor, but evil comes to him who searches for it. Whoever trusts in his riches will fall, but the righteous will flourish like a green leaf. Whoever troubles his own household will inherit the wind, and the fool will be servant to the wise of heart. The fruit of the righteous is a tree of life, and whoever captures souls is wise.

Related Passage — John 4:39–42

Many Samaritans from that town believed in him because of the woman's testimony, "He told me all that I ever did." So when the Samaritans came to him, they asked him to stay with them, and he stayed there two days. And many more believed because of his word. They said to the woman, "It is no longer because of what you said that we believe, for we have heard for ourselves, and we know that this is indeed the Savior of the world."

Questions for Reflection and Application

- Think about some recent times where your actions blessed another person. How were you "enriched" and "watered" as a result?
- The priest and Levite had what they considered good reasons for not helping the beaten man: if the man were dead and they touched him, then they would render themselves "unclean." When have you had what seemed like good reasons for not helping people in need? What were the reasons? In hindsight, were they good enough reasons to not help? Why or why not?
- How can you give your T's—time, talent, and treasure—more freely, starting today?

God, give me the attitude of the Good Samaritan, so that I see everyone as important to you and treat everyone as my neighbor. Amen.

ROTTING BONES

A heart at peace gives life to the body, but envy rots the bones.
—*Proverbs 14:30 (NIV)*

One of the most famous of Jesus' parables is the parable of the Prodigal (or Lost) Son. In the story, the father, who represents God, welcomes back the prodigal, who represents anyone who walks away from God but then repents.

The story does not end at the point of restoration for the younger son. The older son comes in from the field and finds out from a servant that the father is throwing a party for the younger son. Furious, the older son refuses to go inside. When the father comes out and begs the older son to come in, the son answers, "Look, these many years I have served you, and I never disobeyed your command, yet you never gave me a young goat, that I might celebrate with my friends. But when this son of yours came, who has devoured your property with prostitutes, you killed the fattened calf for him!" (Luke 15:29–30).

Consider how the older son, who considers himself the "good" son, treats his father. By refusing to go in, the older son shows great disrespect to his father, forcing his father to come to him. The older son arrogantly tells his father that he has "served" him for years and "never disobeyed." The older son exaggerates the sins of his brother to make himself look better. Finally, the older son implies that his father loves the younger son more.

Anger. Disrespect. Arrogance. Dishonesty. Bitterness. These are the traits of the "good" son, who is envious of the fact that his brother, who walked away from the father, has been welcomed back. In contrast, the former prodigal is at peace, a peace that started the moment he decided to humble himself, return to his father, repent of his sins, and pray that he would be treated as a servant.

The former prodigal has life. His older brother has rotting bones. As Jesus said several times, "Whoever exalts himself will be humbled, and whoever humbles himself will be exalted" (Matthew 23:12).

Passage: Verse in Context — Proverbs 14:26–35

In the fear of the LORD one has strong confidence, and his children will have a refuge. The fear of the LORD is a fountain of life, that one may turn away from the snares of death. In a multitude of people is the glory of a king, but without people a prince is ruined. Whoever is slow to anger has great understanding, but he who has a hasty temper exalts folly. A tranquil heart gives life to the flesh, but envy makes the bones rot. Whoever oppresses a poor man insults his Maker, but he who is generous to the needy honors him.

The wicked is overthrown through his evildoing, but the righteous finds refuge in his death. Wisdom rests in the heart of a man of understanding, but it makes itself known even in the midst of fools. Righteousness exalts a nation, but sin is a reproach to any people. A servant who deals wisely has the king's favor, but his wrath falls on one who acts shamefully.

Related Passage — James 4:10–12

Humble yourselves before the Lord, and he will exalt you. Do not speak evil against one another, brothers. The one who speaks against a brother or judges his brother, speaks evil against the law and judges the law. But if you judge the law, you are not a doer of the law but a judge. There is only one lawgiver and judge, he who is able to save and to destroy. But who are you to judge your neighbor?

Questions for Reflection and Application

- When have you acted like the older son in the parable of the Prodigal Son?
- How often do you compare yourself to others? Judge others? Why?
- What do you envy in others? Why?
- In what situations are you slow to anger, and when does your temper flare quickly?

Father, dissolve the pride that lives within me, that I may humble myself and allow you to lift me up. Amen.

MY DOG'S BETTER

Whoever oppresses a poor man insults his Maker,
but he who is generous to the needy honors him.
—*Proverbs 14:31*

My dog's bigger than your dog / My dog's faster than yours
My dog's better 'cause he eats Ken-L-Ration /
My dog's better than yours.[54]

We like to consider ourselves better than others. When you were a kid, you may have told another kid that your stuff was better, you had cooler friends, or your dad could beat up his dad. As adults, we often compare ourselves to others based on how much we make, how busy we are, what our kids have accomplished, and how our sports teams are doing.

To the Jews of Solomon's day, wealth was a sign of God's favor. If you were wealthy, then you were righteous; if you were poor, then you had done something wrong. Some verses from Proverbs support the idea that poor people are lazy, or worse.

- "How long will you lie there, O sluggard? When will you arise from your sleep? A little sleep, a little slumber, a little folding of the hands to rest, and poverty will come upon you like a robber, and want like an armed man." (6:9–11)
- "Love not sleep, lest you come to poverty; open your eyes, and you will have plenty of bread." (20:13)
- "For the drunkard and the glutton will come to poverty, and slumber will clothe them with rags." (23:21)

Why would Solomon write that oppressing a poor man insults God, whereas being generous with him honors God? Solomon, the richest man in the world, recognized three things: (1) everything he had was a gift from God, (2) God has made all of us in his image, and (3) all of us are sinful and needy.

My dog may be better than your dog, but I'm no better than you. We both need a Savior. And God has provided us with one, because he is generous to the needy. Let's follow his lead.

Passage: Verse in Context — Proverbs 14:26–35

In the fear of the LORD one has strong confidence, and his children will have a refuge. The fear of the LORD is a fountain of life, that one may turn away from the snares of death. In a multitude of people is the glory of a king, but without people a prince is ruined.

Whoever is slow to anger has great understanding, but he who has a hasty temper exalts folly. A tranquil heart gives life to the flesh, but envy makes the bones rot. Whoever oppresses a poor man insults his Maker, but he who is generous to the needy honors him.

The wicked is overthrown through his evildoing, but the righteous finds refuge in his death. Wisdom rests in the heart of a man of understanding, but it makes itself known even in the midst of fools. Righteousness exalts a nation, but sin is a reproach to any people. A servant who deals wisely has the king's favor, but his wrath falls on one who acts shamefully.

Related Passage — Philippians 2:3–4

Do nothing from selfish ambition or conceit, but in humility count others more significant than yourselves. Let each of you look not only to his own interests, but also to the interests of others.

Questions for Reflection and Application

- Which of the blessings in your life do you feel that you deserve, perhaps because of hard work, "keeping your nose clean," or some other action on your part?
- What holds you back from being generous with others, whether it is with your money, time, expertise, or some other thing that you have?
- Consider a time when someone took advantage of your generosity. How did you feel? Why?
- In what situations do you excuse your sinful behavior by comparing it to that of someone who is "worse" in your eyes? How can you break yourself of this habit?

Father, everything I have comes from you—I did nothing to deserve any of it. Amen.

THE FIRST EVANGELIST

Commit your work to the LORD,
and your plans will be established.
—*Proverbs 16:3*

During the three years of Jesus' ministry, his disciple, Philip, did not do much that was noteworthy. When Jesus called him, Philip followed willingly and even recruited Nathanael, telling him that Jesus was the Messiah. But the evening before Jesus was crucified, Philip still seemed confused as to who Jesus really was. After Jesus said that no one comes to the Father except through him, Philip asked Jesus to show the disciples the Father. "Have I been with you so long, and you still do not know me, Philip?" replied Jesus (John 14:9).

When the Holy Spirit came upon the disciples at Pentecost, Philip suddenly understood who Jesus was and is. In response, Philip committed his work to the Lord. When Saul ignited a great persecution of Christians in Jerusalem, Philip ended up in Samaria, where he proclaimed Jesus as the Messiah and performed miracles. Philip's work in Samaria had such an impact that the apostles in Jerusalem sent Peter and John to Samaria to reinforce and strengthen Philip's efforts there.

Then an angel directed Philip to a road leading to Gaza, where Philip met a eunuch who was a court official of the queen of the Ethiopians. After Philip explained that Jesus is the Messiah who fulfilled all prophecies, the eunuch became a Christian. As soon as he baptized the eunuch, Philip was transported fifteen or twenty miles to Azotus, a city on the Mediterranean Sea. Starting there, he preached the gospel along the coast, all the way to Caesarea, fifty miles north.

Consider what happened when Philip submitted himself completely to God. Philip established the church in Samaria. In a remote location, he shared the gospel with a key Ethiopian official who, in turn, presumably started the church in Ethiopia. After God transported Philip to the Mediterranean coast, he preached for fifty miles and converted many.

A confused disciple became the first evangelist outside Jerusalem. All that it took was committing his life to God.

Passage: Verse in Context — Proverbs 16:1–9

The plans of the heart belong to man, but the answer of the tongue is from the LORD. All the ways of a man are pure in his own eyes, but the LORD weighs the spirit. Commit your work to the LORD, and your plans will be established. The LORD has made everything for its purpose, even the wicked for the day of trouble. Everyone who is arrogant in heart is an abomination to the LORD; be assured, he will not go unpunished. By steadfast love and faithfulness iniquity is atoned for, and by the fear of the LORD one turns away from evil. When a man's ways please the LORD, he makes even his enemies to be at peace with him. Better is a little with righteousness than great revenues with injustice. The heart of man plans his way, but the LORD establishes his steps.

Related Passage — Acts 8:35–40

Then Philip opened his mouth, and beginning with this Scripture he told him the good news about Jesus. And as they were going along the road they came to some water, and the eunuch said, "See, here is water! What prevents me from being baptized?" And he commanded the chariot to stop, and they both went down into the water, Philip and the eunuch, and he baptized him. And when they came up out of the water, the Spirit of the Lord carried Philip away, and the eunuch saw him no more, and went on his way rejoicing. But Philip found himself at Azotus, and as he passed through he preached the gospel to all the towns until he came to Caesarea.

Questions for Reflection and Application

- How do you evaluate whether or not your plans or actions are pure and right?
- How can God establish your steps?
- When have you been obedient to God, regardless of the consequences? What happened? Why don't you do that more often? What holds you back?

Father, I want to learn from Philip's example to submit myself completely to your will, even when I don't fully understand your plan for my life. Amen.

WHAT'S IN A NAME?

The name of the LORD is a strong tower;
the righteous man runs into it and is safe.
—*Proverbs 18:10*

I have never liked my name.

My last name almost always is mispronounced. The correct pronunciation is the word "beau" and the word "linger," that is "beau-linger." Most people, thinking that there are two L's in the name, say "ball-injure."

My parents chose my paternal grandmother's maiden name, Robinson, as my middle name, but I have no idea why they chose Christopher for my first name. Maybe they were trying to ensure that my full name, all twenty-seven letters of it, would not fit on any standardized test form. Even the first name wouldn't fit on some, so college marketing materials were addressed to "Christophe," "Christop," and even "Christ." A messiah at seventeen.

I always thought that Christopher sounds pretentious and Chris sounds feminine. I couldn't go by my middle name; in fact, I couldn't even tell people my middle name, because as soon as they heard "Christopher Robin" they saw me as a character from *Winnie the Pooh*. What's in a name? You've gotta be kidding, Shakespeare old boy.

When God spoke to Moses out of a burning bush, Moses had a strange question for God: if the people ask me what your name is, what should I say? It is not clear why Moses thought that the Israelites would quiz him on God's name, but God gave it to him anyway. Actually, God gave him several names. "I am who I am" … "The LORD [Yahweh], the God of your fathers, the God of Abraham, the God of Isaac, and the God of Jacob" (Exodus 3:14–15).

There are other names for God in the Bible. Each gives us a glimpse into the character of God that has been revealed to us. When you hear someone's name, you picture that person. When you hear God's name, you picture the attributes of God. His name is a strong tower. There is power—and reassurance—in his name.

Passage: Verse in Context — Proverbs 18:8–16

The words of a whisperer are like delicious morsels; they go down into the inner parts of the body. Whoever is slack in his work is a brother to him who destroys. The name of the LORD is a strong tower; the righteous man runs into it and is safe. A rich man's wealth is his strong city, and like a high wall in his imagination. Before destruction a man's heart is haughty, but humility comes before honor. If one gives an answer before he hears, it is his folly and shame. A man's spirit will endure sickness, but a crushed spirit who can bear? An intelligent heart acquires knowledge, and the ear of the wise seeks knowledge. A man's gift makes room for him and brings him before the great.

Related Passage — Philippians 2:9–11

Therefore God has highly exalted him and bestowed on him the name that is above every name, so that at the name of Jesus every knee should bow, in heaven and on earth and under the earth, and every tongue confess that Jesus Christ is Lord, to the glory of God the Father.

Questions for Reflection and Application

- How do you feel about your name? What name would you prefer? If God were to give you a new name, then what would you want it to be?
- Look up some of the names for God in the Bible. What characteristics of God does each name reveal?
- What does it mean for the name of God to be "a strong tower"? Where do you need such a tower in your life today?
- Why is there power in the name of Jesus?

Almighty Father, there is power in your name and in the name of Jesus. Thank you for allowing me to call upon your name in my time of need. Amen.

SHARPEN HIS SAW

Iron sharpens iron, and one man sharpens another.
—*Proverbs 27:17*

After noticing the gender gap in many of today's United States churches, David Murrow wrote the best-selling book *Why Men Hate Going to Church*, founded Church for Men, and started training church leaders on how to attract and connect with more men. While conducting pastoral training in Illinois, Murrow asked, "How many of you have more active men than women in your church?"

One hand went up. It belonged to Rev. Dr. Jennifer Wilson, who was the pastor of 160-year-old Grace United Methodist Church in LaSalle, Illinois. Wilson did a variety of things to increase the church's appeal to men, including:

- Changed the church building's décor, replacing quilts, banners, and flowers with earth-tone paint and big-screen TVs.
- Preached guy-centric sermon series with titles such as "Power Play" and "Men and Sex."
- Switched to Scripture versions with male pronouns for God.
- Replaced gender-neutral hymns with guy-friendly songs such as "A Mighty Fortress Is Our God" and "Onward Christian Soldiers."
- When projecting hymn and song lyrics, made sure that the slide backgrounds were images of the great outdoors.

How did the women of Grace UMC feel about the changes? Rather than feeling discriminated against, they were delighted, because the church began to attract dynamic men who understood the gospel and wanted to serve. With worship service attendance growing by leaps and bounds, the church added a third service and then broke out the back of its narthex wall to seat more people.[55]

Usually, the best person to sharpen a man is another man. But the experience of Grace UMC demonstrates that a woman can sharpen a man—or dozens of men—by understanding the needs of men and making a concerted effort to meet those needs.

Before you can sharpen another person, you must know that person and know that person well. Getting to know someone well doesn't take special abilities or spiritual gifts. It just takes an effort.

So get sharpening.

Passage: Verse in Context — Proverbs 27:17–19

Iron sharpens iron, and one man sharpens another. Whoever tends a fig tree will eat its fruit, and he who guards his master will be honored. As in water face reflects face, so the heart of man reflects the man.

Related Passage — 1 Corinthians 12:12–13a, 21–27

For just as the body is one and has many members, and all the members of the body, though many, are one body, so it is with Christ. For in one Spirit we were all baptized into one body—Jews or Greeks, slaves or free—and all were made to drink of one Spirit. …

The eye cannot say to the hand, "I have no need of you," nor again the head to the feet, "I have no need of you." On the contrary, the parts of the body that seem to be weaker are indispensable, and on those parts of the body that we think less honorable we bestow the greater honor, and our unpresentable parts are treated with greater modesty, which our more presentable parts do not require. But God has so composed the body, giving greater honor to the part that lacked it, that there may be no division in the body, but that the members may have the same care for one another. If one member suffers, all suffer together; if one member is honored, all rejoice together. Now you are the body of Christ and individually members of it.

Questions for Reflection and Application

- Who has sharpened you? How? Whom have you sharpened? How?
- Think of some men whom you should be sharpening. How much do you know about them? How can you get to know them better, so that you can be more effective at discipling them?
- Who are some men who should be sharpening you? How much do they know about you? What steps can you take to make them more effective at discipling you?

God, use me to sharpen others. Together, we'll grow stronger as a church. Amen.

TURN, TURN, TURN

For everything there is a season,
and a time for every matter under heaven.
—*Ecclesiastes 3:1*

"What's your favorite Beatles song?" asks Jed King, a young singer in the film *The Song*. "'Turn! Turn! Turn!'" responds Rose Jordan of Sharon, Kentucky. Jed advises her that it's not a Beatles song, but she trumps him with, "The lyrics are in the Bible."

Jed and Rose fall in love. One night Rose asks Jed, "If you could pray for one thing, what would it be?" Jed prays for wisdom, and inspired by the moment, asks Rose to marry him.

The morning after their wedding, Jed writes Rose a love song. It becomes a smash hit, launching Jed's career and sending him on a five-year odyssey of fame, fortune, and long tours away from Rose and their young son, Ray. Rose feels that Jed is choosing his career over her but refuses to leave her ailing father to come on tour. Feeling neglected, Jed succumbs to the temptations of his opening act, sultry singer Shelby Bale, and a one-night mistake becomes a full-blown affair that threatens Jed's marriage, career, and even his life.

Like Jed King, Solomon had a passionate love affair with his wife (the "rose of Sharon"). But Solomon was seduced—by other women and the trappings of fame, fortune, and power—and walked away from the path laid out for him by God. At the end of his life, Solomon wrote, "I have seen everything that is done under the sun, and behold, all is vanity and a striving after wind" (Ecclesiastes 1:14). Solomon wrote the book of Ecclesiastes as a cautionary tale.

Thank God that he did! We can learn from his mistakes and be encouraged that, even in his depression at his failures, he worshiped a God of faithfulness, a God who offers us everything that we need, at the right time … in the appointed season of life.

"Turn! Turn! Turn!" [56] is not a Beatles song, but it's still a great song. After all, the lyrics are in the Bible.

Passage: Verse in Context — Ecclesiastes 3:1–8

For everything there is a season, and a time for every matter under heaven: a time to be born, and a time to die; a time to plant, and a time to pluck up what is planted; a time to break down, and a time to build up; a time to weep, and a time to laugh; a time to mourn, and a time to dance; a time to cast away stones, and a time to gather stones together; a time to embrace, and a time to refrain from embracing; a time to seek, and a time to lose; a time to keep, and a time to cast away; a time to tear, and a time to sew; a time to keep silence, and a time to speak; a time to love, and a time to hate; a time for war, and a time for peace.

Questions for Reflection and Application

- When have you been lured away from God's path for your life? What seduced you to stray? What were the consequences? How have you reconciled with the people you hurt?
- Do you think that Solomon really felt that *everything* that we do is "vanity and a striving after wind" (1:14)? Why or why not? What was he trying to convey?
- Looking at the seasons and times mentioned in the Ecclesiastes passage, in what season or time are you now? How long have you been there? Why does God have you there? Where do you think God will place you next?

Father, whatever season of life I'm in, whatever my circumstances and challenges, you have put me here for a reason. Amen.

BEAUTY AT THE WELL

He has made everything beautiful in its time.
—*Ecclesiastes 3:11a*

She had felt beautiful once. But that was many years and many men ago. Today, like every other day, she had to wait until noon to get water from the well. If she came earlier, then the other women would talk about her. The tramp. The whore. Divorced five times. Now living with whatever man would show her a little kindness, in exchange for … She felt used up. Wretched. Ugly.

As she approached the well, she saw a man sitting there. A Jew. Good. Even if he suspected the worst, he would leave her alone. After all, Jews hated Samaritans.

When she began to draw water, he asked for a drink. She responded tersely, with a little hostility for good measure. Instead of leaving her alone, he said that he had living water to offer. She sighed. Living water? He had been in the sun too long. She asked him if he was greater than Jacob, who made the well. Once again he offered her living water.

He seemed different. He *was* different. Her hope rose. But she had been hurt so many times. Hesitantly, she asked for the living water. He told her to call her husband. When she responded that she didn't have one, he told her that she, after five divorces, was living with a man who was not her husband. Her heart sank. He was a prophet.

She asked him a question, stumbling at the words. While he answered, she didn't listen but looked into his eyes. There she saw love. Not the kind of love that she had received from other men. Real love. This man knew everything about her and he loved her anyway. She didn't feel ugly anymore; she felt beautiful. No. She *was* beautiful. For the first time.

She left her water jar at the well and ran to tell the people of Samaria that the Messiah was there. It didn't matter that they despised her. He didn't. He couldn't. He had made her … and made her beautiful.

Passage: Verse in Context — Ecclesiastes 3:9–13

What gain has the worker from his toil? I have seen the business that God has given to the children of man to be busy with. He has made everything beautiful in its time. Also, he has put eternity into man's heart, yet so that he cannot find out what God has done from the beginning to the end. I perceived that there is nothing better for them than to be joyful and to do good as long as they live; also that everyone should eat and drink and take pleasure in all his toil—this is God's gift to man.

Related Passage — John 4:19–26

The woman said to him, "Sir, I perceive that you are a prophet. Our fathers worshiped on this mountain, but you say that in Jerusalem is the place where people ought to worship." Jesus said to her, "Woman, believe me, the hour is coming when neither on this mountain nor in Jerusalem will you worship the Father. You worship what you do not know; we worship what we know, for salvation is from the Jews. But the hour is coming, and is now here, when the true worshipers will worship the Father in spirit and truth, for the Father is seeking such people to worship him. God is spirit, and those who worship him must worship in spirit and truth." The woman said to him, "I know that Messiah is coming (he who is called Christ). When he comes, he will tell us all things." Jesus said to her, "I who speak to you am he."

Questions for Reflection and Application

- As men, we strive not to be beautiful but to be worthy of respect. Do you believe that God is proud of you? Why or why not?
- What things are most beautiful to you? In what things do you struggle to find beauty?
- The focus of today's Ecclesiastes passage is on finding joy in toil or work. How much joy or beauty do you find in your job? What about in other areas where you toil? What can you do to take true pleasure in all your toil and thus receive God's gift to you?

Father, you know everything about me, and you love me anyway. You see me as beautiful because you have placed your beauty within me. Amen.

SONGS OR TALES

Two are better than one, because they have a good reward for their toil.
For if they fall, one will lift up his fellow.
—*Ecclesiastes 4:9–10a*

One of the heroes of the *Lord of the Rings* trilogy is Frodo Baggins. Even though Frodo is a hobbit, or halfling (about half the height of a man), he is given a quest that even the bravest and strongest man would not want: take the One Ring to the land of Mordor, which is ruled by the evil Lord Sauron, and destroy the Ring in the fires of Mount Doom.

Initially, Frodo is accompanied on his quest by the Fellowship of the Ring, an allegiance of two men, a dwarf, an elf, a wizard, and four hobbits, including Frodo. When the Fellowship is broken by an enemy attack, Frodo ends up with just one companion: friend and fellow hobbit, Samwise Gamgee. As Frodo and Sam near Mordor, Sam becomes philosophical about their quest and wonders if Frodo will ever be put into songs or tales. He suggests that "Frodo and the Ring" will be one of everyone's favorite stories, starring "the most famousest of hobbits."

"You've left out one of the chief characters—Samwise the Brave," advises Frodo. "Frodo wouldn't have got far without Sam."

Frodo's words prove prophetic. Sam proves himself to be incredibly brave, and because he protects and even rescues Frodo, the quest ultimately ends in success. Two have fared better than one could. Their toil and sacrifice bring a great reward to everyone in Middle Earth.

When Jesus sent out his twelve disciples (see Mark 6), he sent them in pairs. When Jesus sent out seventy-two other disciples (see Luke 10), he sent them in pairs. Even when Jesus needed a donkey on which to ride into Jerusalem on Palm Sunday, he sent a pair of disciples. Every step of the way, Jesus taught his followers that two are better than one … even if they are never put into songs or tales.

Passage: Verse in Context — Ecclesiastes 4:9–12

Two are better than one, because they have a good reward for their toil. For if they fall, one will lift up his fellow. But woe to him who is alone when he falls and has not another to lift him up! Again, if two lie together, they keep warm, but how can one keep warm alone? And though a man might prevail against one who is alone, two will withstand him—a threefold cord is not quickly broken.

Related Passage — Mark 6:7–13

And he called the twelve and began to send them out two by two, and gave them authority over the unclean spirits. He charged them to take nothing for their journey except a staff—no bread, no bag, no money in their belts—but to wear sandals and not put on two tunics. And he said to them, "Whenever you enter a house, stay there until you depart from there. And if any place will not receive you and they will not listen to you, when you leave, shake off the dust that is on your feet as a testimony against them." So they went out and proclaimed that people should repent. And they cast out many demons and anointed with oil many who were sick and healed them.

Questions for Reflection and Application

- In what situations do you tend to go it alone instead of partnering with someone? Why do you do that?
- If you are married, then your primary partner is your wife. But your wife cannot be your partner in every situation. What are some situations where it is better for you to partner with another man? In which of those situations are you not partnering with a man today? Why not?
- Each of us has strengths and weaknesses. Your ideal partner is someone with strengths in areas where you have weaknesses. Who is your ideal partner for evangelism? Service to those in need? Teaching? Accountability? Leadership?

Father, open my eyes to the fact that you have placed people in my life for a reason. Do not let me walk this life alone. Amen.

A TENACIOUS CENTER

And though a man might prevail against one who is alone, two will withstand
him—a threefold cord is not quickly broken.

—Ecclesiastes 4:12

KING HENRY V: What treasure, uncle?
EXETER: Tennis-balls, my liege.
– Henry V, Act I, Scene ii

The tennis of Shakespeare's day was very different from the modern game of
tennis. Ancient tennis was played indoors with wooden balls. A player struck
the ball with his hands or with a racket that consisted of a leather glove on the
end of a wooden stick.

The modern game of tennis began in the late 1800s. Rubber balls enabled the
game to be played outdoors, on a grass or dirt court with a net in the middle.
And the tennis racket became a wooden frame with a woven pattern of strings
made of catgut. The source of catgut was cow (cattle) or sheep intestines, not
actual cat guts. Today, some tennis pros still use catgut strings because catgut
helps with ball control, gives the player a good "feel for the ball," and provides
power while minimizing shock to the player's arm.

The primary drawback of catgut is its very high cost.[57] [58] Cheaper alternatives provide less playability and durability. The answer, according to one manufacturer, is to combine two materials in one string, with multifilament polyester
fibers wrapped around a high tenacity center core, which is said to give a player
a gut-like feel.

When it comes to making relationships last, Solomon offered similar advice.
It was common knowledge that a cord of only two strands would break easily,
because the strands would pull apart. A cord of three strands was much stronger. And if two of the strands were wrapped around a center core that offered
"high tenacity," you'd have a very strong cord indeed.

Want a stronger marriage? A stronger bond with a family member? A strong
friendship? Wrap your relationship around God. He's as tenacious as they come.

No cats or cows were harmed in the making of this devotion.

Passage: Verse in Context — Ecclesiastes 4:9–12

Two are better than one, because they have a good reward for their toil. For if they fall, one will lift up his fellow. But woe to him who is alone when he falls and has not another to lift him up! Again, if two lie together, they keep warm, but how can one keep warm alone? And though a man might prevail against one who is alone, two will withstand him—a threefold cord is not quickly broken.

Related Passage — Galatians 2:17–21

But if, in our endeavor to be justified in Christ, we too were found to be sinners, is Christ then a servant of sin? Certainly not! For if I rebuild what I tore down, I prove myself to be a transgressor. For through the law I died to the law, so that I might live to God. I have been crucified with Christ. It is no longer I who live, but Christ who lives in me. And the life I now live in the flesh I live by faith in the Son of God, who loved me and gave himself for me. I do not nullify the grace of God, for if righteousness were through the law, then Christ died for no purpose.

Questions for Reflection and Application

- What areas of your life have unraveled because you did not put God in the center?
- When are you hesitant to build around God? Why?
- What does it mean to you to have been crucified with Christ? How is that reflected in your life today? How do you wish it were reflected? What can you do to allow Christ to shine through you more fully?

Father, be the tenacious center in all my relationships. We cannot easily break when wrapped around you. Amen.

AN UNSPECTACULAR LIFE

Now all has been heard; here is the conclusion of the matter:
Fear God and keep his commandments, for this is the duty of man.
—*Ecclesiastes 12:13*

Solomon lived a spectacular life highlighted by untold riches, one thousand wives and concubines, and the construction of a majestic temple. But at the end of his life, he wrote that, "all is vanity and a striving after wind" (1:14).

At a 2017 high school commencement ceremony, teacher Eric Ling told about someone who lived a far less spectacular life: his father, who had died eighteen months earlier. As Ling grew up, his father spent a lot of time alone in his study. In the house for the first time after his dad's death, Ling went into the study.

"In his desk drawer was a long prayer list of specific people and exactly what they were going through," said Ling, "with a reminder to himself: pray daily. Next to this was a second list; a list of people my father knew who needed help and exactly what that help might be. Several of these he was crossing out, one by one. What a testimony! In his most private and alone times, my father was living out what he believed—not for personal recognition, but for the Kingdom.

"At the funeral, person after person spoke to us of how my father just showed up —whenever someone was in need, he was there. This was significant for many reasons, but mostly because my father was painfully quiet. He would blend into any room, unnoticed, and he actively spurned recognition of any kind.

"He lived, by earthly standards, an unspectacular life and experienced limited professional success. Yet he had a high calling. His vocation was to show God's love to others by being faithful with his gifts. And everyone he encountered, including myself, saw glimpses of the Kingdom through this simple man: humility, self-sacrifice, love of God, love of others, generosity."[59]

May each of us live such an unspectacular life of obedience and faithfulness.

Passage: Verse in Context — Ecclesiastes 12:9–14

Besides being wise, the Preacher also taught the people knowledge, weighing and studying and arranging many proverbs with great care. The Preacher sought to find words of delight, and uprightly he wrote words of truth.

The words of the wise are like goads, and like nails firmly fixed are the collected sayings; they are given by one Shepherd. My son, beware of anything beyond these. Of making many books there is no end, and much study is a weariness of the flesh.

The end of the matter; all has been heard. Fear God and keep his commandments, for this is the whole duty of man. For God will bring every deed into judgment, with every secret thing, whether good or evil.

Related Passage — Ecclesiastes 1:12–15

I the Preacher have been king over Israel in Jerusalem. And I applied my heart to seek and to search out by wisdom all that is done under heaven. It is an unhappy business that God has given to the children of man to be busy with. I have seen everything that is done under the sun, and behold, all is vanity and a striving after wind. What is crooked cannot be made straight, and what is lacking cannot be counted.

Questions for Reflection and Application

- Near the end of his life, the wealthiest man who ever lived said that the duty of every man is to fear God and keep his commandments. Period. What do you tend to add to that very short list?
- At your funeral, for what do you want to be remembered?
- How are you being obedient and faithful today? Where are you struggling to be obedient and faithful?

Father, accomplishments do not measure a man's worth. Help me to be obedient to your extraordinary plan for my ordinary life. Amen.

THE POWER THAT HEALS

Set me as a seal upon your heart.
—*Song of Solomon 8:6a*

"Let him kiss me with the kisses of his mouth! For your love is better than wine; your anointing oils are fragrant; your name is oil poured out; therefore virgins love you" (1:2–3).

So opens Song of Solomon (also known as Song of Songs), which has made more people uncomfortable than any other book in the Bible. The book is unique not just because it is a single poem but because it includes a frank discussion of physical or erotic love between a married couple—Solomon and his wife, who is called "the rose of Sharon" (2:1). Solomon wrote this love song early in his reign, before he ignored God's warning and married many foreign women who turned his heart toward evil.

In the film *The Song*, a modern-day Solomon, singer Jed King, is madly in love with Rose Jordan of Sharon, Kentucky (the rose of Sharon). The morning after their wedding, Jed writes Rose a love song[60] with lyrics from the Song of Solomon. The climax of the song is today's verse. Jed declares that his love for Rose is so strong—stronger than death—that she can set it as a seal upon her heart. No water will ever quench his love, he declares. No power can overcome it.

When the song launches Jed's career as a popular singer and he begins touring endlessly, he begins to drift away from his love for Rose and his first love— his love for God. Recognizing that he is drawn to his sultry opening act, and wanting to remain faithful to his wife, Jed implores Rose to come on tour with him. When she refuses, Jed has an affair that destroys his marriage and, ultimately, his life.

Fortunately for Jed, the last line of his love song comes true in the end when his wife's love for him empowers her to forgive him and give him a second chance. That last line? Love is the power that heals.

It is indeed.

Passage: Verse in Context — Song of Solomon 8:4–7

I adjure you, O daughters of Jerusalem, that you not stir up or awaken love until it pleases.

Who is that coming up from the wilderness, leaning on her beloved?

Under the apple tree I awakened you. There your mother was in labor with you; there she who bore you was in labor.

Set me as a seal upon your heart, as a seal upon your arm, for love is strong as death, jealousy is fierce as the grave. Its flashes are flashes of fire, the very flame of the LORD. Many waters cannot quench love, neither can floods drown it. If a man offered for love all the wealth of his house, he would be utterly despised.

Related Passage — 2 Corinthians 1:20–22

For all the promises of God find their Yes in [Jesus]. That is why it is through him that we utter our Amen to God for his glory. And it is God who establishes us with you in Christ, and has anointed us, and who has also put his seal on us and given us his Spirit in our hearts as a guarantee.

Questions for Reflection and Application

- Does God have his seal on you? What does that seal represent?
- When have you drifted from your first love, your love for God? What was the result?
- For what sins do you need to forgive someone today? What is holding you back from doing that? From where can you obtain the strength that you need to do that?
- Where have you witnessed the healing power of love?

Father, remind me of my first love before I partake in any other relationship. And grant healing to my relationships that have experienced hurt. Amen.

700 YEARS IN THE MAKING

Therefore the LORD himself will give you a sign. Behold, the virgin shall conceive and bear a son, and shall call his name Immanuel.

—*Isaiah 7:14*

The first thirty-nine chapters of the book of Isaiah were written about seven hundred years before the birth of Jesus,[61] yet dozens of the prophecies in those chapters (including a virgin birth and the fact that he would be Immanuel, or God with us) were fulfilled by Jesus.[62]

Consider our world seven hundred long years ago:

- Europe was firmly in the period known as the Middle Ages. There was little long-distance trade, so most people lived and worked in self-sufficient farming communities.
- Marco Polo was back in Italy after a twenty-four-year stay in China. His detailed chronicle of his journey and experiences would inspire Christopher Columbus and other explorers … two hundred years later.
- Natural disasters and diseases could be devastating. A series of fourteenth-century famines caused the world's population to decline. The Black Death of 1348–49 killed about one third of the population of Europe.
- In Western Europe, the Roman Catholic Church was the only Christian church, and it had authority over various kings.
- Church-sanctioned Crusades, or wars with Muslims aimed at recovering the Holy Land from Islamic rule, were in their third century.
- William Wallace, who fought for Scottish independence from England, was captured, taken to London, convicted of treason, and executed. Twenty-three years later, Scotland became independent.
- An Italian surgeon oversaw the first dissection of a corpse and wrote the first manual on anatomy that was founded on practical dissection.
- The production of paper began in Germany.
- The Aztecs founded the city of Tenochtitlan, where Mexico City would develop one day.[63]

Seven hundred years before the birth of Jesus, Isaiah predicted that birth and said that it would be a sign that God wanted a new relationship with us so much that he would come to us and live with us. The first Christmas was a very special day … seven hundred years in the making.

Passage: Verse in Context — Isaiah 7:10–16

Again the LORD spoke to Ahaz: "Ask a sign of the LORD your God; let it be deep as Sheol or high as heaven." But Ahaz said, "I will not ask, and I will not put the LORD to the test."

And [Isaiah] said, "Hear then, O house of David! Is it too little for you to weary men, that you weary my God also? Therefore the LORD himself will give you a sign. Behold, the virgin shall conceive and bear a son, and shall call his name Immanuel. He shall eat curds and honey when he knows how to refuse the evil and choose the good. For before the boy knows how to refuse the evil and choose the good, the land whose two kings you dread will be deserted."

Related Passage — Matthew 1:20–25

But as he considered these things, behold, an angel of the Lord appeared to him in a dream, saying, "Joseph, son of David, do not fear to take Mary as your wife, for that which is conceived in her is from the Holy Spirit. She will bear a son, and you shall call his name Jesus, for he will save his people from their sins." All this took place to fulfill what the Lord had spoken by the prophet: "Behold, the virgin shall conceive and bear a son, and they shall call his name Immanuel" (which means, God with us). When Joseph woke from sleep, he did as the angel of the Lord commanded him: he took his wife, but knew her not until she had given birth to a son. And he called his name Jesus.

Questions for Reflection and Application

- How many times have you heard the Christmas story and the prophecies about the birth of Jesus? If those stories and prophecies have lost their power in your life, then what can you do to regain your sense of wonder at the incarnation and birth of Christ?
- What promises has God made to you that have not been fulfilled yet? How long have you waited for them? How do you remain patient when you have to wait for a long time?

God, you never cease to amaze me. You had a prophet give detailed information about the coming of your Son, Jesus, seven centuries before it happened. Amen.

LIGHTING THE DARKNESS

The people who walked in darkness have seen a great light;
those who dwelt in a land of deep darkness, on them has light shone.

—Isaiah 9:2

When you've been living in darkness for a while, a bright light is more of a shock than a comfort.

Consider the shepherds who were tending their sheep on the hills outside Bethlehem on the first Christmas Eve. They were used to working in the near darkness of a moonless night. When an angel appeared to them, and "the glory of the Lord shone around them" (Luke 2:9), the light wasn't warm and comforting. It was totally unexpected. It was piercing. It was overwhelming. They were terrified.

The single angel was joined by thousands of other angels, all praising God in unison. When the angels were done and the blackness of night returned, the shepherds ran. They ran all the way to the manger to see the holy baby that the angels had announced. Only when they had seen and worshiped Jesus did they go back to the hillside and the flock, glorifying and praising God all the way. It was dark there, but the light still lingered. It would linger forever in their hearts.

In Isaiah 9:2, the prophet writes of the darkness of sin. Some people have lived "in a land of deep darkness" their entire lives. When they see the light for the first time, it will not be warm and comforting. It will be piercing. It will be terrifying because it will expose everything that has been unseen before in the darkness.

When people get over the shock of seeing the light for the first time, some embrace the light. They run, as fast as they can, from the darkness toward the light. Others try to return to the darkness.

Embracing the light can be difficult. It requires us to see ourselves as we really are. But it enables us to see God as he really is and appreciate his stunning love for us. He won't rest until he has led you out of the darkness. For good.

Passage: Verse in Context — Isaiah 9:1–5

But there will be no gloom for her who was in anguish. In the former time he brought into contempt the land of Zebulun and the land of Naphtali, but in the latter time he has made glorious the way of the sea, the land beyond the Jordan, Galilee of the nations.

The people who walked in darkness have seen a great light; those who dwelt in a land of deep darkness, on them has light shone. You have multiplied the nation; you have increased its joy; they rejoice before you as with joy at the harvest, as they are glad when they divide the spoil. For the yoke of his burden, and the staff for his shoulder, the rod of his oppressor, you have broken as on the day of Midian. For every boot of the tramping warrior in battle tumult and every garment rolled in blood will be burned as fuel for the fire.

Related Passage — John 8:12

Again Jesus spoke to them, saying, "I am the light of the world. Whoever follows me will not walk in darkness, but will have the light of life."

Questions for Reflection and Application

- In what parts of your life do you prefer darkness to light? What changes would you make if you knew that God was going to expose these parts to a bright light that would enable other people today to see what is hidden?
- Where in your life have you embraced the light of God? What was the immediate result? What has been the long-term result?
- Whom do you know who needs to experience the light of God, complete with its awesome forgiveness, redemption, and power? What can you do to help that person "see the light"?

Father, although your light may be overwhelming at first, I know it will bring me comfort. Continue to lead me out of darkness until I live completely in your glorious radiance. Amen.

AT THE BACK OF THE STAGE

For to us a child is born, to us a son is given; and the government
shall be upon his shoulder, and his name shall be called Wonderful Counselor,
Mighty God, Everlasting Father, Prince of Peace.
—*Isaiah 9:6*

On the first two Fridays every December, the group performed the "Christmas portion" of Handel's *Messiah*, which includes "For Unto Us" with today's verse as the lyrics. The venue was the famed DAR Constitution Hall in Washington, D.C. The audience each Friday numbered 2,500 to 3,000 people. Admission was free so that no one would be turned away.

The genesis for the group was a 1984 prayer meeting of Patrick Kavanaugh and three couples with a desire to minister to the performing arts community. "We felt God was calling us to have an impact for Christ in the world of performing arts," recalled Kavanaugh, who became executive director of the Christian Performing Artist Fellowship and conductor of the Asaph Ensemble, CPAF's performing group, named after King David's choir director.

Like the Asaph Ensemble's other works, each *Messiah* performance was unique because ballet dancers interpreted the choral and orchestral music. The dancers were led by Robin Sturm and her husband, Robert, both of whom had professional dance experience at the Washington Ballet. In addition to being the principal dancers, the Sturms choreographed the other dancers on the Constitution Hall stage.[64]

Before the curtain went up, the orchestra, chorus, soloists, dancers, and everyone else involved with the production gathered backstage. They were there not to receive last-minute instructions from Kavanaugh but to pray. They prayed that God would be glorified and that attendees would be drawn closer to him. Then they headed for the stage.

To give the dancers the entire stage, the chorus stood on risers at the back of the stage. Standing for over an hour was tough. Staying in sync with a conductor and orchestra that seemed a mile away was tougher. But it was an amazing experience, humbling and exhilarating.

Handel would have been pleased. God certainly was.

Passage: Verse in Context — Isaiah 9:1–7

But there will be no gloom for her who was in anguish. In the former time he brought into contempt the land of Zebulun and the land of Naphtali, but in the latter time he has made glorious the way of the sea, the land beyond the Jordan, Galilee of the nations.

The people who walked in darkness have seen a great light; those who dwelt in a land of deep darkness, on them has light shone. You have multiplied the nation; you have increased its joy; they rejoice before you as with joy at the harvest, as they are glad when they divide the spoil. For the yoke of his burden, and the staff for his shoulder, the rod of his oppressor, you have broken as on the day of Midian. For every boot of the tramping warrior in battle tumult and every garment rolled in blood will be burned as fuel for the fire.

For to us a child is born, to us a son is given; and the government shall be upon his shoulder, and his name shall be called Wonderful Counselor, Mighty God, Everlasting Father, Prince of Peace. Of the increase of his government and of peace there will be no end, on the throne of David and over his kingdom, to establish it and to uphold it with justice and with righteousness from this time forth and forevermore. The zeal of the LORD of hosts will do this.

Questions for Reflection and Application

- When have you been "at the back of the stage," while someone else got the attention, recognition, and even glory? How did you feel about that?
- When have you received attention, recognition, or even glory when it was a team effort and others on the team labored in obscurity? How did you feel about that? What steps did you take to share your accolades with others?
- Which of the names of Jesus—Wonderful Counselor, Mighty God, Everlasting Father, Prince of Peace—resonates the most with you? Why?

God, Handel's masterpiece proclaims amazing news: you sent your Son not just to save us from our sins but also to rule and reign over us. Help me to appreciate that amazing Christmas gift every day of the year. Amen.

JUST OFF RED SQUARE

Behold, God is my salvation; I will trust, and will not be afraid; for the LORD
God is my strength and my song, and he has become my salvation.

—*Isaiah 12:2*

Today's verse is part of the second scene in the Jerome Hines' opera *I Am the Way*, which tells the story of Jesus from the Gospel of John. In 1991, Hines, a famous bass of New York's Metropolitan Opera, felt God calling him to bring his opera to Moscow's famed Bolshoi Theatre. He called Patrick Kavanaugh, director of the DC-area Asaph Ensemble, and asked if he could make Hines' dream a reality.

The next summer, armed with four phone numbers, Kavanaugh went to Moscow on a wing and a prayer. He spoke no Russian, and he knew that the Bolshoi never allowed American operas. After his first three phone calls yielded nothing, Kavanaugh dialed someone who once had been a schoolmate of the Bolshoi's director. Two days later, Kavanaugh was watching an opera at the Bolshoi with the director at his side. When he met with Bolshoi officials, Kavanaugh mystified them by stating that his company would perform the opera for free. When they got over their shock, they gave him an agreement for two performances in July 1993.[65]

Kavanaugh returned to DC and informed his troops that they would be performing an opera on the Bolshoi stage the next summer. After months of preparation, 191 people flew from DC to Moscow and began to rehearse at the Bolshoi.

The first performance got off to a rocky start, with someone jumping on stage and shouting that he was the Messiah! After order was restored, the rest of the performance was a success, as was the second performance two nights later. Almost a thousand Russians gave their lives to Christ at the Bolshoi. A recording of the opera later was shown on Russian national TV, and Kavanaugh was awarded a special medal by Yeltsen's Minister of Culture.

When you trust in God and are not afraid, God can do amazing things.

Passage: Verse in Context — Isaiah 12:1–6

You will say in that day: "I will give thanks to you, O LORD, for though you were angry with me, your anger turned away, that you might comfort me.

"Behold, God is my salvation; I will trust, and will not be afraid; for the LORD God is my strength and my song, and he has become my salvation."

With joy you will draw water from the wells of salvation. And you will say in that day: "Give thanks to the LORD, call upon his name, make known his deeds among the peoples, proclaim that his name is exalted. Sing praises to the LORD, for he has done gloriously; let this be made known in all the earth. Shout, and sing for joy, O inhabitant of Zion, for great in your midst is the Holy One of Israel."

Related Passage — Isaiah 25:8–9

He will swallow up death forever; and the LORD God will wipe away tears from all faces, and the reproach of his people he will take away from all the earth, for the LORD has spoken. It will be said on that day, "Behold, this is our God; we have waited for him, that he might save us. This is the LORD; we have waited for him; let us be glad and rejoice in his salvation."

Questions for Reflection and Application

- Think of a situation where you (or someone you know) had to rely completely on God. What happened? What did you (or the person you know) learn from the experience?
- When are you afraid to trust God and rely on him completely? How can you trust and not be afraid?
- When God comes through for you, how many people do you tell? How do you explain what happened?

Father, give me the faith illustrated by Kavanaugh and his ensemble. I don't have to travel to Russia to share the good news of the gospel. Amen.

THE WILD MAN

O LORD, you are my God; I will exalt you; I will praise your name,
for you have done wonderful things, plans formed of old, faithful and sure.

—*Isaiah 25:1*

In 1997, contemporary Christian singer Rich Mullins was driving to a benefit concert in Wichita, Kansas, when he lost control of his car and was killed. He was forty-one years old.[66] Six years earlier, Mullins had released a song of faith, "Step by Step (Sometimes by Step)," with a chorus based on Isaiah 25:1. That song remains popular on Christian radio to this day.

Before he performed the song in concert one night, Mullins commented that we often try to impress God with "all the right words." You don't have to impress God, Mullins continued, "because He's already knocked out about you. He already loves you more than you can imagine."

Good taste is the enemy of great art, said Mullins. "Good taste has all to do with being cultured and being refined. If art has to do with anything, it has to do with being human. One of the reasons I love the Bible is because the humans in the Bible are not very refined."

When Mullins was a "depressed adolescent," people would try to cheer him up by telling him that God loves him. "I'd always say, 'Big deal, God loves everybody. That don't make me special! That just proves that God ain't got no taste.'

"And I don't think He does. Thank God! 'Cause God takes the junk of our lives and He makes the greatest art in the world out of it. If He was cultured—if He was as civilized as most Christian people wish He was—He would be useless to Christianity. But God is a wild man.

"And I hope that over the course of your life you encounter Him. But let me warn you: you need to hang on for dear life. Or let go for dear life."[67]

As we praise God and learn to walk in his ways, the Wild Man will lead us, step by step.

Passage: Verse in Context — Isaiah 25:1–5

O LORD, you are my God; I will exalt you; I will praise your name, for you have done wonderful things, plans formed of old, faithful and sure. For you have made the city a heap, the fortified city a ruin; the foreigners' palace is a city no more; it will never be rebuilt. Therefore strong peoples will glorify you; cities of ruthless nations will fear you.

For you have been a stronghold to the poor, a stronghold to the needy in his distress, a shelter from the storm and a shade from the heat; for the breath of the ruthless is like a storm against a wall, like heat in a dry place. You subdue the noise of the foreigners; as heat by the shade of a cloud, so the song of the ruthless is put down.

Related Passage — Joel 2:26–27

You shall eat in plenty and be satisfied, and praise the name of the LORD your God, who has dealt wondrously with you. And my people shall never again be put to shame. You shall know that I am in the midst of Israel, and that I am the LORD your God and there is none else. And my people shall never again be put to shame.

Questions for Reflection and Application

- What does it mean for God to be a wild man? What images does it bring to your mind?
- When has God been a wild man in your life? When have you witnessed it in the lives of others?
- How do you exalt and praise God outside of church? How often? What inspires you to do that?
- In the past year, how has God been leading you step by step? What are the next steps on your path?

Father, I don't have to impress you with lofty words because you are "already knocked out" by me. Thank you for looking at me and seeing treasure. Amen.

THE ROLLING THUNDER

For you have been a stronghold to the poor, a stronghold to
the needy in his distress, a shelter from the storm and a shade from the heat.
—*Isaiah 25:4a*

A storm can inspire fear. It also can inspire a famous hymn.

In 1885, Swedish minister Carl Boberg wrote and published a poem, "O Store Gud," or in English, "O Great God." The poem was set to music but remained relatively obscure. In the early 1920s, English missionary Stuart Hine, who was serving in Poland, heard the Russian version of Boberg's poem sung to a Swedish melody and was moved by the poem. While he was ministering in the rugged and beautiful Carpathian mountains, he was inspired to modify and expand the words of the poem in English and to make his own arrangement of the melody. The result was "How Great Thou Art."

Hine composed the first verse when he was caught in a thunderstorm in a Carpathian village:

O Lord, my God, when I in awesome wonder
Consider all the worlds Thy hands have made;
I see the stars, I hear the rolling thunder,
Thy pow'r throughout the universe displayed.

He wrote the second and third verse soon after but did not add the fourth until 1948, when he was back to England. A year later, Hine published the hymn in his own Russian gospel magazine *Grace and Peace*, which was circulated among refugees in fifteen countries. British missionaries began to spread the song to former British colonies in Africa and India. It also found its way to the United States, where it was officially copyrighted, published, and recorded.

Within five years of its appearance in a single magazine, "How Great Thou Art" was one of the most popular hymns in the world.[68] All because a missionary saw God's glory in a thunderstorm.

God is the creator of thunderstorms. He also is our shelter from the storms of life.

Passage: Verse in Context — Isaiah 25:1–5

O LORD, you are my God; I will exalt you; I will praise your name, for you have done wonderful things, plans formed of old, faithful and sure. For you have made the city a heap, the fortified city a ruin; the foreigners' palace is a city no more; it will never be rebuilt. Therefore strong peoples will glorify you; cities of ruthless nations will fear you.

For you have been a stronghold to the poor, a stronghold to the needy in his distress, a shelter from the storm and a shade from the heat; for the breath of the ruthless is like a storm against a wall, like heat in a dry place. You subdue the noise of the foreigners; as heat by the shade of a cloud, so the song of the ruthless is put down.

Related Passage — Psalm 91:1–6

He who dwells in the shelter of the Most High will abide in the shadow of the Almighty. I will say to the LORD, "My refuge and my fortress, my God, in whom I trust." For he will deliver you from the snare of the fowler and from the deadly pestilence. He will cover you with his pinions, and under his wings you will find refuge; his faithfulness is a shield and buckler. You will not fear the terror of the night, nor the arrow that flies by day, nor the pestilence that stalks in darkness, nor the destruction that wastes at noonday.

Questions for Reflection and Application

- Where do you see God's power in your day-to-day life?
- How has God been a shelter from the storm for you? What storms are you experiencing right now? How has God helped you? What more would you like him to do for you?
- Which of the roles of God mentioned in Isaiah 25 (stronghold to the poor, shelter from the storm, and so on) resonates the most with you? Why?

God of rolling thunder, hear my cry in the thunderstorm. Be my shelter. Amen.

PERFECT PEACE FOR "PISTOL"

You keep him in perfect peace whose mind is stayed on you,
because he trusts in you.
—*Isaiah 26:3*

He was one of the greatest basketball players of all time, but the game gave him no peace.

From an early age, "Pistol" Pete Maravich always had a basketball in his hands, and his hard work made him one of the best ball-handlers of all time. And man could he score! Even though he played college ball before the introduction of the three-point shot, Maravich averaged 44.2 points per game for three years at Louisiana State University. He had ten terrific seasons in the NBA, and in 1996 he was honored as one of the fifty greatest players in league history.

Off the court, Maravich's life was a mess. He struggled with alcoholism and depression and, when knee problems forced his retirement in 1980, he considered suicide. After two years of searching for answers, Maravich knelt beside his bed and, weeping, committed his life to Christ. He gave up alcohol, his depression faded, and he pursued his newfound faith just as he had pursued basketball for most of his life.

Maravich started wildly popular basketball camps where he taught kids basketball and nutrition and told them his testimony. He traveled the country to tell his story of transformation at churches, prisons, a Billy Graham Crusade, and even his induction into the Basketball Hall of Fame.

In January 1988, Maravich died while playing in a pickup basketball game at a church gym. An autopsy revealed that rather than having two coronary arteries, Maravich's heart had only one. Doctors said it was nothing short of a miracle that he had lived as long as he had, especially playing one of the most grueling sports.

A few months before he died, Maravich said, "I don't have much time left, and the time that I have I'm giving to the Lord Jesus Christ. I'm giving it to Him, because that's what I'm called to do."[69] [70] Once "Pistol" Pete put his trust in God, God kept him in perfect peace.

Passage: Verse in Context — Isaiah 26:1–6

In that day this song will be sung in the land of Judah: "We have a strong city; he sets up salvation as walls and bulwarks. Open the gates, that the righteous nation that keeps faith may enter in. You keep him in perfect peace whose mind is stayed on you, because he trusts in you. Trust in the LORD forever, for the LORD God is an everlasting rock. For he has humbled the inhabitants of the height, the lofty city. He lays it low, lays it low to the ground, casts it to the dust. The foot tramples it, the feet of the poor, the steps of the needy."

Related Passage — John 14:25–27

"These things I have spoken to you while I am still with you. But the Helper, the Holy Spirit, whom the Father will send in my name, he will teach you all things and bring to your remembrance all that I have said to you. Peace I leave with you; my peace I give to you. Not as the world gives do I give to you. Let not your hearts be troubled, neither let them be afraid."

Questions for Reflection and Application

- What do you approach with the same enthusiasm, determination, and passion as Maravich approached basketball until his retirement? How do you feel when you are doing that? Why has God made you passionate about that?
- What things bring you peace? What things do you pursue (or have you pursued in the past) that do not bring you peace? Why do you (or did you) pursue them?
- If not for his knee problems, Maravich may never have gone searching for a savior and finding his true Savior in Jesus. What difficulties in your life have led you to a stronger relationship with Jesus?

Lord God, like "Pistol" Pete, give me eyes to see what truly brings peace—trusting in you. Amen.

THE ROCK OF AGES

Trust in the LORD forever, for the LORD God is an everlasting rock.

—*Isaiah 26:4*

Augustus Toplady was not a fan of a famous British contemporary of his, John Wesley. After all, Toplady was a staunch Calvinist and Wesley was an Arminian, so the two had very different beliefs on the relationship between God's sovereignty and man's responsibility in the matter of salvation.

Issue	*Calvinism*	*Arminianism*
depravity of man	total	partial
election	unconditional	conditional
atonement	limited	unlimited
God's grace	irresistible	resistible
salvation/security	perseverant/eternal	conditional[71]

Toplady once wrote about Wesley, "I believe him to be the most rancorous hater of the gospel-system that ever appeared on this island." On another occasion, Toplady said, "Wesley is guilty of satanic shamelessness, of acting the ignoble part of a lurking, shy assassin."

In 1776, as another slap at Wesley, Toplady wrote an article about God's forgiveness, ending it with this original poem:

Rock of Ages, cleft for me, let me hide myself in Thee;
Let the water and the blood from Thy wounded side which flowed,
Be of sin the double cure, save from wrath and make me pure.

Set to music by Thomas Hastings, that poem became "the best known, best loved, and most widely useful" hymn in the English language. Unbeknownst to Toplady, it also echoed something that Wesley had written thirty years earlier: "O Rock of Salvation, Rock struck and cleft for me, let those two Streams of Blood and Water which gushed from Thy side, bring down Pardon and Holiness into my soul."[72]

The everlasting rock can save anyone from wrath, even people whom you think are dead wrong.

Passage: Verse in Context — Isaiah 26:1–6

In that day this song will be sung in the land of Judah: "We have a strong city; he sets up salvation as walls and bulwarks. Open the gates, that the righteous nation that keeps faith may enter in. You keep him in perfect peace whose mind is stayed on you, because he trusts in you. Trust in the LORD forever, for the LORD God is an everlasting rock. For he has humbled the inhabitants of the height, the lofty city. He lays it low, lays it low to the ground, casts it to the dust. The foot tramples it, the feet of the poor, the steps of the needy."

Related Passage — Habakkuk 1:12

Are you not from everlasting, O LORD my God, my Holy One? We shall not die. O LORD, you have ordained them as a judgment, and you, O Rock, have established them for reproof.

Related Passage — Acts 4:10–12

"Let it be known to all of you and to all the people of Israel that by the name of Jesus Christ of Nazareth, whom you crucified, whom God raised from the dead—by him this man is standing before you well. This Jesus is the stone that was rejected by you, the builders, which has become the cornerstone. And there is salvation in no one else, for there is no other name under heaven given among men by which we must be saved."

Questions for Reflection and Application

- In the world of social media, we tend to vilify those with whom we disagree. Think about some people with whom you strongly disagree. What common ground do you have with them? How can you reach out to them instead of shouting at them?
- What does it mean to you for God to be your everlasting rock, your Rock of Ages?

Father, be my Rock of Ages. Be the water and the blood that cleanse me. May I put my trust in you and encourage others, including those with whom I disagree, to do the same. Amen.

WAITING FOR GOD

Therefore the LORD waits to be gracious to you, and therefore
he exalts himself to show mercy to you. For the LORD is a God of justice;
blessed are all those who wait for him.
—*Isaiah 30:18*

In 1952, little-known Irish author Samuel Beckett wrote a play called "Waiting for Godot." While a *New York Times* reviewer described it as "an uneventful, maundering, loquacious drama," the play struck a chord with audiences on both sides of the Atlantic. It became the best-known work of Beckett, who won the Nobel Prize for Literature in 1969.

Considered an allegory that conveys "melancholy truths about the hopeless destiny of the human race," the play has two main characters who wait by a withered tree for someone named Godot, who never arrives.[73] In a biography of Beckett, Martin Esslin writes that the two characters are "merely two human beings in the most basic human situation of being in the world and not knowing what they are there for. The two have no evidence that Godot, who clearly represents God, actually exists."[74]

We know that God exists, and waiting for him is not a pointless exercise, but it still can be difficult, because we want God to take immediate action and can get frustrated when he does not. In Isaiah 30:18, the prophet says that those who wait for God are blessed. Why? Why do we have to wait for God?

The answer lies earlier in chapter 30. There, God describes his children as stubborn. They don't ask God for direction and are unwilling to listen to God or follow his instructions, preferring to rebel instead. It is easy to see ourselves in God's description. Often, we find it difficult to wait for God to do what *he* wants, when he is ready and the time is right.

When we truly seek God's will, God comes through for us, because God loves us and wants the best for us. Waiting for God can be challenging, but it's much better than waiting for something exciting to happen in Beckett's famous play.

Passage: Verse in Context — Isaiah 30:15–22

For thus said the LORD God, the Holy One of Israel, "In returning and rest you shall be saved; in quietness and in trust shall be your strength." But you were unwilling, and you said, "No! We will flee upon horses"; therefore you shall flee away; and, "We will ride upon swift steeds"; therefore your pursuers shall be swift. A thousand shall flee at the threat of one; at the threat of five you shall flee, till you are left like a flagstaff on the top of a mountain, like a signal on a hill.

Therefore the LORD waits to be gracious to you, and therefore he exalts himself to show mercy to you. For the LORD is a God of justice; blessed are all those who wait for him.

For a people shall dwell in Zion, in Jerusalem; you shall weep no more. He will surely be gracious to you at the sound of your cry. As soon as he hears it, he answers you. And though the LORD give you the bread of adversity and the water of affliction, yet your Teacher will not hide himself anymore, but your eyes shall see your Teacher. And your ears shall hear a word behind you, saying, "This is the way, walk in it," when you turn to the right or when you turn to the left. Then you will defile your carved idols overlaid with silver and your gold-plated metal images. You will scatter them as unclean things. You will say to them, "Be gone!"

Questions for Reflection and Application

- How often do you find yourself asking God for what you want instead of trying to discern what God wants? How can you improve in this area?
- Why does God give you "the bread of adversity and the water of affliction"?
- Read the parable of the persistent widow (Luke 18:1–8). The woman did not wait patiently for justice; she nagged the judge constantly. Why did Jesus tell this parable? How are you to wait for God?

God, give me patience to wait for you. Remind me of all the times that you have come through for me. Amen.

THE CROOKED STRAIGHT

Every valley shall be lifted up, and every mountain and hill be made low;
the uneven ground shall become level, and the rough places a plain.

—*Isaiah 40:4*

There are twenty-one choral pieces in Handel's *Messiah*, and they have been performed by choirs ranging from a dozen voices to thousands. The first two vocal pieces, however, are sung by a single person, a tenor. The words to the first are from Isaiah 40:1–3; the words to the second are from today's verse, Isaiah 40:4. (Then comes the first choral piece, from Isaiah 40:5.)

George Frideric Handel was a child prodigy who composed operas as a teenager. By his twenties, he was the highest paid composer in the world, and every performance of his in London sold out. In time, audiences began chasing after newer artists, and Handel eventually went bankrupt. He became depressed and stress brought on a palsy that crippled some of his fingers. "Handel's great days are over," wrote Frederick the Great.

Handel's troubles, however, also matured him. His temper mellowed, he softened his formerly sharp tongue, and his music became more heartfelt. One day the more mature Handel received from Charles Jennings a manuscript that was a collection of various biblical texts about Jesus. The opening words, "Comfort ye, comfort ye my people," moved Handel.

On August 22, 1741, Handel started composing music for those words. Twenty-three days later, the entire *Messiah* was complete. "Whether I was in the body or out of the body when I wrote it," he said later, "I know not." Three weeks before Easter in 1743, *Messiah* opened to enormous crowds in London, with Handel leading from the harpsichord.

Handel's fame rose again. Even after going blind, he continued to play the organ for performances of *Messiah* and his other oratorios until his death in 1759.[75]

Once he made Handel's crooked straight and his rough places plain, God was able to elevate Handel's efforts to a pinnacle never before reached.

And the glory of the Lord was revealed.

Passage: Verse in Context — Isaiah 40:1–11

Comfort, comfort my people, says your God. Speak tenderly to Jerusalem, and cry to her that her warfare is ended, that her iniquity is pardoned, that she has received from the LORD's hand double for all her sins. A voice cries: "In the wilderness prepare the way of the LORD; make straight in the desert a highway for our God. Every valley shall be lifted up, and every mountain and hill be made low; the uneven ground shall become level, and the rough places a plain. And the glory of the LORD shall be revealed, and all flesh shall see it together, for the mouth of the LORD has spoken."

A voice says, "Cry!" And I said, "What shall I cry?" All flesh is grass, and all its beauty is like the flower of the field. The grass withers, the flower fades when the breath of the LORD blows on it; surely the people are grass. The grass withers, the flower fades, but the word of our God will stand forever.

Go on up to a high mountain, O Zion, herald of good news; lift up your voice with strength, O Jerusalem, herald of good news; lift it up, fear not; say to the cities of Judah, "Behold your God!" Behold, the LORD God comes with might, and his arm rules for him; behold, his reward is with him, and his recompense before him. He will tend his flock like a shepherd; he will gather the lambs in his arms; he will carry them in his bosom, and gently lead those that are with young.

Questions for Reflection and Application

- Handel's troubles matured him and enabled him to receive and appreciate God's comfort. What has your response been to your troubles? How can you find God's comfort in the midst of life's challenges?
- How has God made your crooked straight and your rough places plain? What work does God still have to do in you?

Father, I know that the comfort that you offered to Handel is available to me. Give me that comfort, that I may glorify you more now than I have in the past. Amen.

THE FORGOTTEN PART

And the glory of the LORD shall be revealed,
and all flesh shall see it together,
for the mouth of the LORD has spoken.
—Isaiah 40:5

When the choir sings the first choral piece in *Messiah*, with today's verse for the words, the first vocal part the audience hears is the alto part.

"When you listen to a choir, you may have trouble picking out the alto part," writes Anna George Meek, who sings professionally with VocalEssence, an ensemble of singers. "Yet if the altos were missing, the piece would feel wrong and empty. Often, the alto line is magical, just below consciousness. The alto line is texture, changing light, tension, weather. …

"As an alto, I have a physical sense of being in the middle of a crowd, embraced on all sides. … Altos might come up under a soprano line for a three or four-note duet and disappear again. We might sing a line in unison with the tenors, not audible as a section, but adding woodsmoke to their sound. Other times, beginning composers won't know where to put the notes leftover in a particular chord, so they give them to the altos. In those cases, our line is a crazy-quilt, a drunken staggering through music that we need to make sound as sober as possible. …

"In your daily life, you may start to see altos. You may recognize an alto because she (or he) is singing a familiar tune, sort of—not badly, just bent through a prism somehow, not quite the notes you know. And altos could be anyone: our neighbors and friends, even family. Even now, altos are walking amongst us, making life richer, though we may barely know it."[76]

In life, a few are called to be soloists, performing alone on the stage. The rest of us are members of a chorus, supported by and working with others around us to deliver music that is richer and sweeter than the sum of our individual efforts.

God has given each of us a vital role to play in this chorus. Especially the altos.

Passage: Verse in Context — Isaiah 40:1–11

Comfort, comfort my people, says your God. Speak tenderly to Jerusalem, and cry to her that her warfare is ended, that her iniquity is pardoned, that she has received from the Lord's hand double for all her sins. A voice cries: "In the wilderness prepare the way of the Lord; make straight in the desert a highway for our God. Every valley shall be lifted up, and every mountain and hill be made low; the uneven ground shall become level, and the rough places a plain. And the glory of the Lord shall be revealed, and all flesh shall see it together, for the mouth of the Lord has spoken."

A voice says, "Cry!" And I said, "What shall I cry?" All flesh is grass, and all its beauty is like the flower of the field. The grass withers, the flower fades when the breath of the Lord blows on it; surely the people are grass. The grass withers, the flower fades, but the word of our God will stand forever.

Go on up to a high mountain, O Zion, herald of good news; lift up your voice with strength, O Jerusalem, herald of good news; lift it up, fear not; say to the cities of Judah, "Behold your God!" Behold, the Lord God comes with might, and his arm rules for him; behold, his reward is with him, and his recompense before him. He will tend his flock like a shepherd; he will gather the lambs in his arms; he will carry them in his bosom, and gently lead those that are with young.

Questions for Reflection and Application

- Where is God calling you to have a role that people easily overlook but, if you were not there, then the effort would not be as effective or compelling? How do you feel about having that role?
- How often do you look for the "altos" around you? Who are the "altos" in your family? At your workplace or school? In your community? In the lives of your children? How do they make your life richer? How can you express your gratitude to them?

Father, even during points in life where you have me sing a "forgotten" part, let me sing to the best of my ability. Every voice is important. Amen.

EXTRA! EXTRA!

Have you not known? Have you not heard? The LORD is the everlasting God,
the Creator of the ends of the earth. He does not faint or grow weary;
his understanding is unsearchable.
—*Isaiah 40:28*

What the prophet shares in Isaiah 40:28 was not exactly a news flash to the average Israelite: We worship a God who has always existed. God created everything. God never gets tired. He knows everything, and everything that he does is perfect. So why does the prophet preface the statements with the equivalent of "Extra! Extra! Read all about it!"?

He was being sarcastic. The sarcasm starts earlier in the chapter. Here's a paraphrase: To what should we compare Almighty God? How about a gold or wood idol that is well-made by a skilled craftsman?

Ludicrous, right? But people who were supposed to be following the true God were following idols instead. And we follow idols today. Not gold or wood figurines, but substitutes for the true God, just the same.

After the sarcasm about idols, the prophet continues his harsh assessment of those who should be honoring and following God. When compared to the all-powerful God—who sits above the earth, who made everything (including the heavens), who brings down princes and other rulers—we are like grasshoppers. But that doesn't stop us from saying things like: "My way is hidden from the Lord, and my right is disregarded by my God" (v. 27).

Sarcasm directed at someone else often is funny. Sarcasm directed at you can seem hurtful. The prophet's sarcasm is designed to shake us out of our pity party— "God doesn't really know me or care about me!"— and back to reality. God *does* know you and love you. He never gets tired of you.

Keep asking for his help. But, more importantly, keep listening to his words. They may not make headlines, but they'll give you the comfort that you need.

Passage: Verse in Context — Isaiah 40:21–28

Do you not know? Do you not hear? Has it not been told you from the beginning? Have you not understood from the foundations of the earth? It is he who sits above the circle of the earth, and its inhabitants are like grasshoppers; who stretches out the heavens like a curtain, and spreads them like a tent to dwell in; who brings princes to nothing, and makes the rulers of the earth as emptiness. Scarcely are they planted, scarcely sown, scarcely has their stem taken root in the earth, when he blows on them, and they wither, and the tempest carries them off like stubble.

To whom then will you compare me, that I should be like him? says the Holy One. Lift up your eyes on high and see: who created these? He who brings out their host by number, calling them all by name; by the greatness of his might and because he is strong in power, not one is missing.

Why do you say, O Jacob, and speak, O Israel, "My way is hidden from the LORD, and my right is disregarded by my God"? Have you not known? Have you not heard? The LORD is the everlasting God, the Creator of the ends of the earth.

Questions for Reflection and Application

- What idols, or substitutes for God, have you followed in the past? Have you been able to leave these idols in the dust, completely? If so, how? If not, why do some still have a hold on you?
- When have you felt that God didn't really know you or care about you? What made you feel that way?
- When have sarcastic comments directed at you caused you to recognize your faults and change your behavior? Why do you suppose the prophet uses sarcasm here?

Lord God, sometimes I forget simple truths and need sarcastic reminders as a kick in the head. Thanks for using sarcasm instead of something that will leave a scar. Amen.

THE VALUE OF STRENGTH

He gives power to the faint, and to him
who has no might he increases strength.
—*Isaiah 40:29*

It is the night before Steve Rogers, a ninety-pound asthmatic from Brooklyn, is to receive an experimental serum that will transform him into a superhuman. Rogers sits alone in the barracks when Dr. Abraham Erskine, a German scientist who created the serum, enters and sits down on a cot across from him. Rogers asks why Erskine chose him.

Erskine replies, "So many people forget that the first country that the Nazis invaded was their own. You know, after the last war, my people struggled. They felt weak. They felt small. And then Hitler comes along … and he hears of me, my work, and he finds me. And he says, you will make us strong. Well, I am not interested. So he sends the head of Hydra, his research division. A brilliant scientist by the name of Johann Schmidt … when he hears about my formula and what it can do, he cannot resist. Schmidt must become that superior man."

"Did it make him stronger?" asks Rogers.

"Yah. But, there were other effects. The serum was not ready. But more important, the man. The serum amplifies everything that is inside. So, good becomes great. Bad becomes worse. This is why you were chosen. Because a strong man, who has known power all his life, will lose respect for that power. But a weak man knows the value of strength, and knows compassion."

"Thanks, I think," says Rogers.

"Whatever happens tomorrow," says Erskine, "you must promise me one thing: that you will stay who you are. Not a perfect soldier, but a good man."

The next day, the serum transforms Rogers, physically. Inside, however, Rogers remains what he always has been, and what Erskine challenged him to be: a good man. A man worthy to assume the identity of Captain America.[77]

When you rely on God for everything, God will make you strong, because you can be trusted with strength.

Passage: Verse in Context — Isaiah 40:27–31

Why do you say, O Jacob, and speak, O Israel, "My way is hidden from the LORD, and my right is disregarded by my God"? Have you not known? Have you not heard? The LORD is the everlasting God, the Creator of the ends of the earth. He does not faint or grow weary; his understanding is unsearchable. He gives power to the faint, and to him who has no might he increases strength. Even youths shall faint and be weary, and young men shall fall exhausted; but they who wait for the LORD shall renew their strength; they shall mount up with wings like eagles; they shall run and not be weary; they shall walk and not faint.

Related Passage — 2 Corinthians 12:7–10

So to keep me from becoming conceited because of the surpassing greatness of the revelations, a thorn was given me in the flesh, a messenger of Satan to harass me, to keep me from becoming conceited. Three times I pleaded with the Lord about this, that it should leave me. But he said to me, "My grace is sufficient for you, for my power is made perfect in weakness." Therefore I will boast all the more gladly of my weaknesses, so that the power of Christ may rest upon me. For the sake of Christ, then, I am content with weaknesses, insults, hardships, persecutions, and calamities. For when I am weak, then I am strong.

Questions for Reflection and Application

- Where have you witnessed a strong man losing respect for power? Where have you witnessed a weak man appreciating the value of strength and demonstrating compassion?
- Jesus was not weak, but he appreciated the value of strength and was compassionate. What other strong and powerful men have done that?
- What made Steve Rogers a good man? What makes you a good man?
- When has God given you power and authority? How well did you use them?

Father, may I rely on you, and you alone, for strength. Amen.

NO MORE WEARINESS

Even youths grow tired and weary, and young men stumble and fall; but those who hope in the LORD will renew their strength. They will soar on wings like eagles; they will run and not grow weary, they will walk and not be faint.

—*Isaiah 40:30–31 (NIV)*

I was tired of waiting to be healed. Tired in general. Weary. Worn out.

One Sabbath day, a group of men, including a rabbi called Jesus, came by. The rabbi said strange things. First, he said that my blindness was so that the works of God might be displayed in me. Then he said that he was the light of the world.

I heard him spit on some dirt, pick it up, and massage it with his hands. He put the mud on my eyes and told me to wash in the pool of Siloam. I practically ran there and went right into the water. The mud fell from my eyes. And then … I saw light. I began to make out shapes.

I tried to find Jesus, but he had left the area. People didn't believe that I had been blind. I got hauled in front of the Pharisees to tell them what had happened. They dragged my parents there too. My parents were terrified of being expelled from the synagogue, so they deferred to me.

I had lived in fear my whole life, but I was done with fear. I stood up to the Pharisees. I told them that Jesus is from God. So they cast me out.

Then Jesus found me. He asked me if I believed in him. Of course I did! I worshiped him, right there. Then he took on the Pharisees too. With me at his side.

It is amazing to see. But it is more amazing to have encountered Jesus. Even when I was blind, he saw me as God's workmanship and a way to show God's power. I feel that power, even now. I feel strong.

I'll never be weary again.

Passage: Verse in Context — Isaiah 40:27–31

Why do you say, O Jacob, and speak, O Israel, "My way is hidden from the LORD, and my right is disregarded by my God"? Have you not known? Have you not heard? The LORD is the everlasting God, the Creator of the ends of the earth. He does not faint or grow weary; his understanding is unsearchable. He gives power to the faint, and to him who has no might he increases strength. Even youths shall faint and be weary, and young men shall fall exhausted; but they who wait for the LORD shall renew their strength; they shall mount up with wings like eagles; they shall run and not be weary; they shall walk and not faint.

Related Passage — Matthew 11:25–30

At that time Jesus declared, "I thank you, Father, Lord of heaven and earth, that you have hidden these things from the wise and understanding and revealed them to little children; yes, Father, for such was your gracious will. All things have been handed over to me by my Father, and no one knows the Son except the Father, and no one knows the Father except the Son and anyone to whom the Son chooses to reveal him. Come to me, all who labor and are heavy laden, and I will give you rest. Take my yoke upon you, and learn from me, for I am gentle and lowly in heart, and you will find rest for your souls. For my yoke is easy, and my burden is light."

Questions for Reflection and Application

- What makes you weary? How does your behavior change when you are exhausted?
- What does it mean to "wait for the Lord"? For what are you waiting right now?
- Of what are you most afraid? How can you overcome that fear?
- Where are you most in need of healing? What would happen if you received the healing that you seek?

Father, like the blind man whom Jesus healed, you gave me eyes to see your wonderful light. My hope is in you. Renew my strength. Amen.

A FIRM FOUNDATION

Fear not, for I am with you; be not dismayed, for I am your God;
I will strengthen you, I will help you, I will uphold you with my
righteous right hand.
—*Isaiah 41:10*

In the late 1700s and early 1800s, a popular hymnal among British Christians and later the United States, had the catchy title of *A Selection of Hymns from the Best Authors, Intended to Be an Appendix to Dr. Watts' Psalms and Hymns.* The editor of the hymnal, John Rippon, was the pastor of Carter's Lane Baptist Church in London. Rippon's assistant was Robert Keene, the Minister of Music at Carter's Lane.

A hymn that first appeared in the Rippon hymnal is "How Firm a Foundation." No one knows who wrote it, but many scholars believe that it was Keene. In the US, the hymn became part of "the history of our common Christianity."[78]

The theme of the hymn is expressed in the first verse:

How firm a foundation, ye saints of the Lord,
Is laid for your faith in His excellent Word!
What more can He say than to you He hath said,
To you who for refuge to Jesus have fled?

The remaining verses are based on other promises made by God in Isaiah 43:2, 2 Corinthians 12:9, Hebrews 13:5, and, verse 2 of the hymn, Isaiah 41:10:

Fear not, I am with thee, O be not dismayed,
For I am thy God, I will still give thee aid.
I'll strengthen thee, help thee, and cause thee to stand,
Upheld by my righteous, Omnipotent hand.

The initial title of the hymn was "Exceedingly Great and Precious Promises."[79] Indeed they are! As with all of God's promises, they are comforting at a deep level. Why fear? God is with you. Why be dismayed? The God of the universe is your God; a God who will strengthen you and help you; a God who will uphold you with a hand that can do anything.

Passage: Verse in Context — Isaiah 41:1–10

Listen to me in silence, O coastlands; let the peoples renew their strength; let them approach, then let them speak; let us together draw near for judgment. Who stirred up one from the east whom victory meets at every step? He gives up nations before him, so that he tramples kings underfoot; he makes them like dust with his sword, like driven stubble with his bow. He pursues them and passes on safely, by paths his feet have not trod. Who has performed and done this, calling the generations from the beginning? I, the LORD, the first, and with the last; I am he.

The coastlands have seen and are afraid; the ends of the earth tremble; they have drawn near and come. Everyone helps his neighbor and says to his brother, "Be strong!" The craftsman strengthens the goldsmith, and he who smooths with the hammer him who strikes the anvil, saying of the soldering, "It is good"; and they strengthen it with nails so that it cannot be moved.

But you, Israel, my servant, Jacob, whom I have chosen, the offspring of Abraham, my friend; you whom I took from the ends of the earth, and called from its farthest corners, saying to you, "You are my servant, I have chosen you and not cast you off"; fear not, for I am with you; be not dismayed, for I am your God; I will strengthen you, I will help you, I will uphold you with my righteous right hand.

Questions for Reflection and Application

- How has God called you from the "farthest corners" of the earth?
- How has God strengthened you? How has God helped you? How has God upheld you?
- Compare the promises that God makes in Isaiah 41:10, Isaiah 43:2, 2 Corinthians 12:9, and Hebrews 13:5. Which are the most meaningful? Which have you witnessed God keeping in your life?

God, you have proven to be a firm foundation to all who trust in you. Amen.

450 VS. 1

For I, the LORD your God, hold your right hand; it is I who say to you,
"Fear not, I am the one who helps you."
—*Isaiah 41:13*

Solomon turned away from God. The kingdom was split in two, with Israel in the north and Judah in the south. Israel suffered under terrible kings: Jeroboam, a former servant of Solomon, reigned for twenty-two years, but he turned from God and did evil, so God made Nadab, his son, king. Nadab had an evil reign of two years and was killed and replaced by Baasha. His twenty-four-year reign was no better. Nor were the reigns of Elah (two years), Zimri (seven days!), and Omri (twelve years).

By the time Elijah came on the scene, the Baal-worshiping Ahab and his wife, Jezebel, were the evil rulers of Israel. They killed God's prophets, except one hundred that were hidden by Obadiah. When a drought prophesied by Elijah continued after three years, Ahab blamed Elijah and wanted him dead.

God had had enough. He sent Elijah to Ahab, and Elijah challenged 450 prophets of Baal to a duel at Mount Carmel. Four hundred and fifty against one. Elijah set the stage with this challenge to the people of Israel who were watching: "If the LORD is God, follow him; but if Baal, then follow him" (1 Kings 18:21).

After cutting up a bull and laying it on wood, the prophets of Baal cried out to Baal—for hours—to light the sacrifice on fire. Nothing happened. After soaking his sacrifice and altar with water, Elijah called out to God, and God sent fire that consumed the sacrifice and, for good measure, the wood, the stones, and all of the water that had drenched everything. Then Elijah, with help from the people of Israel, rounded up and slaughtered the prophets of Baal.

And God sent rain.

Elijah's battle with Ahab and Jezebel was not over. But the duel had shown the people of Israel what Elijah had known all along: God is in charge. When God is on your side, you have nothing to fear.

Passage: Verse in Context — Isaiah 41:11–13

Behold, all who are incensed against you shall be put to shame and confounded; those who strive against you shall be as nothing and shall perish. You shall seek those who contend with you, but you shall not find them; those who war against you shall be as nothing at all. For I, the LORD your God, hold your right hand; it is I who say to you, "Fear not, I am the one who helps you."

Related Passage — Isaiah 43:1–7

But now thus says the LORD, he who created you, O Jacob, he who formed you, O Israel: "Fear not, for I have redeemed you; I have called you by name, you are mine. When you pass through the waters, I will be with you; and through the rivers, they shall not overwhelm you; when you walk through fire you shall not be burned, and the flame shall not consume you.

For I am the LORD your God, the Holy One of Israel, your Savior. I give Egypt as your ransom, Cush and Seba in exchange for you. Because you are precious in my eyes, and honored, and I love you, I give men in return for you, peoples in exchange for your life. Fear not, for I am with you; I will bring your offspring from the east, and from the west I will gather you. I will say to the north, Give up, and to the south, Do not withhold; bring my sons from afar and my daughters from the end of the earth, everyone who is called by my name, whom I created for my glory, whom I formed and made."

Questions for Reflection and Application

- Why did God send a drought that lasted three-and-a-half years? What "droughts" or difficult times have you experienced? Did God cause them, or did God use them to teach you something? What were the lessons that you learned?
- God and his holy messengers, the angels, often tell people not to fear. Why do we fear, even when we know that God is on our side? Why do we need reminders not to fear?

Father, no matter what leaders I find myself under, I know that you have ultimate control. Amen.

A NU THANG

Behold, I am doing a new thing; now it springs forth, do you not perceive it?
I will make a way in the wilderness and rivers in the desert.

—Isaiah 43:19

It was 1990, and rap was in full crossover mode. Top 40 stations blasted M.C. Hammer's "U Can't Touch This," and Hammer's album sold 10 million copies.[80] NBC launched "The Fresh Prince of Bel Air," which starred rap star Will Smith. The show "Yo! MTV Raps," which popularized rap and hip-hop, was in its third season.

Christian rap, however, still struggled to find an audience. The Christian community did not know what to make of it, and the broader market did not take Christian rap seriously.[81] But a trio that had met at Liberty University— Toby McKeehan (tobyMac), Michael Tait, and Kevin Max—changed that. The previous year, the debut album from the group, dcTalk, had sold a surprising one hundred thousand copies. The 1990 sophomore effort, entitled "Nu Thang," put the band, and Christian rap, on the map.

Over the next two years, as the group toured with Michael W. Smith, "Nu Thang" sold over three hundred thousand copies. By the middle of the decade, dcTalk was the biggest group in Christian music, with the trio's fourth album, "Jesus Freak," breaking sales records and giving the band a hit on Top 40 radio.[82]

The title track to "Nu Thang" starts with an infectious, repeated hook that is echoed by a similar hook in the chorus. The verses are raps. In the first, McKeehan says that even though God is doing something new, he doesn't change but remains faithful and solid. In the second and third verses, McKeehan states that Christ is the reason for dcTalk and that Christ can do a "nu thang" in the heart of every listener.

God doesn't change, but he does nu thangs—sorry, new things—all the time. Maybe it's a river in the desert. Maybe it's the use of rap to reach a new audience with the message of God's love. Whatever it is, ya know he's doin' it.

Passage: Verse in Context — Isaiah 43:16–25

Thus says the LORD, who makes a way in the sea, a path in the mighty waters, who brings forth chariot and horse, army and warrior; they lie down, they cannot rise, they are extinguished, quenched like a wick: "Remember not the former things, nor consider the things of old. Behold, I am doing a new thing; now it springs forth, do you not perceive it? I will make a way in the wilderness and rivers in the desert. The wild beasts will honor me, the jackals and the ostriches, for I give water in the wilderness, rivers in the desert, to give drink to my chosen people, the people whom I formed for myself that they might declare my praise.

"Yet you did not call upon me, O Jacob; but you have been weary of me, O Israel! You have not brought me your sheep for burnt offerings, or honored me with your sacrifices. I have not burdened you with offerings, or wearied you with frankincense. You have not bought me sweet cane with money, or satisfied me with the fat of your sacrifices. But you have burdened me with your sins; you have wearied me with your iniquities.

"I, I am he who blots out your transgressions for my own sake, and I will not remember your sins."

Questions for Reflection and Application

- How can God be unchanging and faithful to his Word and yet do new things? Where is God doing new things today?
- Why do you sometimes *not* see the new things that God is doing in your life and the lives of those closest to you? How can you get more perceptive to the new things of God?
- Where in your life should you forget the "former things" and not "consider the things of old"? Where in your life should you remember and revere the past without clinging to it or letting it define who you are today?

Lord, the gospel is for everyone. Give me the inspiration to find creative ways to take your message to those who have not responded to it yet. Amen.

OVERBLOWN?

I will go before you and level the exalted places,
I will break in pieces the doors of bronze and cut through the bars of iron.
—*Isaiah 45:2*

How do you react when you read something such as Isaiah 45:2, which says that God will knock down mountains and cut through prison bars for you? John Eldredge writes what some of us think:

> Doesn't the language of the Bible sometimes sound ... overblown? Really now—God is going to level mountains for us? We'd be happy if he just helped us get through the week. What's all that about breaking down gates of bronze and cutting through bars of iron? I mean, it sounds heroic, but, well, who's really in need of that? This isn't ancient Samaria. We'd settle for a parking place at the mall.

The Bible's language is not overblown, Eldredge continues, if we recognize that we have an enemy:

> You were born into a world at war. When Satan lost the battle against Michael and his angels, "he was hurled to the earth, and his angels with him" (Rev. 12:9). That means that right now, on this earth, there are hundreds of thousands, if not millions, of fallen angels, foul spirits, bent on our destruction. ... So what does [Satan] spend every day and every night of his sleepless, untiring existence doing? "Then the dragon was enraged at the woman and went off to make war against ... those who obey God's commandments and hold to the testimony of Jesus" (v. 17). He has you in his crosshairs, and he isn't smiling. [83]

You have an enemy. But you also have a savior. God sent Jesus to level mountains, knock down doors, cut through iron bars—do whatever is needed to free you from the power of the enemy. The one who was sinless bore the penalty for our sins on the cross, then conquered death by rising from the dead.
It's a little better than a parking place at the mall.

Passage: Verse in Context — Isaiah 45:1–8

Thus says the LORD to his anointed, to Cyrus, whose right hand I have grasped, to subdue nations before him and to loose the belts of kings, to open doors before him that gates may not be closed: "I will go before you and level the exalted places, I will break in pieces the doors of bronze and cut through the bars of iron, I will give you the treasures of darkness and the hoards in secret places, that you may know that it is I, the LORD, the God of Israel, who call you by your name. For the sake of my servant Jacob, and Israel my chosen, I call you by your name, I name you, though you do not know me.

"I am the LORD, and there is no other, besides me there is no God; I equip you, though you do not know me, that people may know, from the rising of the sun and from the west, that there is none besides me; I am the LORD, and there is no other. I form light and create darkness; I make well-being and create calamity; I am the LORD, who does all these things.

"Shower, O heavens, from above, and let the clouds rain down righteousness; let the earth open, that salvation and righteousness may bear fruit; let the earth cause them both to sprout; I the LORD have created it."

Questions for Reflection and Application

- Where is the enemy holding you down or holding you back?
- When has God gone before you and "cleared a path" for you? When has God brought down powerful people to elevate you? When has God rescued you from a place where you were imprisoned? When has God given you "treasures of darkness and the hoards in secret places" (v. 3)?
- Do you pray big prayers to a big God, or do your prayers tend to be small? What big things do you want God to do for you? Why?

God, too often I fail to recognize that I have an enemy and that you and your forces are fighting a war on my behalf, even though I have done nothing to deserve your help. I praise you for being my defender and protector. Amen.

LIKE A FLINT

But the LORD God helps me; therefore I have not been disgraced;
therefore I have set my face like a flint,
and I know that I shall not be put to shame.
—*Isaiah 50:7*

The church building was on the top of a hill, overlooking the sleepy town of Coshocton, Ohio. The congregation was small but faithful. The pastor was a wonderful shepherd of his flock. And his Sunday sermons were boring … until the sermon on Isaiah 50:7.

Everyone could relate to this relatively obscure text for one reason: the ground below the building was solid flint. So the pastor talked about flint for twenty minutes. The properties and beauty of this form of quartz. How it provided a solid foundation for the church building. How the Native Americans had used flint for tools and weapons. How, when the soldiers flogged and beat and spit on Jesus before his crucifixion, as foretold in Isaiah 50:6, Jesus did not hide his face but set it like a flint.

I don't remember another sermon delivered by that pastor, but over forty years later I still hear the closing words of this one: "I have set my face like a flint." It stuck with me because it was a parable that all of us in that church understood. We knew what flint is. We had seen the flint jutting out of the land around the church. It was visible even on winter days when we rode our sleds down that hill. Setting your face like a flint brought an immediate visual image to mind.

Jesus, the best preacher to ever walk the planet, did much of his teaching in parables. Everyday illustrations became metaphors for deep philosophical truths. People could relate, remember, ponder, and discuss. The truth came alive, stayed alive, and was passed on to others.

Want to share truth with someone? Find an applicable parable in the Bible. Or emulate Jesus and come up with one on your own. It will make an impact. Not just for a moment or even for forty years. For eternity.

Passage: Verse in Context — Isaiah 50:4–11

The LORD God has given me the tongue of those who are taught, that I may know how to sustain with a word him who is weary. Morning by morning he awakens; he awakens my ear to hear as those who are taught. The LORD God has opened my ear, and I was not rebellious; I turned not backward. I gave my back to those who strike, and my cheeks to those who pull out the beard; I hid not my face from disgrace and spitting.

But the LORD God helps me; therefore I have not been disgraced; therefore I have set my face like a flint, and I know that I shall not be put to shame. He who vindicates me is near. Who will contend with me? Let us stand up together. Who is my adversary? Let him come near to me. Behold, the LORD God helps me; who will declare me guilty? Behold, all of them will wear out like a garment; the moth will eat them up.

Who among you fears the LORD and obeys the voice of his servant? Let him who walks in darkness and has no light trust in the name of the LORD and rely on his God. Behold, all you who kindle a fire, who equip yourselves with burning torches! Walk by the light of your fire and by the torches that you have kindled! This you have from my hand: you shall lie down in torment.

Questions for Reflection and Application

- What's the last sermon you heard that had such an impact on you that you remember it (or most of it) now? Did that sermon leverage an object or an everyday illustration?
- Why did Jesus use parables when he taught?
- Which of Jesus' parables resonates the most with you? Why?
- When have you used an everyday illustration to make a point? How did your audience respond? Why don't you tell parables more often?

Father, as I read your Word, give me insight and understanding, that the words may burrow themselves into my heart. Amen.

FALSELY ACCUSED

He was despised and rejected by men, a man of sorrows and acquainted with grief; and as one from whom men hide their faces he was despised, and we esteemed him not.

—*Isaiah 53:3*

In 1990, Randy Resh and Bob Gondor were convicted of the 1988 murder of a woman in Randolph Township, Ohio. Resh was sentenced to fifteen years to life for murder and five to fifteen years for attempted rape. Gondor was sentenced to ten to twenty-five years for the involuntary manslaughter and kidnapping and eighteen months for obstructing justice.

There was just one problem: both men were innocent. Nearly seventeen years after they were put in prison, the Ohio Supreme Court set aside their convictions and ordered new trials. In 2007, Resh was retried and acquitted by a jury; the state then dropped all charges for Gondor. Seven years later, a judge found both men factually innocent, paving the way for them to seek compensation from the Ohio Court of Claims.[84]

In March 2017, the state agreed to pay each man $2.3 million. No amount would be enough, Gondor said, for someone who spent seventeen years in prison for something he didn't do. "We lost our lives. We went in at twenty-six and came home at forty-three."[85]

Before their exonerations, Gondor and Resh felt rejected by everyone. They lost their freedom and all aspects of a "normal" life: having a job, raising children, sharing in the lives of friends. They did not deserve the suffering that they incurred; they were innocent of the crime for which they paid the penalty.

So was Jesus. He never sinned and yet he bore the penalty for the sins of everyone else. In spite of his innocence, he was despised and rejected by men, a man of sorrows and acquainted with grief. While Resh and Gondor eventually got out of prison, Jesus went all the way to the cross and died there. He never fought to clear his name but accepted an unjust execution without saying a word in his defense.

He did it for you … and for me.

Passage: Verse in Context — Isaiah 53:1–6

Who has believed what he has heard from us? And to whom has the arm of the LORD been revealed? For he grew up before him like a young plant, and like a root out of dry ground; he had no form or majesty that we should look at him, and no beauty that we should desire him. He was despised and rejected by men, a man of sorrows and acquainted with grief; and as one from whom men hide their faces he was despised, and we esteemed him not.

Surely he has borne our griefs and carried our sorrows; yet we esteemed him stricken, smitten by God, and afflicted. But he was pierced for our transgressions; he was crushed for our iniquities; upon him was the chastisement that brought us peace, and with his wounds we are healed. All we like sheep have gone astray; we have turned—every one—to his own way; and the LORD has laid on him the iniquity of us all.

Related Passage — Psalm 118:19–23

Open to me the gates of righteousness, that I may enter through them and give thanks to the LORD. This is the gate of the LORD; the righteous shall enter through it. I thank you that you have answered me and have become my salvation. The stone that the builders rejected has become the cornerstone. This is the LORD's doing; it is marvelous in our eyes.

Questions for Reflection and Application

- When have you been falsely accused? How did you respond? What was the final result?
- What happened between Palm Sunday, when Jesus was hailed as a king, and Good Friday, when Jesus was despised, rejected, and crucified? How have you despised and rejected Jesus?
- Could Jesus have cleared his name? Why didn't he?

Lord Jesus, you stood falsely accused and still bore the burden reserved for me. I can never thank you enough. Amen.

NOT A BEAST

Surely he has borne our griefs and carried our sorrows;
yet we esteemed him stricken, smitten by God, and afflicted.
—*Isaiah 53:4*

One of the toughest commands in the Bible is Galatians 6:2: "Bear one another's burdens, and so fulfill the law of Christ." Bearing someone else's burdens can take a lot out of you and seem like a thankless job. You may side with Mick Jagger of the Rolling Stones when he sings that he'll never be a beast of burden for the woman he loves.[86]

When you think about what Christ did for each of us—taking the punishment for our sins and all of the grief and sorrow that accompanied that punishment—taking on someone else's load doesn't seem so daunting. But what about those situations where we can't bear someone else's burden?

Such a situation is presented in *The Lord of the Rings* trilogy. Frodo Baggins is assigned the task of taking the One Ring to Mordor and destroying it in the fires of Mount Doom. Bearing the Ring is a terrible burden for Frodo, and his companion Sam hates to see his friend suffering, but Sam knows that he cannot bear the burden for Frodo.

When the pair finally reaches Mount Doom, Frodo collapses, unable to go any further. Worse, he begins to see their dreaded enemy, Sauron, because of the Ring. Even though he is exhausted, Sam springs to life. "Then let us be rid of it, once and for all," he says. "Come on, Mr. Frodo. I can't carry it for you ... but I can carry you!" He puts Frodo on his shoulder and, with his last bit of strength, Sam carries Frodo through an opening in the side of the active volcano so that Frodo can cast the Ring into the fire.

It really doesn't matter if your feet are hurting, your back is hurting, or you just don't feel like it. Help others with their heavy loads. It doesn't make you a beast of burden. It makes you an emulator of Jesus.

Passage: Verse in Context — Isaiah 53:1–6

Who has believed what he has heard from us? And to whom has the arm of the LORD been revealed? For he grew up before him like a young plant, and like a root out of dry ground; he had no form or majesty that we should look at him, and no beauty that we should desire him. He was despised and rejected by men, a man of sorrows and acquainted with grief; and as one from whom men hide their faces he was despised, and we esteemed him not.

Surely he has borne our griefs and carried our sorrows; yet we esteemed him stricken, smitten by God, and afflicted. But he was pierced for our transgressions; he was crushed for our iniquities; upon him was the chastisement that brought us peace, and with his wounds we are healed. All we like sheep have gone astray; we have turned—every one—to his own way; and the LORD has laid on him the iniquity of us all.

Related Passage — Philippians 2:5–8

Have this mind among yourselves, which is yours in Christ Jesus, who, though he was in the form of God, did not count equality with God a thing to be grasped, but emptied himself, by taking the form of a servant, being born in the likeness of men. And being found in human form, he humbled himself by becoming obedient to the point of death, even death on a cross.

Questions for Reflection and Application

- What did it mean for Jesus to bear your griefs and carry your sorrows?
- What burdens are you currently bearing for others? What burdens could you be bearing? How else could you be helping those in your life who have heavy burdens to bear?
- How are you resisting or preventing others from helping you with your burdens? Why?

Father, give me the strength to carry my brothers and sisters who have no strength left. Amen.

AMAZING LOVE!

But he was pierced for our transgressions;
he was crushed for our iniquities; upon him was the chastisement
that brought us peace, and with his wounds we are healed.
—*Isaiah 53:5*

And can it be that I should gain an int'rest in the Savior's blood?
Died He for me, who caused His pain? For me, who Him to death pursued?
Amazing love! How can it be that Thou, my God, shouldst die for me?

That is the opening to the hymn "And Can It Be," written by Charles Wesley in 1738. Born in 1707, Charles was a bright child who became a King's Scholar at Westminster and a strong student at Oxford. There, he and his brother, John, sought to live the Christian life so methodically that they were dubbed "Methodists" by other students.

After graduation, the brothers went to the American colony of Georgia as missionaries, but Charles was a failure. Demanding and autocratic, he insisted on baptizing infants by immersing them three times. One angry woman fired a gun at him.

Charles returned to England ill and depressed, joined by John a short time later. The brothers began attending meetings led by a Moravian Christian, Peter Boehler. Those meetings uplifted the brothers and renewed their spirits. On May 21, 1738, Charles wrote, "I now found myself at peace with God, and rejoiced in hope of loving Christ. I saw that by faith I stood." He considered himself a convert to Christianity on that day.

Two days later, Charles began writing a hymn. Many historians believe that it was "And Can It Be" because of the testimony in verse 4: "Long my imprisoned spirit lay, Fast bound in sin and nature's night; Thine eye diffused a quick'ning ray, I woke, the dungeon flamed with light; My chains fell off, my heart was free; I rose, went forth, and followed Thee."[87]

Jesus was pierced, crushed, wounded, and killed for the sins of Charles Wesley … and you … and me. Amazing love!

Passage: Verse in Context — Isaiah 53:4–11

Surely he has borne our griefs and carried our sorrows; yet we esteemed him stricken, smitten by God, and afflicted. But he was pierced for our transgressions; he was crushed for our iniquities; upon him was the chastisement that brought us peace, and with his wounds we are healed. All we like sheep have gone astray; we have turned—every one—to his own way; and the LORD has laid on him the iniquity of us all.

He was oppressed, and he was afflicted, yet he opened not his mouth; like a lamb that is led to the slaughter, and like a sheep that before its shearers is silent, so he opened not his mouth. By oppression and judgment he was taken away; and as for his generation, who considered that he was cut off out of the land of the living, stricken for the transgression of my people? And they made his grave with the wicked and with a rich man in his death, although he had done no violence, and there was no deceit in his mouth.

Yet it was the will of the LORD to crush him; he has put him to grief; when his soul makes an offering for guilt, he shall see his offspring; he shall prolong his days; the will of the LORD shall prosper in his hand. Out of the anguish of his soul he shall see and be satisfied; by his knowledge shall the righteous one, my servant, make many to be accounted righteous, and he shall bear their iniquities.

Questions for Reflection and Application

- How does the crucifixion of Jesus bring you peace? How do the wounds of Jesus—which he received before and during his crucifixion—heal you?
- What went wrong for Charles Wesley in Georgia? In what areas of your Christian life have you become so methodical that you are missing the essence and vitality of your faith? What changes do you need to make?
- What "chains" are keeping you from joy and wonder in your walk with Jesus? How can you shed them?

Lord Jesus, I do not deserve your act of amazing love for me. I praise you for your atoning sacrifice. Amen.

PAUL THE SHEEP

All we like sheep have gone astray; we have turned—every one—
to his own way; and the LORD has laid on him the iniquity of us all.

—*Isaiah 53:6*

No one would compare the apostle Paul to a sheep. Except Paul himself.

Paul wrote two letters to the church at Corinth. In the second letter, Paul compared himself to false prophets who had captivated some in Corinth. Sarcastically calling them "super-apostles," Paul wrote that he is "not in the least inferior" to them and listed his qualifications as an apostle (2 Corinthians 11:5). Hebrew. Israelite. Offspring of Abraham. A "better" servant of Christ with "far greater labors, far more imprisonments, with countless beatings, and often near death" (v. 23). He had been whipped five times. Beaten with rods three times. Shipwrecked three times. Stoned and left for dead. He had been "in danger from rivers, danger from robbers, danger from my own people, danger from Gentiles, danger in the city, danger in the wilderness, danger at sea, danger from false brothers" (v. 26).

Paul was boasting to make a point, not out of arrogance. The Christians in Corinth knew this because of what Paul had written in his first letter to them: "For I am the least of the apostles, unworthy to be called an apostle, because I persecuted the church of God. But by the grace of God I am what I am, and his grace toward me was not in vain. On the contrary, I worked harder than any of them, though it was not I, but the grace of God that is with me" (1 Corinthians 15:9–10).

As a young man, Paul had been a sheep, led astray by pride, as he shared in his letter to the Philippians. His "confidence in the flesh" and "righteousness under the law" (3:4, 6) caused him to persecute Christians. Fortunately for him and for us, Paul encountered Jesus on the road to Damascus and became a Christian.

Paul still was a sheep but instead of being led astray by pride, he faithfully followed his new shepherd … The Good Shepherd.

Passage: Verse in Context — Isaiah 53:3–6

He was despised and rejected by men, a man of sorrows and acquainted with grief; and as one from whom men hide their faces he was despised, and we esteemed him not.

Surely he has borne our griefs and carried our sorrows; yet we esteemed him stricken, smitten by God, and afflicted. But he was pierced for our transgressions; he was crushed for our iniquities; upon him was the chastisement that brought us peace, and with his wounds we are healed. All we like sheep have gone astray; we have turned—every one—to his own way; and the LORD has laid on him the iniquity of us all.

Related Passage — 1 Peter 2:21–25

Christ also suffered for you, leaving you an example, so that you might follow in his steps. He committed no sin, neither was deceit found in his mouth. When he was reviled, he did not revile in return; when he suffered, he did not threaten, but continued entrusting himself to him who judges justly. He himself bore our sins in his body on the tree, that we might die to sin and live to righteousness. By his wounds you have been healed. For you were straying like sheep, but have now returned to the Shepherd and Overseer of your souls.

Questions for Reflection and Application

- Why did God lay your iniquity on Jesus? How should you respond?
- Paul forever was humbled by the fact that he had persecuted Christians, resulting in their imprisonment and even death. What sins have you committed that seem unforgiveable? How can you be assured that God really has forgiven you for them?
- How have you gone "astray" in the past week? Month? Year? What can you do, starting today, to get back on track? Who can help you to stay on track? How?

Father, I like Paul have gone astray as a sheep, led away by false teachers. But I also, as a sheep, seek to follow my Good Shepherd. Guide me as I go. Amen.

NO SEPARATION

No weapon that is fashioned against you shall succeed,
and you shall refute every tongue that rises against you in judgment.
—Isaiah 54:17a

"The finest trick of the devil is to persuade you that he does not exist."

This quote from Charles Baudelaire, made famous when paraphrased by Roger "Verbal" Kint near the end of the film *The Usual Suspects*, tells us a lot about our primary adversary. The devil has many weapons, but his primary weapon against us is lies. Jesus described the devil as "a liar and the father of lies" (John 8:44). The devil's lies began in the garden of Eden, when he persuaded Adam and Eve that God was keeping something good from them. The result was sin and separation from God.

Satan's lies not only can cause us to doubt God's goodness but also can confuse us as to what is true. Jesus explained that there is no truth in the devil (John 8:44). The devil has servants who seem to profess truth but subtly distort it and deceive the faithful (1 Timothy 4:1–3). These false prophets, or wolves in sheep's clothing (Matthew 7:15), can lead believers astray.

When people are persuaded by the devil, their minds can become blind to the truth, and they can be prevented "from seeing the light of the gospel of the glory of Christ, who is the image of God" (2 Corinthians 4:4). Such people can be led to commit sins because their thoughts are "led astray from a sincere and pure devotion to Christ" (2 Corinthians 11:3).

How do we ensure that no weapon that is fashioned by the devil against us shall succeed and that we can refute every tongue that rises against us in judgment? Jesus said, "If you abide in my word, you are truly my disciples, and you will know the truth, and the truth will set you free" (John 8:31b–32).

Thanks to the work of Christ, Satan, our accuser, cannot separate us from the love of God in Christ Jesus our Lord (see Romans 8:31–39).

Passage: Verse in Context — Isaiah 54:11–17

"O afflicted one, storm-tossed and not comforted, behold, I will set your stones in antimony, and lay your foundations with sapphires. I will make your pinnacles of agate, your gates of carbuncles, and all your wall of precious stones.

"All your children shall be taught by the LORD, and great shall be the peace of your children. In righteousness you shall be established; you shall be far from oppression, for you shall not fear; and from terror, for it shall not come near you. If anyone stirs up strife, it is not from me; whoever stirs up strife with you shall fall because of you.

"Behold, I have created the smith who blows the fire of coals and produces a weapon for its purpose. I have also created the ravager to destroy; no weapon that is fashioned against you shall succeed, and you shall refute every tongue that rises against you in judgment.

"This is the heritage of the servants of the LORD and their vindication from me, declares the LORD."

Questions for Reflection and Application

- What are some ways that the devil is convincing our culture that he does not exist? What are some distorted truths that you have encountered recently?
- What lies has the devil attempted to make you believe? Which did you end up believing, even for a short time? What was the result?
- When have you encountered false accusations against you because of what you believe or how you live out your faith? How did you respond? What was the result?
- How can you become more effective at thwarting the devil and his schemes against you and those you love?

Father, no weapon of the devil can separate me from you. Amen.

ARE YOU THE ONE?

The Spirit of the LORD God is upon me, because the LORD
has anointed me to bring good news to the poor; he has sent me to
bind up the brokenhearted, to proclaim liberty to the captives,
and the opening of the prison to those who are bound.
—*Isaiah 61:1*

What was the mission of Jesus? After Jesus was baptized and tempted in the wilderness, he returned to Galilee, teaching in synagogues and healing people. When he taught on the Sabbath in his hometown of Nazareth, he read Isaiah 61:1–2, then started teaching with, "Today this Scripture has been fulfilled in your hearing" (Luke 4:21).

Later, when John the Baptist was in prison, he sent two of his disciples to Jesus with a question: "Are you the one who is to come, or shall we look for another?" (7:19). Jesus answered, "Go and tell John what you have seen and heard: the blind receive their sight, the lame walk, lepers are cleansed, and the deaf hear, the dead are raised up, the poor have good news preached to them. And blessed is the one who is not offended by me" (vv. 22–23).

By including "the poor have good news preached to them," Jesus clearly was pointing John to Isaiah 61:1. John would have remembered that just after he baptized Jesus, the Holy Spirit descended on Jesus in bodily form, like a dove; and a voice came from heaven, "You are my beloved Son; with you I am well pleased" (3:22). That was the anointing foretold in Isaiah 61:1.

At the end of Isaiah 61, the prophet foretells that Jesus would be clothed with the garments of salvation and covered with the robe of righteousness. The good news that Jesus preached was this: God offers salvation and righteousness through his Beloved Son.

In prison and facing certain death, John the Baptist had a moment of doubt about Jesus. Through his disciples, John asked Jesus, "Are you the one?" By pointing John to Isaiah 61, Jesus reassured John with an emphatic "Yes!"

Jesus does the same for us today.

Passage: Verse in Context — Isaiah 61:1–3

The Spirit of the LORD God is upon me, because the LORD has anointed me to bring good news to the poor; he has sent me to bind up the brokenhearted, to proclaim liberty to the captives, and the opening of the prison to those who are bound; to proclaim the year of the LORD's favor, and the day of vengeance of our God; to comfort all who mourn; to grant to those who mourn in Zion—to give them a beautiful headdress instead of ashes, the oil of gladness instead of mourning, the garment of praise instead of a faint spirit; that they may be called oaks of righteousness, the planting of the LORD, that he may be glorified.

Related Passage — Luke 4:16–21

And he came to Nazareth, where he had been brought up. And as was his custom, he went to the synagogue on the Sabbath day, and he stood up to read. And the scroll of the prophet Isaiah was given to him. He unrolled the scroll and found the place where it was written, "The Spirit of the Lord is upon me, because he has anointed me to proclaim good news to the poor. He has sent me to proclaim liberty to the captives and recovering of sight to the blind, to set at liberty those who are oppressed, to proclaim the year of the Lord's favor."

And he rolled up the scroll and gave it back to the attendant and sat down. And the eyes of all in the synagogue were fixed on him. And he began to say to them, "Today this Scripture has been fulfilled in your hearing."

Questions for Reflection and Application

- Even John the Baptist struggled with his faith. How can God use doubt to reveal his glory?
- Why did Jesus answer John's doubts by quoting Isaiah 61?
- What doubts have you had about your faith? How has God reassured you?

Lord Jesus, like John the Baptist, I sometimes doubt you and need your reassurance … and you provide it, every time I ask. Amen.

FEELING GOD'S PLEASURE

Before I formed you in the womb I knew you.
—*Jeremiah 1:5a*

The film *Chariots of Fire* profiles two sprinters who represent the United Kingdom in the 1924 Paris Olympic Games: Harold Abrahams and Eric Liddell. Both train and compete fiercely. Both are driven to succeed. But their motivations are wildly different.

Abrahams, a Jew, runs with a chip on his shoulder, but overcoming prejudice is not his primary goal. He places his entire identity on his success on the track. Liddell, a Christian and the son of a missionary, runs to glorify God. Even though he earns a spot in the 100 meters, he refuses to compete in the event because the qualifying heats take place on a Sunday.

Liddell ends up making the finals of the 400 meters, which is an event for which he has not trained. When he runs the race, he recalls a conversation that he had with his sister, who feared that his running was getting in the way of his true calling, that of being a missionary in China. "Jenny, I believe God made me for a purpose, for China," Eric had said in response. "But he also made me fast. And when I run, I feel his pleasure. To give that up would be to hold him in contempt. You were right: it's not just fun. To win is to honor him." Liddell wins the 400 and, shortly after the Games, goes to China.

Before Eric Liddell was conceived, God knew him. Knew that he would become a missionary. And knew that he would be a fantastic sprinter. Before Liddell went to China, his success on the track made him somewhat of a celebrity, and his popularity gave him opportunities to talk to people about God. He became a missionary not just in China but in the UK as well.

God has given you a purpose, but he also has blessed you with certain gifts. When you make the most of those gifts, you honor God. And God honors you in return.

Passage: Verse in Context — Jeremiah 1:1–10

The words of Jeremiah, the son of Hilkiah, one of the priests who were in Anathoth in the land of Benjamin, to whom the word of the LORD came in the days of Josiah the son of Amon, king of Judah, in the thirteenth year of his reign. It came also in the days of Jehoiakim the son of Josiah, king of Judah, and until the end of the eleventh year of Zedekiah, the son of Josiah, king of Judah, until the captivity of Jerusalem in the fifth month.

Now the word of the LORD came to me, saying, "Before I formed you in the womb I knew you, and before you were born I consecrated you; I appointed you a prophet to the nations."

Then I said, "Ah, LORD God! Behold, I do not know how to speak, for I am only a youth." But the LORD said to me, "Do not say, 'I am only a youth'; for to all to whom I send you, you shall go, and whatever I command you, you shall speak. Do not be afraid of them, for I am with you to deliver you, declares the LORD."

Then the LORD put out his hand and touched my mouth. And the LORD said to me, "Behold, I have put my words in your mouth. See, I have set you this day over nations and over kingdoms, to pluck up and to break down, to destroy and to overthrow, to build and to plant."

Questions for Reflection and Application

- What are the primary gifts with which God has blessed you? How are you using those gifts for the kingdom and the glory of God?
- Before Liddell left for China, his prowess as a sprinter gave him opportunities to share his faith. How are your gifts giving you opportunities in the workplace and elsewhere?
- Where are you struggling to use your gifts? Is God calling you to change something—your job, your church, your location—or to get more creative in your current situation? How do you know?

Father, I want to do what you have created me to do, and I want my actions to bring glory to you. When I run the race of life, I want to feel your pleasure. Amen.

BACK IN KINDERGARTEN

But the LORD said to me, "Do not say, 'I am only a youth';
for to all to whom I send you, you shall go,
and whatever I command you, you shall speak."
—*Jeremiah 1:7*

ALL I REALLY NEED TO KNOW about how to live and what to do and how to be I learned in kindergarten. Wisdom was not at the top of the graduate school mountain, but there in the sandpile at Sunday school.

A 1986 book containing wisdom from Robert Fulghum's childhood—such as share everything, play fair, clean up your own mess, and say you're sorry when you hurt somebody—sold seven million copies. *All I Really Need to Know I Learned in Kindergarten* resonated with people because it reminded them that, even when we are very young, we know a lot of things that apply throughout our lives.

We may get wiser as we get older, but being young has its advantages, as God makes clear at the beginning of the book of Jeremiah. God tells the young Jeremiah that his destiny is to be a prophet. Jeremiah's response is, essentially, that prophets are old men, so maybe God should come back in a few decades.

Rather than getting upset, God tells Jeremiah that he'll be a terrific prophet *because* he is young. You'll be able to go anywhere and talk to anyone, Jeremiah, because you have energy and stamina, and you won't be daunted by any task. God closes by reassuring Jeremiah that God will make him strong and will be with him every step of the way.

When God calls you to something, he wants you to trust him and rely on him as if you were a child. Certainly, he wants you to do everything you can to be prepared for the task, but you should not rely entirely on your own knowledge, abilities, and experience. When compared to what God brings to the table, everything you know is the equivalent of a kindergarten education.

Passage: Verse in Context — Jeremiah 1:6–10

Then I said, "Ah, LORD God! Behold, I do not know how to speak, for I am only a youth." But the LORD said to me, "Do not say, 'I am only a youth'; for to all to whom I send you, you shall go, and whatever I command you, you shall speak. Do not be afraid of them, for I am with you to deliver you, declares the LORD."

Then the LORD put out his hand and touched my mouth. And the LORD said to me, "Behold, I have put my words in your mouth. See, I have set you this day over nations and over kingdoms, to pluck up and to break down, to destroy and to overthrow, to build and to plant."

Related Passage — 1 Timothy 4:11–16

Command and teach these things. Let no one despise you for your youth, but set the believers an example in speech, in conduct, in love, in faith, in purity. Until I come, devote yourself to the public reading of Scripture, to exhortation, to teaching. Do not neglect the gift you have, which was given you by prophecy when the council of elders laid their hands on you. Practice these things, immerse yourself in them, so that all may see your progress. Keep a close watch on yourself and on the teaching. Persist in this, for by so doing you will save both yourself and your hearers.

Questions for Reflection and Application

- What did Jesus mean when he said that "whoever does not receive the kingdom of God like a child shall not enter it" (Mark 10:15)?
- Jeremiah's excuse was that he was too young. Moses' excuse was that he was not an eloquent speaker. What are your primary excuses when God calls you to something?
- How has God used your weaknesses to further his kingdom?

Father, let me come into your kingdom like a child—full of wonder and trust. Amen.

HEALING IN THE DARK

Heal me, O LORD, and I shall be healed; save me,
and I shall be saved, for you are my praise.
—*Jeremiah 17:14*

LeBron James. The kid from Akron who had broken the hearts of Cleveland sports fans when he took his talents to South Beach, had come back home. And now he had his team—*my* team, the Cleveland Cavaliers—in a deciding Game 7 against the awesome Golden State Warriors.

And I couldn't watch. My heart had been broken too many times by Cleveland teams.

I caught pieces anyway. My daughters were watching in the family room, so I saw glimpses whenever I emerged from my hiding place in my bedroom. When my wife decided to watch the second half in the bedroom, I had to get out of the house. So I went for a long walk in the dark, and I talked to God.

My talk was a rambling affair where I reminded him of how much a championship would mean, not just to me but also to everyone who is in or from northeast Ohio. But mostly I prayed. "It's not fair to ask that their shots go in," I told God. "But please give them that little extra bit of energy to play defense. To get a hand in the passing lane. To play team defense." I even prayed that Kevin Love would move his feet on defense.

When I got home, it was 89-89, with about 3:00 on the clock. I escaped back outside. On my first walk, I had heard shouts of joy in my neighborhood whenever the Cavs did something good. On my second walk, I heard only one shout. Just one. "Uh oh," I thought.

When I got home the second time, there were 10.6 seconds left. LeBron was on the floor, holding his wrist. But it was 92-89. The Cavs had held Golden State scoreless that entire time.

Answered prayers. The Cavs had won it with defense. God had healed me … and millions of long-suffering Cleveland sports fans.

Passage: Verse in Context — Jeremiah 17:7–8, 12–18

"Blessed is the man who trusts in the LORD, whose trust is the LORD. He is like a tree planted by water, that sends out its roots by the stream, and does not fear when heat comes, for its leaves remain green, and is not anxious in the year of drought, for it does not cease to bear fruit." …

A glorious throne set on high from the beginning is the place of our sanctuary. O LORD, the hope of Israel, all who forsake you shall be put to shame; those who turn away from you shall be written in the earth, for they have forsaken the LORD, the fountain of living water.

Heal me, O LORD, and I shall be healed; save me, and I shall be saved, for you are my praise. Behold, they say to me, "Where is the word of the LORD? Let it come!" I have not run away from being your shepherd, nor have I desired the day of sickness. You know what came out of my lips; it was before your face. Be not a terror to me; you are my refuge in the day of disaster. Let those be put to shame who persecute me, but let me not be put to shame; let them be dismayed, but let me not be dismayed; bring upon them the day of disaster; destroy them with double destruction!

Questions for Reflection and Application

- Why do many of us identify with sports teams and athletes?
- When do you find it most difficult to trust in God?
- Jeremiah likens someone who trusts in God to a tree with deep roots near water. Think of three other analogies for someone who trusts in God.
- How long have you waited to be healed of something? How do you keep from getting frustrated with God when healing does not come?

Father, you answer prayers for big issues and small ones, and your answers bring healing when I need it most. Amen.

THE GOOD OLD DAYS

Behold, the days are coming, declares the LORD, when I will raise up
for David a righteous Branch, and he shall reign as king and deal wisely,
and shall execute justice and righteousness in the land.
—*Jeremiah 23:5*

Exiled in Babylon, God's chosen people longed for the "good old days." They longed to return to their homeland, rebuild Jerusalem and its Temple, and live in peace and harmony under righteous kings such as David and Solomon.

But David had been dead for nearly four hundred years. The kingdom had been divided for centuries. And the people of Israel (and Judah) had disobeyed God for generations. The darkness of their present situation had caused them to turn their past into an idol.

Through Jeremiah, God told his people that he had allowed them to be scattered because they had been disobedient. God promised to gather a remnant of them from foreign lands and "bring them back to their fold" (v. 3) to "dwell in their own land" (v. 8). It wasn't enough for the sheep to live in a familiar place, though. They needed a shepherd who would care for them. So God promised to raise up a righteous king, a descendant of David, who would save his people and rule them with justice and righteousness.

That king, of course, was Jesus. He would not come for over five hundred years, and his kingdom was, and is, not of this world.

Like the people of Jeremiah's time, we have a tendency to romanticize the past. Regardless of how good things were then, the past is over, never to return. And, as Billy Joel reminds us in his song "Keeping the Faith," the "good old days" weren't always good, and the future isn't as daunting as we may think.

God doesn't want us to dwell on the past. He wants us to focus on the present and walk behind him into the future. If we let him take the lead and follow him faithfully, then our Good Shepherd never will lead us astray.

Passage: Verse in Context — Jeremiah 23:1–8

"Woe to the shepherds who destroy and scatter the sheep of my pasture!" declares the LORD. Therefore thus says the LORD, the God of Israel, concerning the shepherds who care for my people: "You have scattered my flock and have driven them away, and you have not attended to them. Behold, I will attend to you for your evil deeds, declares the LORD. Then I will gather the remnant of my flock out of all the countries where I have driven them, and I will bring them back to their fold, and they shall be fruitful and multiply. I will set shepherds over them who will care for them, and they shall fear no more, nor be dismayed, neither shall any be missing, declares the LORD.

"Behold, the days are coming, declares the LORD, when I will raise up for David a righteous Branch, and he shall reign as king and deal wisely, and shall execute justice and righteousness in the land. In his days Judah will be saved, and Israel will dwell securely. And this is the name by which he will be called: 'The LORD is our righteousness.'

"Therefore, behold, the days are coming, declares the LORD, when they shall no longer say, 'As the LORD lives who brought up the people of Israel out of the land of Egypt,' but 'As the LORD lives who brought up and led the offspring of the house of Israel out of the north country and out of all the countries where he had driven them.' Then they shall dwell in their own land."

Questions for Reflection and Application

- What are some of your fondest memories? What are some events from the past that you would prefer to forget?
- How are your recollections of the "good old days" preventing you from enjoying the present?
- What does God want you to accomplish in the next three to five years? What should you be doing right now to prepare yourself?

Father, help me to leave the past in the past. With you at the helm of my life, the best days lie ahead of me. Amen.

THE MASTER PLANNER

> "For I know the plans I have for you," declares the LORD, "plans to prosper you and not to harm you, plans to give you hope and a future."
> —*Jeremiah 29:11 (NIV)*

For the Israelites exiled in Babylon, the good news was that God would bring them back to their homeland. The bad news was that it would take *seventy years*. Those who were taken to Babylon would spend their entire lives there. To ensure that they had the best possible lives there, God told them to follow this plan: Build houses and live in them. Plant gardens and eat their produce. Get married. Have children. Instruct them to do the same. Seek the welfare of your city of exile, and pray on its behalf.

God's plan was a tough pill to swallow. But being disobedient to God had led to the ruin of God's chosen people, so the exiles decided to follow God's plan. They prospered. They found hope and a future.

In the business world, formulating a strategy and a plan for realizing that strategy always has been tough, but the rapid pace of change in today's world makes it next to impossible. With markets, technologies, and competitors in constant flux, formerly successful business models no longer work, and businesses have to adjust and even remake their plans frequently.

Planning can be difficult in our personal lives at every stage. What college major should I pursue? How can I get started in my career? Should I change jobs? Change companies? Change careers? Should I marry this person? When should we start a family? Is this the best neighborhood for us? Am I raising my kids the right way? Do I have the right balance in my life? When should I retire? The questions never stop.

Regardless of how well you plan, you'll never outdo the Master Planner. He knows the future, and he has a plan to give you a good one. Ask him about it. His door is always open.

Passage: Verse in Context — Jeremiah 29:1, 4–13

These are the words of the letter that Jeremiah the prophet sent from Jerusalem to the surviving elders of the exiles, and to the priests, the prophets, and all the people, whom Nebuchadnezzar had taken into exile from Jerusalem to Babylon. …

"Thus says the LORD of hosts, the God of Israel, to all the exiles whom I have sent into exile from Jerusalem to Babylon: Build houses and live in them; plant gardens and eat their produce. Take wives and have sons and daughters; take wives for your sons, and give your daughters in marriage, that they may bear sons and daughters; multiply there, and do not decrease. But seek the welfare of the city where I have sent you into exile, and pray to the LORD on its behalf, for in its welfare you will find your welfare. For thus says the LORD of hosts, the God of Israel: Do not let your prophets and your diviners who are among you deceive you, and do not listen to the dreams that they dream, for it is a lie that they are prophesying to you in my name; I did not send them, declares the LORD.

"For thus says the LORD: When seventy years are completed for Babylon, I will visit you, and I will fulfill to you my promise and bring you back to this place. For I know the plans I have for you, declares the LORD, plans for welfare and not for evil, to give you a future and a hope. Then you will call upon me and come and pray to me, and I will hear you. You will seek me and find me, when you seek me with all your heart."

Questions for Reflection and Application

- How much effort do you put into planning? What are some plans of your own that God has rerouted?
- Think about an aspect of your life that frustrates you and from which you would like to escape. How does God want you to redeem it instead?
- Who are some people you avoid because they are "different"? What is God calling you to do with them? How will you do that?

God, forgive my arrogance for trying to plan and manage my own life. You made me and you have a plan for me. Help me to understand and follow that plan. Amen.

THE ONE THING

Call to me and I will answer you, and will tell you great
and hidden things that you have not known.
—Jeremiah 33:3

All of us want to know the meaning of our lives. Why am I here? What is my purpose? Why are these things happening to me?

In the film *City Slickers*, three Manhattan friends experiencing personal crises decide to go on a two-week vacation driving cattle from New Mexico to Colorado. On the way, Mitch, a radio ad salesman, talks with Curly, the harsh cowboy who is leading the cattle drive. After Curly describes the beauty of "bringing in the herd," Mitch expresses envy at how "your life makes sense to you." Curly laughs at how "city folk" worry about every detail.

"You all … spend about fifty weeks a year getting knots in your rope," says Curly, "and then you think two weeks up here will untie them for you. None of you get it. Do you know what the secret of life is?"

"No, what?"

"One thing. Just one thing. You stick to that and everything else don't mean s---."

"That's great, but what's the one thing?"

"That's what you've got to figure out."

Mitch is mystified and frustrated by Curly's response, and Curly dies before Mitch can get him to elaborate. Abandoned by the other trail hands, Mitch and his friends must finish the cattle drive on their own. On the way, Mitch finds meaning in his life.

God promises us that when we call to him, he will answer and will tell us "great and hidden things." Like Mitch, many of us want an easy answer to every one of life's tough questions. But God knows that easy answers don't satisfy. He wants our search for meaning to be a running dialog with him, not a single question to a mountaintop guru. Let's get the conversation going.

Passage: Verse in Context — Jeremiah 33:1–9

The word of the LORD came to Jeremiah a second time, while he was still shut up in the court of the guard: "Thus says the LORD who made the earth, the LORD who formed it to establish it—the LORD is his name: Call to me and I will answer you, and will tell you great and hidden things that you have not known.

"For thus says the LORD, the God of Israel, concerning the houses of this city and the houses of the kings of Judah that were torn down to make a defense against the siege mounds and against the sword: They are coming in to fight against the Chaldeans and to fill them with the dead bodies of men whom I shall strike down in my anger and my wrath, for I have hidden my face from this city because of all their evil.

"Behold, I will bring to it health and healing, and I will heal them and reveal to them abundance of prosperity and security. I will restore the fortunes of Judah and the fortunes of Israel, and rebuild them as they were at first. I will cleanse them from all the guilt of their sin against me, and I will forgive all the guilt of their sin and rebellion against me. And this city shall be to me a name of joy, a praise and a glory before all the nations of the earth who shall hear of all the good that I do for them. They shall fear and tremble because of all the good and all the prosperity I provide for it."

Questions for Reflection and Application

- What are some tough questions for which you:
  - Settled for easy answers? What happened as a result?
  - Received an answer from God? How?
  - Are still waiting for an answer?
- During what activities do you feel closest to God? What is it about those activities that opens the lines of communication with God?
- What is the secret of life?

Father, I know that you are the source of all knowledge and understanding. Forgive me for not turning to you enough. Prod me to study your Word and talk to you more often. Amen.

THE GIFT OF TODAY

The steadfast love of the LORD never ceases; his mercies never come to an end;
they are new every morning; great is your faithfulness.
—*Lamentations 3:22–23*

"Don't you just love New Year's? You can start all over. Everybody gets a second chance."

So says Lenore, a "friend" of Lieutenant Dan, in the waning seconds of 1971 in the film *Forrest Gump*. Her statement foreshadows a fresh start for Lieutenant Dan in 1974. The man who had become a bitter alcoholic after losing his legs in Vietnam decides to follow Forrest to Louisiana and become his first mate on a shrimp boat. When Hurricane Carmen destroys all shrimping boats except Forrest's, the pair makes a fortune, and Dan makes his peace with God.

Many of us can't wait a few years, or even a year, for a fresh start. But we don't have to. God offers us the opportunity for one every morning, as Chris Rice reminds us in his song "Life Means So Much."

In the first verse, Rice compares today to the latest page in your journal. What will you write in that journal? A curse or a blessing? In the second verse, Rice compares today to the latest deposit of time in your bank account. Everyone is paid the same: twenty-four hours each. How will you spend your currency? Will you help someone else or look out only for yourself?

After each verse comes Rice's prayer as the chorus: "Teach us how to make each day count, God, because life means so much."

One man understood and demonstrated the value of life, sings Rice near the end of the song. That man gave his life for you, to demonstrate the value of your life.

God is faithful. His love is steadfast. He offers us unending mercies, including new mercies—and a fresh start—every morning.

Every day of your life is a gift. Make the most of it, starting today.

Passage: Verse in Context — Lamentations 3:19–27

Remember my affliction and my wanderings, the wormwood and the gall! My soul continually remembers it and is bowed down within me. But this I call to mind, and therefore I have hope: The steadfast love of the LORD never ceases; his mercies never come to an end; they are new every morning; great is your faithfulness. "The LORD is my portion," says my soul, "therefore I will hope in him."

The LORD is good to those who wait for him, to the soul who seeks him. It is good that one should wait quietly for the salvation of the LORD. It is good for a man that he bear the yoke in his youth.

Related Passage — Psalm 30:1–5

I will extol you, O LORD, for you have drawn me up and have not let my foes rejoice over me. O LORD my God, I cried to you for help, and you have healed me. O LORD, you have brought up my soul from Sheol; you restored me to life from among those who go down to the pit. Sing praises to the LORD, O you his saints, and give thanks to his holy name. For his anger is but for a moment, and his favor is for a lifetime. Weeping may tarry for the night, but joy comes with the morning.

Questions for Reflection and Application

- In what area or areas of your life are you longing for a fresh start? Why?
- If today were January 1, then what would your New Year's resolution be?
- How are God's mercies new every morning? How can you take advantage of that?
- How can you make the most of today? Tomorrow? Every day after?

God, teach me to count the days and make the days count. I often forget how precious every moment of life is. Amen.

PERSEVERANCE

The LORD is good to those who wait for him, to the soul who seeks him.
—*Lamentations 3:25*

"If you're going through hell, keep going."

"Success is not final, failure is not fatal: it is the courage to continue that counts."

"We shall defend our island, whatever the cost may be, we shall fight on the beaches, we shall fight on the landing grounds, we shall fight in the fields and in the streets, we shall fight in the hills; we shall never surrender." —Winston Churchill

On May 10, 1940, a month after Germany seized Norway and the same day that Germany invaded the Benelux Countries, Winston Churchill became the British Prime Minister. With Britain's allies falling like dominos, Churchill committed himself and the nation to all-out war until victory was achieved. He reassured and rallied his countrymen during the Battle of Britain in the summer of 1940, and the British victory became an early turning point in the war.[88]

Great Britain was still standing, but it would take five more years before final victory was achieved. For Churchill's England, perseverance was essential to survival.

Jesus spoke about perseverance in one of his parables. A widow repeatedly demands justice from a judge who neither fears God nor respects men. After ignoring her for a while, the judge finally gave her justice, just to get her to stop bothering him.

"And will not God give justice to his elect, who cry to him day and night?" asked Jesus. "Will he delay long over them? I tell you, he will give justice to them speedily" (Luke 18:7–8).

How often do we lose heart when we pray for a while and don't receive a response? What will the Righteous Judge do for us if we persist in asking for justice, or mercy, or help, or strength, or comfort, or any other good thing?

God is good to those who wait for him and who earnestly seek him.

Passage: Verse in Context — Lamentations 3:19–27

Remember my affliction and my wanderings, the wormwood and the gall! My soul continually remembers it and is bowed down within me. But this I call to mind, and therefore I have hope: The steadfast love of the Lord never ceases; his mercies never come to an end; they are new every morning; great is your faithfulness. "The Lord is my portion," says my soul, "therefore I will hope in him."

The Lord is good to those who wait for him, to the soul who seeks him. It is good that one should wait quietly for the salvation of the Lord. It is good for a man that he bear the yoke in his youth.

Related Passage — Psalm 27:11–14

Teach me your way, O Lord, and lead me on a level path because of my enemies. Give me not up to the will of my adversaries; for false witnesses have risen against me, and they breathe out violence. I believe that I shall look upon the goodness of the Lord in the land of the living! Wait for the Lord; be strong, and let your heart take courage; wait for the Lord!

Questions for Reflection and Application
- Why did David believe that he would see "the goodness of the Lord in the land of the living"?
- What is the longest stretch of time where you have prayed consistently for something? What happened?
- Why doesn't God answer all of our prayers quickly? Why does he seem to demand perseverance from us?
- Other than in your prayer life, what are some areas of your life where God wants you to be more perseverant?

God, give me the perseverance I need to persist in my praying. I want to build a strong and lasting relationship with you. Amen.

MINUTE BY MINUTE

But you, O LORD, reign forever;
your throne endures to all generations.
—*Lamentations 5:19*

The word "forever" appears over four hundred times in the Bible, usually in reference to God. It is reassuring to know that God always has been in charge and always will be in charge. But for us temporal beings, whose lives can be consumed by the tyranny of the urgent, the whole concept of forever may seem out of our reach. Why bother with forever when we struggle to get through today?

Just as a journey of a thousand miles begins with a single step, the pathway to forever takes place one minute at a time. Every minute offers us a choice in how we will live. Every minute offers us an opportunity.

How many minutes are there in a year? If you've ever heard the song "Seasons of Love" from the musical "Rent," then you know the answer: 525,600. According to the song, you evaluate a year on how you spent those minutes. How many were spent in laughter? In tears? In celebration? In strife? In love? The song implores you to measure your life in the seasons—and the minutes—that are spent loving others. Remember the love, it repeats. Measure in love.

Life is a marathon, not a sprint, but both races consist of a series of steps. Our challenge is to focus not just on the next step but consider it in an eternal context, as Hebrews 12 explains: "Let us run with endurance the race that is set before us, looking to Jesus, the founder and perfecter of our faith, who for the joy that was set before him endured the cross, despising the shame, and is seated at the right hand of the throne of God. Consider him who endured from sinners such hostility against himself, so that you may not grow weary or fainthearted. In your struggle against sin you have not yet resisted to the point of shedding your blood" (vv. 1–4).

Measure your life in love. One minute at a time.

Passage: Verse in Context — Lamentations 5:14–21

The old men have left the city gate, the young men their music. The joy of our hearts has ceased; our dancing has been turned to mourning. The crown has fallen from our head; woe to us, for we have sinned! For this our heart has become sick, for these things our eyes have grown dim, for Mount Zion which lies desolate; jackals prowl over it.

But you, O LORD, reign forever; your throne endures to all generations. Why do you forget us forever, why do you forsake us for so many days? Restore us to yourself, O LORD, that we may be restored! Renew our days as of old.

Related Passage — Revelation 4:8–11

And the four living creatures, each of them with six wings, are full of eyes all around and within, and day and night they never cease to say, "Holy, holy, holy, is the LORD God Almighty, who was and is and is to come!" And whenever the living creatures give glory and honor and thanks to him who is seated on the throne, who lives forever and ever, the twenty-four elders fall down before him who is seated on the throne and worship him who lives forever and ever. They cast their crowns before the throne, saying, "Worthy are you, our Lord and God, to receive glory and honor and power, for you created all things, and by your will they existed and were created."

Questions for Reflection and Application

- It's pretty hard to run a race of endurance if there is no finish line. In your Christian walk (or race), what are your goals for this week? This month? This year?
- How can you measure your life in love?
- A consistent theme in the Bible is the importance of passing on faith from one generation to the next. How did your dad pass on his faith to you? How are you passing (or will you pass) your faith on to your children?

God, the idea of forever can be overwhelming to me, but I take comfort in the fact that you are with me every minute and every step of the way. Amen.

YOUR TRUE NAME

And I will give you a new heart, and a new spirit I will put within you.
And I will remove the heart of stone from your flesh
and give you a heart of flesh.
—Ezekiel 36:26

When God made a covenant with Abram, God also gave him a new name: Abraham, which means "father of a multitude." After Jacob wrestled a "man" all night and refused to give in, even when the "man" put Jacob's hip out of joint, God gave Jacob a new name, Israel, which means, "he strives with God."

According to John Eldredge, only God can give you your true name, because only God sees who you truly are. And who you truly are is not your sin. God has washed away your sin. It is as far from you as the east is from the west. When God looks at you, he does not see your sin.

But that's not all, continues Eldredge. You have a new heart. That's the promise of the new covenant.

"Too many Christians today are living back in the old covenant. They've had Jeremiah 17:9 drilled into them and they walk around believing *my heart is deceitfully wicked*. Not anymore it's not. Read the rest of the book." In Jeremiah 31:33, God says that he will put his Law in your minds and write it on our hearts. He will be our God, and we will be his people. In Romans 2:29, Paul writes that "circumcision is circumcision of the heart, by the Spirit" (NIV).

"You have a new heart," writes Eldredge. "Did you hear me? Your heart is *good*."

What God sees when he sees you is the *real* you, the true you, the man he had in mind when he made you.[89]

No one loves you as God does because no one knows you—the real you—as God does. God has given you a new heart. And he has a new name for you. Your true name.

Passage: Verse in Context — Ezekiel 36:22–30

"Therefore say to the house of Israel, Thus says the LORD God: It is not for your sake, O house of Israel, that I am about to act, but for the sake of my holy name, which you have profaned among the nations to which you came. And I will vindicate the holiness of my great name, which has been profaned among the nations, and which you have profaned among them. And the nations will know that I am the LORD, declares the LORD God, when through you I vindicate my holiness before their eyes. I will take you from the nations and gather you from all the countries and bring you into your own land. I will sprinkle clean water on you, and you shall be clean from all your uncleannesses, and from all your idols I will cleanse you.

"And I will give you a new heart, and a new spirit I will put within you. And I will remove the heart of stone from your flesh and give you a heart of flesh. And I will put my Spirit within you, and cause you to walk in my statutes and be careful to obey my rules. You shall dwell in the land that I gave to your fathers, and you shall be my people, and I will be your God. And I will deliver you from all your uncleannesses. And I will summon the grain and make it abundant and lay no famine upon you. I will make the fruit of the tree and the increase of the field abundant, that you may never again suffer the disgrace of famine among the nations."

Questions for Reflection and Application

- What does it mean to have a new heart? What is different about your life since you got a new heart?
- What does it mean to have the Holy Spirit within you? What is different about your life since the Holy Spirit took up residence?
- Why did God give you a new heart? Why did God give you a new spirit? What changes should you make to reflect these realities?

Father, you love me so much that you have given me a new heart, a new spirit, and a new name. Amen.

FROM A BIRMINGHAM JAIL

> If this be so, our God whom we serve is able to deliver us from the
> burning fiery furnace, and he will deliver us out of your hand, O king.
> But if not, be it known to you, O king, that we will not serve your gods
> or worship the golden image that you have set up.
> —*Daniel 3:17–18*

The Civil War had ended nearly a century earlier but in some places in the South, African-Americans still did not have the same rights as whites. For example, in Birmingham, Alabama, there were "White Only" and "Black Only" restrooms and drinking fountains. Some lunch counters served whites only, and some local businesses refused to hire blacks. So in 1963, Martin Luther King Jr. and other Civil Rights leaders began a desegregation campaign in Birmingham that included mass meetings, lunch counter and library sit-ins, marches on City Hall, and a boycott of downtown merchants. Hundreds were arrested.

A week after the start of the campaign, the city government obtained a court injunction against the protests. King and other leaders decided to disobey the court order, even though bail funds were depleted and they could be jailed for a long time. King was arrested on Good Friday and placed in solitary confinement. After reading in the *Birmingham News* that eight Birmingham clergymen had condemned the protests, he wrote a response in the margins of a copy of that newspaper. That response became known as "Letter from a Birmingham Jail."

In his letter, King maintained that he had broken unjust laws to arouse the conscience of the community. So too, wrote King, had Shadrach, Meshach, and Abednego, refusing to obey the laws of Nebuchadnezzar "on the grounds that a higher moral law was at stake."

Just as Daniel's friends did not know that they would survive the fiery furnace and cause Nebuchadnezzar to accept their God, King did not know that his efforts would lead to a major desegregation in Birmingham.[90] [91] All of them did what was right and let God take care of the rest. Obedience led to courage.

Passage: Verse in Context — Daniel 3:14–18, 23–25

Nebuchadnezzar answered and said to them, "Is it true, O Shadrach, Meshach, and Abednego, that you do not serve my gods or worship the golden image that I have set up? Now if you are ready when you hear the sound of the horn, pipe, lyre, trigon, harp, bagpipe, and every kind of music, to fall down and worship the image that I have made, well and good. But if you do not worship, you shall immediately be cast into a burning fiery furnace. And who is the god who will deliver you out of my hands?"

Shadrach, Meshach, and Abednego answered and said to the king, "O Nebuchadnezzar, we have no need to answer you in this matter. If this be so, our God whom we serve is able to deliver us from the burning fiery furnace, and he will deliver us out of your hand, O king. But if not, be it known to you, O king, that we will not serve your gods or worship the golden image that you have set up." …

And these three men, Shadrach, Meshach, and Abednego, fell bound into the burning fiery furnace. Then King Nebuchadnezzar was astonished and rose up in haste. He declared to his counselors, "Did we not cast three men bound into the fire?" They answered and said to the king, "True, O king." He answered and said, "But I see four men unbound, walking in the midst of the fire, and they are not hurt; and the appearance of the fourth is like a son of the gods."

Questions for Reflection and Application

- What laws today do you consider unjust enough that you would risk an indefinite jail sentence to disobey them? Against what practices in our culture would you speak out openly, even if it cost you your job, friends, or reputation?
- Consider the courage it took for Daniel's friends to state that, even if God did not save them, he still was God. For which of your beliefs would you be willing to give up your life?

Lord God, teach me obedience. When I am obedient, you grant me the courage and strength I need to see the battle through to the end. Amen.

NEW AND IMPROVED

*His dominion is an everlasting dominion, which shall not pass away,
and his kingdom one that shall not be destroyed.*
—Daniel 7:14b

In the 1980s, Procter & Gamble, long the king of marketing consumer products, was losing share of the $4 billion United States paper diaper market to its rival Kimberly-Clark. The K-C's Huggies® brand had become the market leader, surpassing P&G's Pampers® brand. What was P&G to do?

Pampers became New Pampers. Then Ultra Pampers. Then Ultra Pampers Plus. Unable to top the combination of "Ultra" and "Plus" in the product name, P&G went back to Pampers but made it gender-specific: Pampers for boys and Pampers for girls. Then it was Pampers Phases, which P&G called the world's first "developmental diapers."[92]

Consumer products companies such as P&G know that we crave the new. If we can't have brand new, then we want new and improved. Except when we don't.

Beginning in 1975, PepsiCo began hammering its rival Coca-Cola's flagship cola product with the "Pepsi Challenge." Consumers did blind taste-tests of Coke® and Pepsi®, and the majority of the time they picked Pepsi. As Pepsi gained market share, Coca-Cola decided to reformulate Coke. The new, sweeter Coke hit the shelves in April 1985, horrifying loyal Coke drinkers and leading to nationwide protests. Just seventy-eight days after the introduction of "New Coke," the company brought back its original formula, renamed Coca-Cola Classic, and phased out New Coke.[93]

God doesn't need to pore over market research studies before deciding what to do. He is all-knowing, so he knows not only what we want but also, more importantly, what is best for us. Everything that he does is perfect, so he never has to change anything. He is the same yesterday, today, and forever (Hebrews 13:8).

In his visions, Daniel saw "the Ancient of Days" (God) put the Son of Man (Jesus) over all people (Daniel 7:9). His dominion will never end and his kingdom will never be destroyed.

God's dominion and kingdom are not new or new and improved. But they are reassuring. Every day.

Passage: Verse in Context — Daniel 7:9–10, 13–14

"As I looked, thrones were placed, and the Ancient of Days took his seat; his clothing was white as snow, and the hair of his head like pure wool; his throne was fiery flames; its wheels were burning fire. A stream of fire issued and came out from before him; a thousand thousands served him, and ten thousand times ten thousand stood before him; the court sat in judgment, and the books were opened. …

"I saw in the night visions, and behold, with the clouds of heaven there came one like a son of man, and he came to the Ancient of Days and was presented before him. And to him was given dominion and glory and a kingdom, that all peoples, nations, and languages should serve him; his dominion is an everlasting dominion, which shall not pass away, and his kingdom one that shall not be destroyed."

Related Passage — Hebrews 13:5–8

Keep your life free from love of money, and be content with what you have, for he has said, "I will never leave you nor forsake you." So we can confidently say, "The Lord is my helper; I will not fear; what can man do to me?" Remember your leaders, those who spoke to you the word of God. Consider the outcome of their way of life, and imitate their faith. Jesus Christ is the same yesterday and today and forever.

Questions for Reflection and Application

- When has an "improved" product or an "improvement" in your life disappointed you? Alternatively, when has an improvement proved superior to its predecessor? What were the primary differences between detriments and enhancements?
- When you hear or read "Ancient of Days," what images come to mind?
- What things in your life have stood the test of time? Why?

God, I thank you that I can rely on you to be the same—yesterday, today, and tomorrow. Amen.

EXTRAVAGANT GRACE

The LORD our God is merciful and forgiving,
even though we have rebelled against him.
—*Daniel 9:9 (NIV)*

David, whom God called "a man after my heart" (Acts 13:22), ruled well because he followed God. Solomon did the same, for a while. But then Solomon turned away from God, and his successors did the same. Israel was divided into two kingdoms—Israel and Judah—and both kingdoms strayed from God and eventually were conquered by foreign enemies. Exiled in Babylon, Daniel and many other Israelites realized that their downfall had been caused by turning away from God.

But God still longed for their return. And when we stray, no matter how far we stray or how much we rebel, God longs for our return, as Jesus explained in the parable of the Prodigal Son.

In the story, a man has two sons, and the younger one tells his father that he wants his inheritance. Now. This is worse than telling the father, "I wish you were dead." It is treating the father as if he is dead already.

After rebelling and getting an inheritance that he doesn't deserve, the younger son leaves for a foreign land and squanders all his money in a short time. In absolute ruin, he decides to go back to his father, repent, and ask to be treated as a hired servant, because no Jewish father would suffer the absolute humiliation of accepting back such a disrespectful son.

What the younger son doesn't know is that, while he has been gone, his father has been longing for his return. The father has been scanning the horizon for the son every day. When he spots the son a long way off, the father runs to him, embraces him, and kisses him. As soon as the son repents, the father restores him to sonship and invites everyone to celebrate the return of the "lost" son who has been "found."

God waits for his rebellious children to return so that he can show us his mercy and forgiveness. His grace is extravagant.

Passage: Verse in Context — Daniel 9:4–10, 17–18

I prayed to the LORD my God and made confession, saying, "O LORD, the great and awesome God, who keeps covenant and steadfast love with those who love him and keep his commandments, we have sinned and done wrong and acted wickedly and rebelled, turning aside from your commandments and rules. We have not listened to your servants the prophets, who spoke in your name to our kings, our princes, and our fathers, and to all the people of the land. To you, O LORD, belongs righteousness, but to us open shame, as at this day, to the men of Judah, to the inhabitants of Jerusalem, and to all Israel, those who are near and those who are far away, in all the lands to which you have driven them, because of the treachery that they have committed against you. To us, O LORD, belongs open shame, to our kings, to our princes, and to our fathers, because we have sinned against you.

To the LORD our God belong mercy and forgiveness, for we have rebelled against him and have not obeyed the voice of the LORD our God by walking in his laws, which he set before us by his servants the prophets. … Now therefore, O our God, listen to the prayer of your servant and to his pleas for mercy, and for your own sake, O LORD, make your face to shine upon your sanctuary, which is desolate. O my God, incline your ear and hear. Open your eyes and see our desolations, and the city that is called by your name. For we do not present our pleas before you because of our righteousness, but because of your great mercy.

Questions for Reflection and Application

- How have you rebelled against God in the past few weeks? The past few years? Why do you continue to rebel against God?
- The prodigal son was willing to give up his status as a son. What would you be willing to give up to be accepted by God (even though, because of God's grace, you don't have to)?
- Why is God merciful and forgiving toward us when we keep turning away from him?

Father, your grace for me knows no bounds. Like the prodigal son, I have gone astray, but you call me and welcome me back. Amen.

FALLOW GROUND

Break up your fallow ground, for it is the time to seek the LORD,
that he may come and rain righteousness upon you.
—Hosea 10:12b

God told Hosea to take a prostitute as his wife. When she returned to her former profession, God instructed Hosea to buy her back, forgive her, and love her as his wife again. Through Hosea, God demonstrated that even though the people of Israel repeatedly had abandoned him, God continued to love his people and long for their return to him. Their hearts were hard and cold to God, like soil that had lain fallow for years, but if they softened their hearts then God would rain righteousness on them.

Jesus' parable of the sower uses a similar analogy about soil. The sower throws seeds everywhere. Some fall along the path and the birds eat them. Others fall on rocky ground with little soil and they wither in the sun. Other seeds fall among thorns and are choked by them. The seeds that fall on good soil produce an abundance of grain. When the disciples asked him to explain the parable, he told them this:

- **Path:** He who hears the word of the kingdom but does not understand it has the evil one snatch away what has been sown in his heart.
- **Rocky ground:** He who "has no root in himself" receives the word with joy but falls away when tribulation or persecution arises (Matthew 13:21).
- **Thorns:** The cares of the world and the deceitfulness of riches choke the word.
- **Good soil:** He hears the word, understands it, and bears fruit.

In the message of Hosea, God is ready to rain righteousness on his wayward people but waits until they ready their hearts and earnestly seek him. The parable of the sower portrays a God who is even more extravagant in his love and grace. Rather than limiting the seed to the "ready" soil, the sower scatters seed everywhere.

God's rain is falling now. Don't miss the opportunity. Break up your fallow ground.

Passage: Verse in Context — Hosea 10:1–2, 9–14a

Israel is a luxuriant vine that yields its fruit. The more his fruit increased, the more altars he built; as his country improved, he improved his pillars. Their heart is false; now they must bear their guilt. The LORD will break down their altars and destroy their pillars. …

From the days of Gibeah, you have sinned, O Israel; there they have continued. Shall not the war against the unjust overtake them in Gibeah? When I please, I will discipline them, and nations shall be gathered against them when they are bound up for their double iniquity.

Ephraim was a trained calf that loved to thresh, and I spared her fair neck; but I will put Ephraim to the yoke; Judah must plow; Jacob must harrow for himself. Sow for yourselves righteousness; reap steadfast love; break up your fallow ground, for it is the time to seek the LORD, that he may come and rain righteousness upon you.

You have plowed iniquity; you have reaped injustice; you have eaten the fruit of lies. Because you have trusted in your own way and in the multitude of your warriors, therefore the tumult of war shall arise among your people, and all your fortresses shall be destroyed.

Questions for Reflection and Application

- Put yourself in Hosea's place. Could you marry a prostitute? After she returned to that lifestyle, could you rescue her, forgive her, and love her as your wife again? Why or why not?
- On whom does God send his rain of righteousness? On what type of ground did the sower in Jesus' parable sow his seed? Why does God send his blessings on people who do not have "good soil"?
- If a farmer had to break up the soil after a tough Midwest winter, then what tools would he use? How fallow is your "ground"? How can you break it up?

Father, break apart my hard heart so that I can receive your rain of righteousness. Amen.

A BETTER MAN

Return to the LORD your God, for he is gracious and merciful,
slow to anger, and abounding in steadfast love.
—Joel 2:13b

In the film *As Good As It Gets*, Melvin Udall is a self-absorbed loner with a severe case of obsessive-compulsive disorder. He is rude to everyone except Carol Connelly, the only server at his daily restaurant who can put up with him. He regularly berates Simon Bishop, a gay artist in the apartment next to his.

After Simon is assaulted and hospitalized, Melvin is intimidated into caring for Simon's dog and becomes emotionally attached to it. Not wanting to give up the dog, Melvin invites Simon to move into his guest room. To keep Carol working at the restaurant, Melvin pays the medical expenses for her acutely asthmatic son.

Simon is unable to pay his medical bills and approaching bankruptcy, so Melvin agrees to drive him to Baltimore so that Simon can ask his estranged parents for money. Carol comes along. At a restaurant, Melvin gives Carol the best compliment of her life—because of her, he has started doing something he hates: taking pills for his OCD. "You make me want to be a better man," he says. But a few minutes later, he once again says something rude, driving her away.

When they return to New York, Carol tells Melvin that she does not want him in her life anymore. Simon convinces Melvin to go see Carol, and the two walk to a nearby bakery. Outside it, Melvin tells Carol that she is the "greatest woman alive" and kisses her. As he opens the door of the bakery for Carol, Melvin looks down to see that he has stepped on a crack. Unphased, he proceeds into the bakery.

Melvin's love for Carol makes him a better man. Our love for God can make us better men too. God knows our hearts. When we stray, he encourages us to return to him, for he is gracious and merciful, slow to anger, and abounding in steadfast love.

God is as good as it gets.

Passage: Verse in Context — Joel 2:10–17

The earth quakes before them; the heavens tremble. The sun and the moon are darkened, and the stars withdraw their shining. The LORD utters his voice before his army, for his camp is exceedingly great; he who executes his word is powerful. For the day of the LORD is great and very awesome; who can endure it?

"Yet even now," declares the LORD, "return to me with all your heart, with fasting, with weeping, and with mourning; and rend your hearts and not your garments." Return to the LORD your God, for he is gracious and merciful, slow to anger, and abounding in steadfast love; and he relents over disaster. Who knows whether he will not turn and relent, and leave a blessing behind him, a grain offering and a drink offering for the LORD your God?

Blow the trumpet in Zion; consecrate a fast; call a solemn assembly; gather the people. Consecrate the congregation; assemble the elders; gather the children, even nursing infants. Let the bridegroom leave his room, and the bride her chamber.

Between the vestibule and the altar let the priests, the ministers of the LORD, weep and say, "Spare your people, O LORD, and make not your heritage a reproach, a byword among the nations. Why should they say among the peoples, 'Where is their God?'"

Questions for Reflection and Application

- Before Joel's call to return to God, there is an implied warning. What is it?
- When do you judge others by their outward actions? Why? How do you feel when others judge you by your actions without knowing your background, situation, and intent?
- What are some ways that God has made you a "better man"? Where would you like God's help to improve?

God, you make me a "better man" when I spend time in your presence. Amen.

TRUSTING AND OBEYING

And it shall come to pass that everyone
who calls on the name of the LORD shall be saved.
—Joel 2:32a

Chapter 13 of Isaiah describes the day of the Lord as one of tremendous destruction, where people are in anguish as God punishes the world for its evil and the wicked for their iniquity. The sun, moon, and stars do not give light, the heavens tremble, and the earth is shaken. Chapter 2 of Joel paints a similarly terrifying picture of that day: God's unstoppable army spreads inescapable fire and destruction. As that army descends, the earth quakes, the heavens tremble, and the sun, moon, and stars are darkened.

The only ones who endure the day of the Lord are those who call on the name of the Lord. What does it mean to do that?

When the disciples received the Holy Spirit on Pentecost (see Acts 2), Peter quoted from Joel, including "everyone who calls on the name of the Lord shall be saved." Later in Acts, when Paul was asked if he wanted to stand trial in Jerusalem, he replied, "I appeal to Caesar" (25:11). The word "appeal" (*epikaloumai*) is the same word that is translated "call" when Peter quoted Joel. In appealing to (or calling on) Caesar, Paul was submitting to the authority of Caesar and resting his fate on Caesar's judgment. When we call on the name of the Lord, we agree to be obedient to God, trusting fully and completely in him.

When we trust in and obey God, we not only endure the day of the Lord, but we experience true joy, as a famous hymn reminds us:

When we walk with the Lord in the light of His Word, What a glory He sheds on our way!

While we do His good will He abides with us still, And with all who will trust and obey.

Trust and obey, for there's no other way To be happy in Jesus, But to trust and obey.[94]

Passage: Verse in Context — Joel 2:23–32

"Be glad, O children of Zion, and rejoice in the LORD your God, for he has given the early rain for your vindication; he has poured down for you abundant rain, the early and the latter rain, as before. "The threshing floors shall be full of grain; the vats shall overflow with wine and oil. I will restore to you the years that the swarming locust has eaten, the hopper, the destroyer, and the cutter, my great army, which I sent among you. "You shall eat in plenty and be satisfied, and praise the name of the LORD your God, who has dealt wondrously with you. And my people shall never again be put to shame. You shall know that I am in the midst of Israel, and that I am the LORD your God and there is none else. And my people shall never again be put to shame.

"And it shall come to pass afterward, that I will pour out my Spirit on all flesh; your sons and your daughters shall prophesy, your old men shall dream dreams, and your young men shall see visions. Even on the male and female servants in those days I will pour out my Spirit.

"And I will show wonders in the heavens and on the earth, blood and fire and columns of smoke. The sun shall be turned to darkness, and the moon to blood, before the great and awesome day of the LORD comes. And it shall come to pass that everyone who calls on the name of the LORD shall be saved. For in Mount Zion and in Jerusalem there shall be those who escape, as the LORD has said, and among the survivors shall be those whom the LORD calls."

Questions for Reflection and Application

- Before you were an adult, in what areas did you struggle to obey your parents and other authority figures? As an adult, where do you struggle to obey? Why?
- In what areas of your life are you trusting and obeying God? In what areas are you not doing that?
- How do you feel about the day of the Lord? What do you hope to do before it arrives?

Lord God, remind me that if I trust and obey you, then the day of the Lord will be a day of great joy, not sorrow. Amen.

GOOD FORTUNE

For the LORD God does nothing without revealing
his secret to his servants the prophets.

—*Amos 3:7*

There are over forty-three thousand Chinese restaurants in the United States. Some feature Cantonese cuisine, which is mild and often fried or steamed. Others offer Hunan and Szechuan dishes that have strong and spicy flavors. Nearly all have one thing in common: the fortune cookie.

Based on a Japanese cookie called *sujiura senbei* that is sold at the beginning of the year for good luck, the fortune cookie gets its unique flavor from the combination of vanilla and sesame oil. Round when it is removed from the oven, the cookie is folded around a thin strip of paper that has a "fortune" written on it. There are databases of thousands of fortunes, and some of these databases are accessible online.

Fortune cookies are popular because they rarely, if ever, convey bad news about the future. God's prophets, on the other hand, were not so, um, fortunate. They often were charged with conveying unpleasant and unpopular messages from God, sometimes costing the prophets their lives. Jesus characterized the religious leaders of his day, the scribes and Pharisees, as descendants of those who had killed the prophets. A short time later, the scribes and Pharisees orchestrated the crucifixion of Jesus.

In Amos' day, things were not going well for the Jews. They cried out to God, asking for an explanation. God responded through his prophet Amos: "Does disaster come to a city, unless the LORD has done it?" (v. 6). In case they still didn't get it, God revealed his "secret" to Amos: the people were suffering the consequences of turning their backs on God. Later, God gave the people hope, again speaking through Amos: "Seek me and live. … Seek good, and not evil, that you may live; and so the LORD, the God of hosts, will be with you" (5:4, 14).

God doesn't keep secrets from us. He doesn't hide predictions for our lives in crispy yellow cookies. He speaks plainly to us in his Word. And there he offers us unbelievable and undeserved hope.

Passage: Verse in Context — Amos 3:3–8

"Do two walk together, unless they have agreed to meet? Does a lion roar in the forest, when he has no prey? Does a young lion cry out from his den, if he has taken nothing? Does a bird fall in a snare on the earth, when there is no trap for it? Does a snare spring up from the ground, when it has taken nothing? Is a trumpet blown in a city, and the people are not afraid? Does disaster come to a city, unless the LORD has done it? For the LORD God does nothing without revealing his secret to his servants the prophets. The lion has roared; who will not fear? The LORD God has spoken; who can but prophesy?"

Related Passage — Matthew 13:10–15

Then the disciples came and said to him, "Why do you speak to them in parables?" And he answered them, "To you it has been given to know the secrets of the kingdom of heaven, but to them it has not been given. For to the one who has, more will be given, and he will have an abundance, but from the one who has not, even what he has will be taken away. This is why I speak to them in parables, because seeing they do not see, and hearing they do not hear, nor do they understand. Indeed, in their case the prophecy of Isaiah is fulfilled that says: 'You will indeed hear but never understand, and you will indeed see but never perceive.' For this people's heart has grown dull, and with their ears they can barely hear, and their eyes they have closed, lest they should see with their eyes and hear with their ears and understand with their heart and turn, and I would heal them."

Questions for Reflection and Application

- Do you like fortune cookies? Why or why not? Can you recall a favorite fortune from one?
- Several popular books speak of secret codes in the Bible. Why are these books popular?
- If God speaks plainly to us in the Bible, then why are some parts of the Bible so difficult to understand? What do you do when you encounter a Bible passage that is unclear?

God, I thank you that you speak plainly and directly to me in your Word. Amen.

SHAMEFUL JOY

But do not gloat over the day of your brother in the day of his misfortune.
—Obadiah 12a

We may not admit it, but when it comes to *schadenfreude*, many of us have too much of Homer Simpson in us. When Homer's insufferably nice neighbor Ned Flanders starts the Leftorium, a store for left-handed people, Homer hopes that the store will fail. When his wish begins to come true, Homer is beside himself with glee, prompting a conversation with his daughter Lisa.

Lisa asks Homer if he knows what *schadenfreude* is and then explains that it is a German term for "shameful joy," taking pleasure in the suffering of others. Homer replies, "Oh, come on, Lisa. I'm just glad to see him fall flat on his butt! He's usually all happy and comfortable, and surrounded by loved ones, and it makes me feel … What's the opposite of that shameful joy thing of yours?" "Sour grapes," says Lisa. "Boy," says Homer, "those Germans have a word for every-thing!"[95]

We take pleasure in the misfortunes of others for the same reason that we compare ourselves to others: we think that we'll look better if others look worse. God, however, does not compare us to others. He measures us by a perfect stan-dard and we all fail. Badly. Utterly. We score a zero. (See Psalm 14.)

Thankfully, God offers us a solution, as Paul writes in Romans 3: "For all have sinned and fall short of the glory of God, and are justified by his grace as a gift, through the redemption that is in Christ Jesus, whom God put forward as a propitiation by his blood, to be received by faith. This was to show God's righteousness, because in his divine forbearance he had passed over former sins" (vv. 23–25).

When your brother suffers misfortune, remember the paraphrase of the statement first uttered by preacher and martyr John Bradford nearly five hun-dred years ago: "There, but for the grace of God, go I." Lift up your brother. You'll want him to do the same when you stumble.

Passage: Verse in Context — Obadiah 12–15

But do not gloat over the day of your brother in the day of his misfortune; do not rejoice over the people of Judah in the day of their ruin; do not boast in the day of distress. Do not enter the gate of my people in the day of their calamity; do not gloat over his disaster in the day of his calamity; do not loot his wealth in the day of his calamity. Do not stand at the crossroads to cut off his fugitives; do not hand over his survivors in the day of distress. For the day of the LORD is near upon all the nations. As you have done, it shall be done to you; your deeds shall return on your own head.

Related Passage — Philippians 2:1–4

So if there is any encouragement in Christ, any comfort from love, any participation in the Spirit, any affection and sympathy, complete my joy by being of the same mind, having the same love, being in full accord and of one mind. Do nothing from selfish ambition or conceit, but in humility count others more significant than yourselves. Let each of you look not only to his own interests, but also to the interests of others.

Questions for Reflection and Application

- Outside of sports events, when is the last time that you hoped someone would fail? Why?
- How often do you compare yourself to others? Why do you do that? How can you stop?
- Jesus commands us to love not just our friends but our enemies as well (see Matthew 5:43–48). When someone you really don't like fails or reaches a low point in life, what are some ways that you can demonstrate God's love to him?

Father, may I not take pleasure in the misfortunes of others but instead be a hand to lift them up. Amen.

IN THE BELLY

Then Jonah prayed to the LORD his God from the belly of the fish, saying,
"I called out to the LORD, out of my distress, and he answered me;
out of the belly of Sheol I cried, and you heard my voice."
—*Jonah 2:1–2*

The story of Jonah and the whale seems so ridiculous that it should be an animated film. And it was. In 2002, Artisan Entertainment released *Jonah: A VeggieTales Movie*, complete with a theme song by Newsboys, "In the Belly of the Whale."

Imagine however, that the story really happened and you are Jonah. God commands you to go to the capital city of an enemy country and tell the people that because of their evil behavior he will destroy the city in forty days. You don't want to warn the people because you know that if they repent of their evil ways, then God will not destroy them. So you board a ship heading in the opposite direction.

Once the ship gets out to sea, a tremendous storm hits, and the ship is buffeted relentlessly by the wind and the waves. When you see the fear in the eyes of the captain, you know that the situation is really bad. You tell the sailors that you are fleeing from God and convince them to throw you overboard. As you sink, you sense that the storm has ended. At least you can die in peace. The last thing you remember is being on the bottom.

Then you wake and it's pitch black. The ground is damp and sticky. The place smells absolutely horrible. But you're alive. You sense that you are moving. You hear the rushing of water outside the walls. You're … in the belly of a fish. How is that possible? You don't care. You pray and you thank God for saving you.

It's an unbelievable story. But so is yours. God can save anyone, anytime, in any way that he chooses. The wind and the waves obey him. So do the fish. So should we.

Passage: Verse in Context — Jonah 1:13–2:6

Nevertheless, the men rowed hard to get back to dry land, but they could not, for the sea grew more and more tempestuous against them. Therefore they called out to the LORD, "O LORD, let us not perish for this man's life, and lay not on us innocent blood, for you, O LORD, have done as it pleased you." So they picked up Jonah and hurled him into the sea, and the sea ceased from its raging. Then the men feared the LORD exceedingly, and they offered a sacrifice to the LORD and made vows.

And the LORD appointed a great fish to swallow up Jonah. And Jonah was in the belly of the fish three days and three nights.

Then Jonah prayed to the LORD his God from the belly of the fish, saying, "I called out to the LORD, out of my distress, and he answered me; out of the belly of Sheol I cried, and you heard my voice. For you cast me into the deep, into the heart of the seas, and the flood surrounded me; all your waves and your billows passed over me. Then I said, 'I am driven away from your sight; yet I shall again look upon your holy temple.' The waters closed in over me to take my life; the deep surrounded me; weeds were wrapped about my head at the roots of the mountains. I went down to the land whose bars closed upon me forever; yet you brought up my life from the pit, O LORD my God."

Questions for Reflection and Application

- When God told Jonah to go to Nineveh, why did Jonah go the other way? What are things that God wants you to do that you have resisted? Of what are you afraid?
- Has God ever put you, in a metaphorical sense, in the belly of a fish? If so, how did you handle that situation? What would you do differently?
- The story of Jonah is unbelievable. But so is yours. What are some unbelievable things in your story?

God, you transform lives in unbelievable ways. Transform mine that I may serve you well. Amen.

CRUSHING YOUR SINS

He will again have compassion on us; he will tread our iniquities underfoot.
You will cast all our sins into the depths of the sea.
—Micah 7:19

Chapter 7 of the book of Micah tells us that because God has compassion on us, he wants to do more than forgive our sins. He wants to trample our iniquities under his feet, effectively grinding them into dust. But the passage goes on to say that God will throw our sins into the depths of the sea. Why would God do that?

In the western Pacific Ocean—1,600 miles south of Japan and 1,500 miles east of the Philippines—is the island of Guam. Two hundred miles southwest of Guam is the deepest part of any ocean on earth: Challenger Deep. This spot, at the southern end of the Mariana Trench, is 36,200 feet deep. That's nearly seven miles deep.

Only four types of living creatures have been found in Challenger Deep: amphipods (shrimp-like crustaceans), sea cucumbers, amoeba-like protists called forams, and jellyfish.

These are the only life forms that can withstand the pressure of Challenger Deep, which is over one thousand times the pressure at the surface. That pressure is crushing, literally. Calcium carbonate, which is the basis of nearly all shelled animals, is dissolved at that depth.[96]

When something is crushed and dissolved in the deepest part of the ocean, it is forgotten. This idea is the basis for the song "Ocean Floor," which was a Christian radio hit for the group Audio Adrenaline in 2003. The singer lists his sins: hurting others, selfishness, pride, greed, and even secret sins that he has tried to hide from others and from God. He then celebrates the fact that because God has thrown his sins into the depths of the sea, they are not just forgiven but forgotten.

As your sins drift to the bottom of the ocean, they are crushed before they get to the bottom. Disintegrated. Erased. No more.

That's just the way God wants it.

Passage: Verse in Context — Micah 7:18–20

Who is a God like you, pardoning iniquity and passing over transgression for the remnant of his inheritance? He does not retain his anger forever, because he delights in steadfast love. He will again have compassion on us; he will tread our iniquities underfoot. You will cast all our sins into the depths of the sea. You will show faithfulness to Jacob and steadfast love to Abraham, as you have sworn to our fathers from the days of old.

Related Passage — Psalm 103:6–13

The LORD works righteousness and justice for all who are oppressed. He made known his ways to Moses, his acts to the people of Israel. The LORD is merciful and gracious, slow to anger and abounding in steadfast love. He will not always chide, nor will he keep his anger forever. He does not deal with us according to our sins, nor repay us according to our iniquities. For as high as the heavens are above the earth, so great is his steadfast love toward those who fear him; as far as the east is from the west, so far does he remove our transgressions from us. As a father shows compassion to his children, so the LORD shows compassion to those who fear him.

Questions for Reflection and Application

- What does it mean for God to crush your sins under his feet and cast them into the depths of the sea?
- What are some sins that you have committed that you can't forget? What does God want you to do with them?
- What are some sins committed against you that you can't forget? What does God want you to do with them?

Father, you have crushed my sins as if they were sitting on the ocean floor. You have erased them. Dissolved them. Hallelujah! Amen.

NO MORE MR. NICE GUY

The LORD is good, a stronghold in the day of trouble.
—*Nahum 1:7a*

"Aslan is a lion—*the* Lion, the great lion."…

"Then he isn't safe?" said Lucy.

"Safe?" said Mr. Beaver, "don't you hear what Mrs. Beaver tells you? Who said anything about safe? 'Course he isn't safe. But he's good. He's the King, I tell you."[97]

Aslan, the Christ-figure in C. S. Lewis' children's books, is not safe. But he's good. Jesus, the true Christ, is not safe either. Or nice, as Paul Coughlin writes in his controversial book *No More Christian Nice Guy*. "Jesus' behavior was so different from how the average guy in church is expected to behave that if you look at the record honestly, we wouldn't pray to such a person. We would pray *for* such as person."

For example, Jesus said things to people that simply weren't nice. He called people "hypocrites" (Matthew 6:2), "whitewashed tombs" (23:27), "fools" (v. 17), and "a brood of vipers" (v. 33). To their faces.

God often wasn't very nice in the Old Testament. He is portrayed not as a warm and cuddly grandfather but as a warrior, fighting for those who depend on him and against those who rebel against him—including Israel. And when God speaks, his language can be, well, off-putting. Consider how God responds after Job, who has lost everything and is at the end of his rope, demands answers: "Why do you talk without knowing what you're talking about? … Where were you when I created the earth? Tell me, since you know so much!" (38:2–11 MSG) … "Do you presume to tell me what I'm doing wrong?" (40:8–14 MSG).

God was not offended by Job. He was direct with Job because that's what Job needed. Jesus was direct with people because that's what they needed.

A nice person is wishy-washy, touchy, easily offended, blown about by the wind. A good person—like our good God—is solid and firm, honest and straightforward, bold, authentic, and holy.

God is not safe. God is not nice. But he's good. Let's follow his lead.

Passage: Verse in Context — Nahum 1:3–7

The LORD is slow to anger and great in power, and the LORD will by no means clear the guilty. His way is in whirlwind and storm, and the clouds are the dust of his feet. He rebukes the sea and makes it dry; he dries up all the rivers; Bashan and Carmel wither; the bloom of Lebanon withers. The mountains quake before him; the hills melt; the earth heaves before him, the world and all who dwell in it.

Who can stand before his indignation? Who can endure the heat of his anger? His wrath is poured out like fire, and the rocks are broken into pieces by him. The LORD is good, a stronghold in the day of trouble; he knows those who take refuge in him.

Related Passage — Matthew 23:1–5a, 27–28

Then Jesus said to the crowds and to his disciples, "The scribes and the Pharisees sit on Moses' seat, so do and observe whatever they tell you, but not the works they do. For they preach, but do not practice. They tie up heavy burdens, hard to bear, and lay them on people's shoulders, but they themselves are not willing to move them with their finger. They do all their deeds to be seen by others. … Woe to you, scribes and Pharisees, hypocrites! For you are like whitewashed tombs, which outwardly appear beautiful, but within are full of dead people's bones and all uncleanness. So you also outwardly appear righteous to others, but within you are full of hypocrisy and lawlessness."

Questions for Reflection and Application

- Why didn't God answer Job's questions? Why did Jesus call Pharisees and other church leaders "hypocrites," "whitewashed tombs," "fools," and "a brood of vipers"?
- Who puts pressure on you to be "nice"? How do you respond? Do you agree with Coughlin that a Christian man is called to be good instead of nice? Why or why not?
- If you are not nice, then how do you avoid being labelled a "jerk"?

God, I praise you that you are good and that when things get rough, you remain my stronghold. Show me how to be good and strengthen me to follow through. Amen.

PAY-IT-FORWARD JOY

Yet I will rejoice in the LORD;
I will take joy in the God of my salvation.
—Habakkuk 3:18

As the book of Habakkuk opens, Habakkuk is tired. Tired of seeing violence and destruction that go unchecked. Tired of seeing iniquity and wrong actions that go unpunished. Tired of watching those in authority do nothing or, worse, pervert justice. So Habakkuk opens his book with an angry plea: "O LORD, how long shall I cry for help, and you will not hear?" (1:2). Maybe you've heard someone utter a similar plea. Maybe you've said it yourself.

After Habakkuk lists his grievances, God responds. After Habakkuk complains again, God responds again. Then Habakkuk considers what God has done and his tune changes. Even if there are no crops in the fields, no fruit on the vines, and no flocks or herds—a recipe for starvation—Habakkuk will choose to rejoice. He knows that even if he has nothing, God will take care of him. Perhaps by having another person meet his needs.

Meeting the needs of others is a daily occurrence at Rosa's Fresh Pizza in Philadelphia. Patrons regularly pay $1 to leave a Post-It® note on a board. When a homeless person doesn't have a dollar, he can use a Post-It note to pay for a slice of pizza. The program started in 2014 with one patron's request to pay it forward with a dollar. Today, the generosity of paying customers provides fifty to one hundred meals a day for the homeless. Owner Mason Wartman no longer tracks prepaid slices via Post-It notes, but donators and those who benefit continue to adorn the wall with notes of encouragement and notes of thanks, such as this one: "I just want to thank everyone that donated to Rosa's; it gave me a place to eat every day and the opportunity to get back on my feet. I start a new job tomorrow!"[98]

Rejoice in the Lord, regardless of your situation or circumstances. When you take joy in the God of your salvation, you can spread that joy to others.

It's pay-it-forward joy.

Passage: Verse in Context — Habakkuk 3:1–6, 17–19

A prayer of Habakkuk the prophet, according to Shigionoth.

O LORD, I have heard the report of you, and your work, O LORD, do I fear. In the midst of the years revive it; in the midst of the years make it known; in wrath remember mercy. God came from Teman, and the Holy One from Mount Paran.

His splendor covered the heavens, and the earth was full of his praise. His brightness was like the light; rays flashed from his hand; and there he veiled his power. Before him went pestilence, and plague followed at his heels. He stood and measured the earth; he looked and shook the nations; then the eternal mountains were scattered; the everlasting hills sank low. His were the everlasting ways. …

Though the fig tree should not blossom, nor fruit be on the vines, the produce of the olive fail and the fields yield no food, the flock be cut off from the fold and there be no herd in the stalls, yet I will rejoice in the LORD; I will take joy in the God of my salvation. God, the LORD, is my strength; he makes my feet like the deer's; he makes me tread on my high places.

Questions for Reflection and Application

- How do you maintain your faith in God and even rejoice in the Lord during lean times?
- In what can you rejoice today?
- When have you been the beneficiary of a pay-it-forward scheme? When have you blessed someone else by paying it forward?
- What do you think of the term "pay-it-forward joy"? How can you spread joy to others today?

Father, even when I'm down to nothing, I still have you, and that is enough for you are all I need. I will trust in you. Amen.

FROM A DISTANCE

The LORD your God is in your midst,
a mighty one who will save.
—*Zephaniah 3:17a*

In 1990, Bette Midler's version of the song "From a Distance," which suggested that God watches us from a distance, went to number one on the Adult Contemporary chart and number two on the Billboard Hot 100. The song generated a great deal of discussion about the nature of God. Is God benevolent? Is God active in our lives? Or does God watch us from a distance?

In the book of Acts, the apostles performed "many wonders and signs" (5:12). Two of the apostles, Peter and John, encountered a man who was lame since birth. Invoking the name of Jesus, Peter healed him. Recognizing the formerly lame beggar, the people in the temple ran toward the trio. Peter told the crowd that faith in the name of Jesus had made the lame man strong.

Religious leaders arrested Peter and John. The next day these leaders, along with the high priest, demanded to know by what power or name Peter and John acted. Peter answered that it was "by the name of Jesus Christ of Nazareth, whom you crucified, whom God raised from the dead" (4:10). The leaders were astonished that two uneducated common men had such boldness and had healed a man. When the leaders commanded Peter and John not to speak or teach at all in the name of Jesus, the pair flatly refused. Because the people were praising God for the healing of a lame man, the religious leaders let Peter and John go.

The night that Jesus was arrested, Peter denied him three times. After Jesus was crucified, Peter, John, and the other disciples hid, afraid that they would suffer a similar fate. Even after the disciples saw Jesus alive and watched him ascend, they remained timid and unsure. But when they received the Holy Spirit, they started and built the church, one bold step at a time.

God does not watch us from a distance. The Mighty One is in our midst, alive and active.

Passage: Verse in Context — Zephaniah 3:11–19

"On that day you shall not be put to shame because of the deeds by which you have rebelled against me; for then I will remove from your midst your proudly exultant ones, and you shall no longer be haughty in my holy mountain. But I will leave in your midst a people humble and lowly. They shall seek refuge in the name of the LORD, those who are left in Israel; they shall do no injustice and speak no lies, nor shall there be found in their mouth a deceitful tongue. For they shall graze and lie down, and none shall make them afraid."

Sing aloud, O daughter of Zion; shout, O Israel! Rejoice and exult with all your heart, O daughter of Jerusalem! The LORD has taken away the judgments against you; he has cleared away your enemies. The King of Israel, the LORD, is in your midst; you shall never again fear evil. On that day it shall be said to Jerusalem: "Fear not, O Zion; let not your hands grow weak. The LORD your God is in your midst, a mighty one who will save; he will rejoice over you with gladness; he will quiet you by his love; he will exult over you with loud singing. I will gather those of you who mourn for the festival, so that you will no longer suffer reproach. Behold, at that time I will deal with all your oppressors. And I will save the lame and gather the outcast, and I will change their shame into praise and renown in all the earth."

Questions for Reflection and Application

- Peter and John went from being common fishermen to bold apostles who stood up to the religious leaders of their time. What significant changes have occurred in your life since you started following Jesus?
- What has been your personal experience with the Holy Spirit? What would you like it to be?
- When have you witnessed God being alive and active in your midst?
- Why does it seem like God is watching from a distance sometimes? How can you combat that perception?

God, I thank you that you do not observe me from a distance but love me enough to send the Comforter, the Holy Spirit, to live within me. Amen.

YOUR GLORY DAYS

*The latter glory of this house shall be greater than the former,
says the Lord of hosts.*
—Haggai 2:9

The more challenges you have faced in adulthood, the more that high school may seem like your glory days, as captured in the song "Glory Days" by Bruce Springsteen. In the song, Springsteen portrays a blue-collar guy who never left his hometown. Like most of his friends, Springsteen's character reached his peak in high school. Now the only way to get through the monotony of middle age is to drink with his high-school friends and reminisce about their days as teenagers, when they were impressive on the baseball field and attractive to the opposite sex. The passage of time, sings Springsteen, leaves you with nothing but boring stories of your glory days.

In the video for the song, Springsteen portrays a high-school pitcher mentioned in the song. The video opens with Springsteen's character at a construction site, daydreaming of playing baseball. After work, he heads to a local ball field, where he sets up a plywood strike zone behind the plate and carries a basket of baseballs to the mound. He hurls pitch after pitch at the plywood until the song starts and the image changes to his band performing the song in a bar. At the end of the song, we return to the baseball field, where the son of Springsteen's character belts one of his pitches into center field, and then his wife comes to pick them up and take them home.

The Jews of Haggai's day had a proud history but an uncertain future. Returning to Jerusalem from exile in Babylon, they found the city, and its Temple, in ruins. Many believed that their best days, and those of their nation, were in their rearview mirror. Perhaps you feel the same way about your life. But God promised them—and he promises you—that the true glory days lay ahead because God is the Author of the future.

Glory days won't pass you by. They're on the road ahead. Just follow the Guide.

Passage: Verse in Context — Haggai 2:3–9

"Who is left among you who saw this house in its former glory? How do you see it now? Is it not as nothing in your eyes? Yet now be strong, O Zerubbabel, declares the LORD. Be strong, O Joshua, son of Jehozadak, the high priest. Be strong, all you people of the land, declares the LORD. Work, for I am with you, declares the LORD of hosts, according to the covenant that I made with you when you came out of Egypt. My Spirit remains in your midst. Fear not.

"For thus says the LORD of hosts: Yet once more, in a little while, I will shake the heavens and the earth and the sea and the dry land. And I will shake all nations, so that the treasures of all nations shall come in, and I will fill this house with glory, says the LORD of hosts. The silver is mine, and the gold is mine, declares the LORD of hosts. The latter glory of this house shall be greater than the former, says the LORD of hosts. And in this place I will give peace, declares the LORD of hosts."

Questions for Reflection and Application

- When you see your former classmates on social media, what are your thoughts? How do you think they react when they see you on social media?
- When were the glory days of your life? Why were those your best days?
- When you read that your glory days are ahead of you, how do you react?
- How has God been working in your life in the past few years? The past few months? The past few days? For what is God preparing you?
- What step can you take today to follow your Guide?

God, I praise you that you have given me a hope and a future, one where you are in charge. I eagerly anticipate my glory days with you. Amen.

SHOUTING AT JESUS

Rejoice greatly, O daughter of Zion! Shout aloud, O daughter of Jerusalem!
Behold, your king is coming to you; righteous and having salvation is he,
humble and mounted on a donkey, on a colt, the foal of a donkey.
—*Zechariah 9:9*

Like Haggai, Zechariah returned to Jerusalem with Jewish exiles from Babylon. When Zechariah prophesied about judgment for Israel's enemies, the people gained hope that the nation of Israel once again would rise to prominence. And when Zechariah followed that up with a prophecy about a righteous king bringing salvation and peace, the people saw that king as a military leader who would lead Israel to victory over its enemies.

Over five hundred years later, the people of Israel remained a relatively small band with little control over their destiny. Now Rome ruled. The Jews desperately wanted to overthrow their oppressors and re-establish their nation. They needed an anointed king to lead them in this quest.

Could it be Jesus of Nazareth? Clearly he was chosen by God. He performed miracles. He spoke with authority about a new kingdom. He attracted huge crowds.

And now he was approaching Jerusalem. Thousands of people lined the streets. The noise grew to a deafening level. People threw palm branches and their cloaks on the road, as if they were lining it for a king. And Jesus was *mounted on a donkey, on a colt, the foal of a donkey*. It was Zechariah's prophecy! He was the promised king! *Hosanna!* the people shouted over and over. *Save us!*

Five days later, he was dead, hanging on a cross. The hoped-for Messiah was just another pretender. Just another fake.

Except that he wasn't. In Zechariah's day, and in Jesus' day, the people wanted salvation from their political oppressors. What God promised and delivered was salvation from a bigger enemy. *The* enemy. And Jesus brought that salvation by dying on a cross and rising to life on the third day … Easter Sunday.

Are you shouting at Jesus to save you? Or are you rejoicing that he already has?

Passage: Verse in Context — Zechariah 9:9–10, 14–17

Rejoice greatly, O daughter of Zion! Shout aloud, O daughter of Jerusalem! Behold, your king is coming to you; righteous and having salvation is he, humble and mounted on a donkey, on a colt, the foal of a donkey. I will cut off the chariot from Ephraim and the war horse from Jerusalem; and the battle bow shall be cut off, and he shall speak peace to the nations; his rule shall be from sea to sea, and from the River to the ends of the earth. …

Then the LORD will appear over them, and his arrow will go forth like lightning; the LORD God will sound the trumpet and will march forth in the whirlwinds of the south. The LORD of hosts will protect them, and they shall devour, and tread down the sling stones, and they shall drink and roar as if drunk with wine, and be full like a bowl, drenched like the corners of the altar.

On that day the LORD their God will save them, as the flock of his people; for like the jewels of a crown they shall shine on his land. For how great is his goodness, and how great his beauty! Grain shall make the young men flourish, and new wine the young women.

Questions for Reflection and Application

- When has God disappointed you? What were you expecting God to do? What happened instead?
- From what has Jesus saved you? What do you want Jesus to do now? Why?
- When have you turned to someone other than Jesus to save you? From what? What happened?
- When have you relied on your own abilities rather than asking God for help? Why do you do that?
- How can you rejoice in God's goodness today?

Father, forgive me for not rejoicing enough about the amazing gift that you have given to me. Amen.

WHOLE AGAIN

"But for you who fear my name,
the sun of righteousness shall rise with healing in its wings."
—*Malachi 4:2a*

Most of us need healing.

The expression "time heals all wounds" is bunk. Time doesn't heal anything. Only the Great Physician can heal us. As Malachi tells us, God has the healing that we need in his wings. All we have to do is ask. Jesus said, "Ask, and it will be given to you. ... If you then, who are evil, know how to give good gifts to your children, how much more will your Father who is in heaven give good things to those who ask him!" (Matthew 7:7, 11).

But we don't ask. Instead we project an image that everything is fine and, privately, try to fix ourselves and everything else on our own. This is captured in the song "Missing Love" by the group PFR. The song laments the fact that life becomes about surviving wounds and protecting our hearts from further damage. We long to live in freedom from fear, shame, and the lie that we'll never change. But in our hiding we end up missing the love and the healing that Christ offers. Thankfully, our Savior pursues us relentlessly and does not rest until we are healed and whole.

The Gospel of Mark includes the story of a blind man named Bartimaeus. As Jesus was leaving Jericho, Bartimaeus, who was begging on the roadside, called out to Jesus, asking for mercy. People nearby told him to be quiet, but he yelled louder, "Son of David, have mercy on me!" Jesus stopped and called Bartimaeus, who threw off his cloak, sprang up, and came to Jesus. Jesus asked Bartimaeus, "What do you want me to do for you?" Bartimaeus replied, "Rabbi, let me recover my sight." Jesus said to him, "Go your way; your faith has made you well" (Mark 10:48–51). Immediately, Bartimaeus could see. And he followed Jesus out of Jericho.

Jesus has the same question for you: "What do you want me to do for you?" Ask for healing. He'll make you whole again.

Passage: Verse in Context — Malachi 4:1–6

"For behold, the day is coming, burning like an oven, when all the arrogant and all evildoers will be stubble. The day that is coming shall set them ablaze, says the LORD of hosts, so that it will leave them neither root nor branch. But for you who fear my name, the sun of righteousness shall rise with healing in its wings. You shall go out leaping like calves from the stall. And you shall tread down the wicked, for they will be ashes under the soles of your feet, on the day when I act, says the LORD of hosts.

"Remember the law of my servant Moses, the statutes and rules that I commanded him at Horeb for all Israel.

"Behold, I will send you Elijah the prophet before the great and awesome day of the LORD comes. And he will turn the hearts of fathers to their children and the hearts of children to their fathers, lest I come and strike the land with a decree of utter destruction."

Questions for Reflection and Application

- If Jesus were to ask you, "What do you want me to do for you?", how would you respond? Would Jesus do what you ask? Why or why not?
- Where has your trust been broken? Where are you protecting your heart? Where are you living as a captive instead of as one who is free? What lies about you have you taken to heart?
- Where else do you need healing in your life? Where do you go for healing?
- What is one step you can take to model yourself after Bartimaeus when asking for healing?

Jesus, I want you to heal me and make me whole. Amen.

NOTES

1 Maria Temming, "How Many Stars Are There," *Sky & Telescope* (July 15, 2014).

2 Lee Strobel, *The Case for a Creator* (Zondervan, 2005).

3 Carl Wiser, "Tom Bailey of Thompson Twins." (August 12, 2014): http://www.songfacts.com /blog/interviews/tom_bailey_of_thompson_twins.

4 Jeffrey Kluger, "The New Science of Siblings," *Time* (July 10, 2006).

5 Amy Zipkin, "A Personal Sort of Time Travel: Ancestry Tourism," *The New York Times* (July 29, 2016).

6 Kenneth E. Bailey, *Jesus Through Middle Eastern Eyes: Cultural Studies in the Gospels* (IVP Academic, 2008).

7 "Winning the Race: Lance Armstrong Shares His Struggle to Survive Cancer…and Thrive!" *NIH MedLinePlus*, (Summer 2006): https://medlineplus.gov/magazine/issues/summer06 /articles/summer06pg6-9.html.

8 Feargal McKay, "Lance Armstrong Foundation – Every Cent Counts," *PodiumCafe.com*, (September 23, 2008).

9 "The Rise and Fall of Lance Armstrong." *Forbes* (January 2013): https://www.forbes.com /pictures/54f4e70fda47a54de8245129/1995-wins-tour-dupont/#6965412412ee.

10 Nina Mandell, "Lance Armstrong's advice to his 18-year-old self: Treat people better," *USA Today* (December 10, 2015).

11 Clint O'Connor, "Fathers, sons, and *Field of Dreams*: Dwier Brown's stint as John Kinsella continues to stir emotions," *Akron Beacon Journal* (June 18, 2017).

12 C. S. Lewis, *Mere Christianity* (Macmillan, 1952).

13 Ethan Siegel, "The Physics of Santa Claus," *Forbes* (December 20, 2015).

14 *Encyclopedia Britannica*, 15th ed. (1998), s.v. "Ezra."

15 Richie Allen, "Michael Phelps Workout and Diet," (December 11, 2011): MuscleProdigy.com.

16 Joseph Hooper, "Get into Olympic Shape with Michael Phelps," *Men's Journal* (July 2004).

17 Ana Gascon, "The Sanctuaries of Twila Paris," *Contemporary Christian Music Magazine* (November 1991).

18 Rudyard Kipling, "If", 1910.

19 Lewis Carroll, *Alice's Adventures in Wonderland*, 1865.

20 Eric Metaxas, "The Secret of Jackie Robinson's Greatness: Turning the Other Cheek," *CNS-News* (April 15, 2016): https://www.cnsnews.com/commentary/eric-metaxas/secret-jackie -robinsons-greatness-turning-other-cheek.

21 John Eldredge, *Waking the Dead: The Glory of a Heart Fully Alive* (Thomas Nelson Inc, 2006).

22 John Eldredge, *Waking the Dead: The Glory of a Heart Fully Alive* (Thomas Nelson Inc, 2006).

23 C. S. Lewis, *Mere Christianity* (Macmillan, 1952).

24 Robert J. Morgan, *Then Sings My Soul: 150 of the World's Greatest Hymn Stories* (Thomas Nelson Inc, 2003).

25 Robert J. Morgan, *Then Sings My Soul: 150 of the World's Greatest Hymn Stories* (Thomas Nelson Inc, 2003).

26 C. Michael Hawn, "History of Hymns: 'It Is Well with My Soul'," Discipleship Ministries–The United Methodist Church: https://www.umcdiscipleship.org/resources/history-of-hymns-it-is-well-with-my-soul.

27 "History of 'In God We Trust'," US Department of the Treasury (March 8, 2011): https://www.treasury.gov/about/education/Pages/in-god-we-trust.aspx.

28 "John Wayne Biography", Biography.com, and several online sources (for quotes from films).

29 The editors of Encyclopaedia Britannica, "Requiem Mass," (May 30, 2016): https://www.britannica.com/art/requiem-mass.

30 Program notes from the Coshocton Community Choir concert "I'm Gonna Sing" (April 2017).

31 Hymn lyrics attributed to William Kethe; Music composed by Louis Bourgeois.

32 Richard Pallardy, "Oskar Schindler," *Encyclopedia Britannica* (April 21, 2018): https://www.britannica.com/biography/Oskar-Schindler and the Danish website Auschwitz.dk.

33 National Center for Health Statistics, "Health, United States, 2015: With Special Features on Racial and Ethnic Health Disparities," U.S. Department of Health and Human Services (2015): https://www.cdc.gov/nchs/data/hus/hus15.pdf.

34 Amanda MacMillian, "15 Things Nobody Tells You About Losing Weight," *Health* (February 10, 2015): http://www.health.com/health/gallery/0,,20888773,00.html.

35 Alex Williams, "Feeling the Hunger for the Next Diet Book," *The New York Times* (April 17, 2005).

36 "William Wilberforce," British Broadcasting Company (updated July 5, 2011): http://www.bbc.co.uk/religion/religions/christianity/people/williamwilberforce_1.shtml.

37 "Who Was William Wilberforce?", BeliefNet: http://www.beliefnet.com/entertainment/movies/amazing-grace/who-was-william-wilberforce.aspx.

38 Susan Krauss Whitbourne PhD, "Nine Signs You're Really an Introvert," *Psychology Today* (March 25, 2014): https://www.psychologytoday.com/us/blog/fulfillment-any-age/201403/nine-signs-you-are-really-introvert.

39 https://www.secretservice.gov/.

40 Frank Vaisvilas, "Agent who took bullet for president remembers Nancy Reagan," *Chicago Tribune* (March 6, 2016).

41 Kenneth W. Osbeck, *101 Hymn Stories: The Inspiring True Stories Behind 101 Favorite Hymns* (Kregel Publications, 2010).

42 Robert J. Morgan, *Then Sings My Soul: 150 of the World's Greatest Hymn Stories* (Thomas Nelson Inc, 2003).

43 Bob Smietana, "Running out of Miracles," *Christianity Today* (May 1, 2004): https://www.christianitytoday.com/ct/2004/may/4.44.html.

44 Phil Vischer, Speech at Moody Founder's Week, February 4, 2015. https://www.youtube.com/watch?v=EoSbZ2pETT4.

45 *"Kyrie by Mr. Mister," SongFacts: http://www.songfacts.com/detail.php?id=1196.*

46 Josh Belcher, "Richard Page of Mr. Mister and the Story Behind 'Kyrie'," *Rockin' God's House* (January 18, 2014): http://rockingodshouse.com/richard-page-of-mr-mister-and-the-story-behind-kyrie.

47 Franklin Graham, "After 'Unbroken': The remarkable story of Louis Zamperini's faith," FoxNews (December 24, 2014): http://www.foxnews.com/opinion/2014/12/24/after-unbroken-remarkable-story-louis-zamperini-faith.html.

48 Ira Berkow, "Louis Zamperini, Olympian and 'Unbroken' War Survivor, Dies at 97," *The New York Times* (July 3, 2014).

49 John Eldredge, *The Journey of Desire: Searching for the Life You've Always Dreamed Of*, (Thomas Nelson, 2000).

50 Sean Robson and Thomas Manacapilli, "Enhancing Performance Under Stress: Stress Inoculation Training for Battlefield Airmen," RAND Corporation (2014).

51 Richard Adams, *Watership Down*, 1972.

52 Book Builders LLC, *Encyclopedia of British Writers, 19th and 20th Centuries* (Facts on File, 2003).

53 Laura Thompson, "Agatha Christie's private life would have stumped even Poirot," *The Telegraph* (August 22, 2009).

54 Words to a jingle in Ken-L-Ration television commercials beginning in the 1960s.

55 David Murrow, in discussion with the author, September 2014.

56 "Turn! Turn! Turn!" written by Pete Seeger, 1959.

57 Warren King, "Shakespeare & The Ancient Game of Tennis," NoSweatShakespeare (July 4, 2014): https://www.nosweatshakespeare.com/blog/shakespeare-ancient-tennis.

58 "History of Tennis Strings," Tennis Reviewer (2018): http://www.tennisreviewer.com/best-tennis-strings/history-of-tennis-strings.

59 Eric Ling, Cuyahoga Valley Christian Academy Commencement Address (May 28, 2017).

60 "The Song (Awaken Love)," lyrics by Jill Paquette (2014).

61 Eugene E. Carpenter and Wayne McCown, "Structure, Authorship, and Date of Isaiah," *Asbury Bible Commentary* (Zondervan, 1992). https://www.biblegateway.com/resources/asbury-bible-commentary/Structure-Authorship-Date.

62 "353 Prophecies Fulfilled in Jesus Christ," According to the Scriptures (January 20, 2015): http://www.accordingtothescriptures.org/prophecy/353prophecies.html.

63 Tim Lambert, "Daily Life in the Middle Ages," (2017): http://localhistories.org/middle.html; Tim O'Neill, "Myths about the Middle Ages," (August 6, 2015): Quora.com.

64 Carey Kinsolving, "An Alliance of Talent and Prayer," *The Washington Post* (November 30, 1991).

65 Carey Kinsolving, "American Gets Calling to Bring Opera On Christ's Life to Russia," *Chicago Tribune* (August 7, 1992).

66 "Rich Mullins Killed in Crash," *Christianity Today* (October 27, 1997).

67 Rich Mullins, "Step by Step (Sometimes by Step)," Recording of live performance.

68 Robert J. Morgan, *Then Sings My Soul: 150 of the World's Greatest Hymn Stories* (Thomas Nelson Inc, 2003).

69 Pat Williams, *Triumph!: Powerful Stories of Athletes of Faith* (Barbour Publishing, 2014).

70 Michael Foust, "How the Pistol found purpose," *Baptist Press* (March 30, 2007).

71 Many Arminians believe in eternal security.

72 Robert J. Morgan, *Then Sings My Soul: 150 of the World's Greatest Hymn Stories* (Thomas Nelson Inc, 2003).

73 Brooks Atkinson, "Beckett's 'Waiting for Godot,'" *The New York Times* (April 20, 1956).

74 Martin J. Esslin. "Samuel Beckett: Irish Author." In *Encyclopedia Britannica* (1998).

75 Robert J. Morgan, *Then Sings My Soul: 150 of the World's Greatest Hymn Stories* (Thomas Nelson Inc, 2003).

76 Anna George Meek, "An alto's-eye view of choral music," *Classical MPR* (February 5, 2014): https://www.classicalmpr.org/story/2014/02/04/alto-eye-view.

77 Joe Johnston director, *Captain America: The First Avenger*, Distributed by Paramount Pictures (2011).

78 Louis F. Benson, *Classic Hymn Stories* (1903), chapter IV.

79 Robert J. Morgan, *Then Sings My Soul: 150 of the World's Greatest Hymn Stories* (Thomas Nelson Inc, 2003).

80 Whitney Pastorek, "20 years ago: MC Hammer's 'U Can't Touch This,'" *Entertainment Weekly* (January 8, 2010): http://ew.com/article/2010/01/11/flashback-mc-hammer-drops-u-cant-touch-this.

81 Sketch the Journalist, "The History of Christian Hip Hop & Christian Rap," *Holy Culture* (January 22, 2009): http://www.holyculture.net/blog/2009/01/22/the-history-of-christian-hip-hop-christian-rap.

82 W.K. McNeil (editor), *Encyclopedia of American Gospel Music* (Routledge, 2003).

83 John Eldredge, *Waking the Dead: The Glory of a Heart Fully Alive* (Thomas Nelson Inc, 2006).

84 "Robert Gondor," The National Registry of Exonerations (March 25, 2017): https://www.law.umich.edu/special/exoneration/Pages/casedetail.aspx?caseid=3245.

85 Stephanie Warsmith, "Bob Gondor and Randy Resh to receive more than $2 million each for wrongful imprisonment; Gondor says amount will be less after debts," *Akron Beacon Journal* (March 23, 2017).

86 "Beast of Burden", written by Keith Richards and Mick Jagger (1977).

87 Robert J. Morgan, *Then Sings My Soul: 150 of the World's Greatest Hymn Stories* (Thomas Nelson Inc, 2003).

88 Herbert G. Nicholas, "Winston Churchill: Prime Minister of the United Kingdom," In *Encyclopedia Britannica* (1998).

89 John Eldredge, *Wild at Heart: Discovering the Secret of a Man's Soul* (Thomas Nelson, 2001).

90 "Explore: The Birmingham Campaign," PBS: http://www.pbs.org/black-culture/explore/civil-rights-movement-birmingham-campaign/#.Wx3EpiAh200.

91 "Birmingham Campaign," The Martin Luther King, Jr. Research and Education Institute at Stanford University: https://kinginstitute.stanford.edu/encyclopedia/birmingham-campaign.

92 "Paper-diaper business gets down and dirty," *The Economist* (November 28, 1991).

93 Abbey Klaassen, "New Coke: One of Marketing's Biggest Blunders Turns 25," *Ad Age* (April 23, 2010).

94 "Trust and Obey", written by John H. Sammis and Daniel B. Towner (1887).

95 Jon Vitti, "When Flanders Failed," *The Simpsons,* television series, directed by Jim Reardon (1991).

96 Jennifer Frazer, "What Lives at the Bottom of the Mariana Trench? More Than You Might Think," *Scientific American* (April 14, 2013).

97 C. S. Lewis, *The Lion, the Witch & The Wardrobe,* 1950.

98 Elizabeth Fiedler, "Philadelphia Pizza Lovers Pay It Forward One Slice at a Time," NPR (January 14, 2015): https://www.npr.org/sections/thesalt/2015/01/14/377033772/philadelphia-pizza-lovers-pay-it-forward-one-slice-at-a-time.

ABOUT THE AUTHOR

Chris Bolinger is an "average Joe" Christian who writes for guys like him. After a twenty-seven-year career in high tech—including stints as a software engineer, product manager, and entrepreneur—Chris left the tech world to focus on providing resources to small church leaders and other Christians. While *Daily Strength for Men* is his first book, he has written more than a hundred articles for newspapers and other publications. He has interviewed Christian authors and church leaders for his radio show and was an executive producer of the film *The Song*.

Chris is a competitive tennis player from a family of athletes and has coached basketball and tennis at the junior high and high school levels. A native of Akron who moved back to northeast Ohio in 1999, Chris sheepishly admits to being a fan of the hapless Cleveland Browns.

Connect with Chris at DAILYSTRENGTHFORMEN.COM.

NOTES

NOTES

NOTES

NOTES

NOTES

DAILYSTRENGTHFORMEN.COM